Ramana Maharshi

The Crown Jewel of Advaita

John Allen Grimes

Albion
Andalus
Boulder, CO
2012

"The old shall be renewed,

and the new shall be made holy."

— Rabbi Avraham Yitzhak Kook

Albion-Andalus, Inc.
P. O. Box 19852
Boulder, CO 80308
www.albionandalus.com

Design and composition by Albion-Andalus, Inc.

Cover design by Sari Wisenthal-Shore

Manufactured in the United States of America

ISBN-13: 978-0615632681 (Albion-Andalus Books)

ISBN-10:0615632688

To

Bhagavan Sri Ramana Maharshi

& Professor R. Balasubramanian

Who imparted the timeless wisdom of Advaita
To myself and oh so many others.

Contents

Preface

Some thirty years ago now, from 1978-1985, I attended the Radhakrishnan Institute for Advanced Study in Philosophy as a M.A. and Ph.D. student. I went there for a number of reasons. First, I had a deep and abiding interest in Advaita Vedānta philosophy and the Radhakrishnan Institute had a glowing reputation as an advanced study centre specializing in Advaita. Beginning with Suryanarayana Sastri, and continuing through T.M.P. Mahadevan, R. Balasubramanian, and P.K. Sundaram, one cannot imagine the depth of knowledge and immense joy I had in studying there. Secondly, partly due to its location, and partly due to the interests and devotion of these professors to Advaita, there was an intimate connection between the Institute, Ramaṇa and the Ramaṇāśramam, and the Paramacarya Sri Candrasekarendra Sarasvati and the Kāñcī Maṭha, just an hour or two down the road.

Ramaṇa has often been called an Advaitin's Advaitin. He has been praised as one of the greatest living embodiments of Advaita Vedānta, as great as the greatest of that illustrious group. Such a wonder the world seldom sees. He has often been described as "an incarnation of Advaita". The description is an intriguing philosophical oxymoron as the thunderous truth of Advaita boldly declares that no one has ever been born, lived, or died, and yet it is, without doubt, an astonishingly powerful image in conveying the profound affinity that exists between the teachings of Advaita and Ramaṇa. As one passes the philosophically relevant portions of Ramaṇa's teachings through the lens of Advaita, they will be seen to be in perfect accord with the essence of Advaita's philosophical teachings. What is all the more astonishing is that Ramaṇa's teachings emerged spontaneously as the fruit of his sudden "Great Awakening" and only subsequently, almost by accident, did he learn of the ancient Upaniṣadic and Advaitic teachings.

This book is an attempt to view, to see *(darśan)* the life and teachings of Bhagavān Śrī Ramaṇa Maharshi through the lens of the philosophical system *(darśana)* known as Advaita Vedānta. Replying to a question from a visitor to Śrī Ramaṇāśramam, Ramaṇa said: "To have *darśan* (being in the presence) of a Sage is sure to bring good to you. Thousands of people pass by Tiruvannamalai in trains every day, but few alight here and fewer still visit the *āśrama.* About *darśan* of, and association with, a Sage, the scriptures say that it is a vessel that enables you to cross the vast ocean of birth and death *(samsāra).* What more benefit do you want?"

Not only does the word *"darśan"* mean "being in the presence" of a Sage or deity, but it is also the nearest equivalent Sanskrit word for "philosophy". *Darśana,* from the Sanskrit root *drś,* meaning "to see" implies not only vision (which includes insight, intuition, and vision of the truth), but also the instrument of vision (such as viewpoint, worldview, doctrine, philosophical system). In a word, *darśana* implies "sight" in all its myriad connotations, and the term, like many Sanskrit terms, is multi-significant, multi-valent. Thus, besides expressing viewpoints or perspectives, the term also suggests the idea of right vision or realization *(mokṣa).* The former meaning customarily refers to the six great orthodox Indian philosophical systems *(ṣaḍdarśana).* Here, it is not so much a search for the truth as it is an exposition, elaboration, clarification, vindication and conceptual fixation of what has been received. The latter meaning, on the other hand, refers to the person experiencing a vision of or insight. In this case, it is direct, personal and experiential. In other words, the "seeing" implied by the term *darśana* includes both conceptual knowledge and perceptual observation, critical exposition and intuitional experience, logical enquiry and spiritual insight, concrete and abstract, gross and subtle. The English expression "I see" contains a hint of this multi-valence in that it denotes both a direct vision as well as a correct understanding.

Darśana, as a systematic elaboration of the truth, encompasses fundamental interpretations of reality more commonly known as the classical philosophical systems. In this technical sense, the term embraces the different streams of philosophical thought running parallel to one another and which were engaged in mutual dialogue, discussion, debate, criticism, and counter-criticism for the past two thousand years.

Thus, the word *"darśan"* is rich with meaning. To study, understand, interpret, and continue the scholarship of the Indian *darśanas* it is imperative that one realize that it holistically both implies thinking and living, theory and practice, an ancient, continuous, and seamless tradition. It has been able to combine, in an almost unique manner, conformity to tradition with an adventurous, enquiring mind.

I cannot express in words my heart-felt gratitude to Professor R. Balasubramanian for suggesting that I should write a book on Ramaṇa and philosophy. Only a spiritual aspirant can truly understand the immense joy that comes from reading, reflecting, and reveling in Ramaṇa's teachings. Truly, this is *satsaṅg*. Further, I couldn't have written this book without having been a student all those years under R. Balasubramanian at the Radhakrishnan Institute. Though I have studied Advaita for many, many years, I am really not competent to write about a Sage such as Ramaṇa. This is not mere lip-service. As has often been said, only a *mukta* can truly understand another *mukta*. All else is but intellectual gymnastics. This being said, I have done my best and I pray that Ramaṇa, as well as the reader, will forgive whatever blemishes appear in this work. They are all traceable to my own personal limitations for which I sincerely implore your and Ramaṇa's pardon.

I am so immensely thankful to Chris Quilkey, Editor of the *Mountain Path* at Ramaṇāśramam, for providing me with materials on the life and teachings of Ramaṇa. They made my work so much easier. Only a research scholar can truly know how invaluable his help was. I must also offer my gratitude to Arthur Osborne and David Godman for their selfless service in providing topical collections of exemplary conversations Ramaṇa had with spiritual seekers. Finally, I want to thank Martin Wolff for helping to proofread the manuscript and for making valuable suggestions.

John Allen Grimes
Chennai, India 2012

Abbreviations

BG	*Bhagavad-gītā*
BS	*Brahmasūtra*
BSB	*Brahmasūtrabhāsya* of Śrī Śaṅkarācārya
BU	*Bṛhadāraṇyaka Upaniṣad*
BUBV	*Bṛhadāraṇyakopaniṣad-bhāṣya-vārtikā*
CU	*Chāndogya Upaniṣad*
KU	*Katha Upaniṣad*
KeU	*Kena Upaniṣad*
MU	*Maitri Upaniṣad*
MK	*Māṇḍūkya-kārikā*
MaU	*Māṇḍūkya Upaniṣad*
MuU	*Muṇḍaka Upaniṣad*
NS	*Naiṣkarmya-siddhi*
PD	*The Pañcadaśī of Vidyāraṇya*
PP	*Periya-purāṇam*
SU	*Śvetāśvatara Upaniṣad*
TU	*Taittirīya Upaniṣad*
VP	*Vedānta-paribhāṣā of Dharmarāja*
V	*Vivekacūdāmaṇi*

Timeline of Ramana Maharsi's Life

1879	Born December 30 in Tiruchuzhi
1891	Moves to Dindigul
1892	Death of Father; moves to Madurai
1895	Hears of "Arunācala"
1896	Mid-July – Great Experience
	August 29 – leaves for Arunācala
	September 1 – arrives in Arunācala
	Stays in Thousand-pillared Hall; Pātāla Liṅgam
1898	Moves to Gurumūrtam; Mango Grove
1898	Moves to Pavalakkunru
	Mother visits in December
1899	Moves to Virupākṣa Cave
1900-02	Replies to Gambiram's questions
1907	Named "Ramaṇa Maharshi" by Gaṇapati Muni
1912	Death experience at Tortoise Rock
1916	Moves to Skandāśrama
1917	Mother settles at Skandāśrama
1922	Mother's *Mahāsamādhi*
1922	Moves to Ramaṇāśrama
1926	Stopped going round the hill
1950	April 14 – Ramaṇa's *Mahāsamādhi*

I

The Life of Ramana

A Sage is simply an embodiment, a momentary appearance of the nameless, formless Reality. It may appear as if a Sage has a birth, a personality, a history, speaks, acts, teaches—all the raw material which informs a biography—but know that all this is but a tale that a mind that is possessed by the defect of duality tells. In whatever way one perceives a Sage, the Sage remains what the Sage is, always has been, and always will be.

Early Life

As the story is told, on a cool pre-dawn December morning in 1879 in the little non-descript South Indian town of Tiruchuzhi, an incomparable Sage was born. It was 1:00 a.m. on Monday, December 30th, during the Tamil month of Mārgazhi. For the Hindus it was an auspicious day—the *Ārudra-darśanam* day—the day when the temple image of Lord Śiva is taken in procession in order to celebrate the divine grace of the Lord. It was an auspicious time as the movable image *(utsava)* of Śiva was just about to re-enter the temple precincts when Veṅkaṭ arāman (his birth name) was born to Sundaram Iyer and Alagammāḷ. That which is formless had taken a form. That which is birthless had been birthed. That which is timeless entered into time so that the world would benefit. Some call it the descent of divine grace. The moon was suspended high in the sky like a ball of light resting on the tip of eternity. The cool rays of the Sage's thunderous silence were soon to illumine the entire universe.

The Self that dances as unbroken bliss in devotees' hearts, Śiva unique, the Light Supreme that shines unceasing in bright Tiruchuzhi, bestow your grace on me and shine as the Heart within my heart.

There, in that room, in that house, the Sage was born into what, for all appearances, was a normal South Indian middle-class *brahmin* family. Sundaram Iyer was a well-known, well-respected *vakil* (pleader) in the town. Life was normal, favorable, uneventful, and happy for the parents and their four children: Veṅkaṭarāman, his elder brother, his younger brother and sister. There were no distractions in this sequestered town, and the wants of its inhabitants were few. Perhaps the only unusual thing that can be said about this family was a story that an ascetic had once been refused alms by one of Sundaram Iyer's ancestors and thus the ascetic had cursed the family so that in every generation one member of the family would become an ascetic, renounce the world, and live on alms secured by begging. Whether one believes in curses or not, it is true that one of Sundaram Iyer's paternal uncles had become a wandering monk and that his elder brother had suddenly left home one day never to be seen again. Now it was the turn of the next generation to continue the curse, if curse it was, for what is a curse to one may be a blessing to another. In this instance, a generation lost a family member while humanity gained a Sage.

In this peaceful, quiet climate, as a simple country child in tune with his environment, Veṅkaṭarāman began his life. There was nothing particularly distinctive about Veṅkaṭarāman's early years. There was no obvious indication that he would become Ramaṇa Maharshi, the Sage of Aruṇācala. He attended the local elementary school that was held in a small low-roofed house that formed part of the temple complex. Next to the school was a large banyan tree around which the children used to play. At the age of eleven, for just one year, he went to school in Dindigul, the nearest sizable town. Then, in 1892 his father died, and the children went to live in the house of their paternal uncle in Madurai. There, Veṅkaṭarāman attended Scott's Middle School and then the American Mission High School. Through his school years Veṅkaṭarāman, though intelligent, was an incorrigibly indifferent scholar and displayed little interest for studies.

Although he was similar to his fellow-students in many ways, it may be noted that he differed from most small town boys in that he had a prodigiously retentive memory (which not only served to get him through school, but which would be utilized in the future in regards to things he would hear or read but once), an alert mind, a greater than average natural athletic ability, a fierce, tenacious strength, and an uncanny ability to sink into extremely deep sleep.

Regarding this deep sleep, later in his life Ramaṇa narrated the following incidents on observing the presence of a relative who was visiting Tiruvannamalai:

> Seeing you reminds me of something that happened in Dindigul when I was a boy. Your uncle, Periappa Seshayyar, was then living there. Some function was going on in the house and everyone attended it and then in the night went to the temple. I was left alone in the house. I was sitting reading in the front room, but after a while I locked the front door and fastened the windows and went to sleep. When they returned from the temple, no amount of shouting or banging at the door or window would wake me. At last they managed to open the door with a key from the opposite house and then they tried to wake me up by beating me. All the boys beat me to their heart's content, and your uncle did too, but without effect. I knew nothing about it until they told me in the morning . . . the same sort of thing happened to me in Madurai also. My classmates didn't dare touch me when I was awake, but if they had any grudge against me they would come when I was asleep and carry me wherever they liked and beat me as much as they liked and then put me back to bed, and I would know nothing about it until they told me the next morning.[1]

[1] Devaraja Mudaliar, *Day by Day with Bhagavan*, 129.

Why do biographers attach so much significance to the fact that he was such a heavy sleeper? As we shall see, in the philosophical teachings of Advaita Vedānta, deep sleep is often likened (though they are not identical) to the experiential mystical state of non-duality *(nirvikalpa-samādhi)*. Deep sleep is employed as a powerful metaphorical analogy which conveys the message that in certain existential encounters with the ultimate Reality one loses all sense of duality including the understanding that a knowing subject, someone, is experiencing a known object, something, which is other than the knower. There, in the mystical experience of non-duality, there is no knower, no known, and no act of knowing. To those who declare that such a non-dual experience is not only inconceivable, but impossible even to imagine, the universal daily example of the state of deep dreamless sleep is cited by philosophers.

Not only was Veṅkaṭarāman an indifferent student, his religious education was also extremely minimal. Having attended mission schools, he did have a marginal awareness of some of the teachings of the *Bible*. However, he knew next to nothing of the Hindu scriptures. His first real enquiry into the meaning of life and death occurred when his father died. Paul Brunton related what Ramaṇa said to him: "On the day his father died, he felt puzzled by death and pondered over it, whilst his mother and brothers wept. He thought for hours and after the corpse was cremated he got by analysis to the point of perceiving that it was the 'I' which makes the body see, run, walk, and eat. 'I' now know this 'I', but my father's 'I' had left the body."[1]

Then, some three years later, at the end of his fifteenth year, two events happened which awoke, seemingly without any prior preparation, strong religious yearnings in the boy. The first incident has been somewhat erroneously reproduced in virtually all the biographies of Ramaṇa. The earliest biographer, B.V. Narasimha Swami, wrote in 1930 that the boy Veṅkaṭarāman had no reverence to Aruṇācala until a relative announced that he had recently returned from there and, upon hearing the name, a thrill went through his veins. In actuality, Veṅkaṭarāman had

---

[1] Paul Brunton and Munagala Venkataramiah, *Conscious Immortality*, 68.

been hearing the verse: "the mere remembrance of Aruṇācala confers liberation," from his childhood and had a child's simple reverence for Aruṇācala.

Seemingly accidentally and innocently, the first thrill from Aruṇācala came, not because he heard the name, but because a mere mortal had returned from there. One day an elderly relative of his that he had known in Tiruchuzhi visited the family, and the boy asked the relative where he had come from. The relative replied, "from Aruṇācala." This acted as a magic potion overwhelming Veṅkaṭarāman because, though the boy had no definite idea as to what Aruṇācala signified, he had a vague idea that it was the name of the holiest form of God. When his relative casually said that he had returned from Aruṇācala, the very thought of a mere mortal returning from God was a thrilling revelation to him. So, with evident excitement, he put his next question to the elderly gentleman, "What! From Aruṇācala! Where is it?" He got the reply that Aruṇācala was a mountain at Tiruvannamalai, a town that Veṅkaṭarāman already knew about. The thrill vanished, and he remarked, "I did not understand its meaning." Referring to this incident the Sage was later to compose a hymn:

> Look, oh, great wonder! There it stands as if insentient. Mysterious is the way it works, beyond all human understanding. From my unthinking childhood the immensity of Aruṇācala had shone in my awareness, but even when I learned from someone that it was only Tiruvannamalai, I did not realize its meaning. When it stilled my mind and drew me to itself, and I came near, I saw that it was the Immovable, stillness absolute.

A second seemingly innocent incident occurred at this time that contributed to the turning of the boy's mind towards spirituality. A copy of Sekkilār's *Periya-purāṇam*, a Tamil book narrating the lives of the sixty-three Śaivite saints *(nāyanmārs)*, came into his hands. "The book happened to be in our house and coming across it, I looked into it out of curiosity and then becoming interested, read the whole book."[1] He was enthralled

---

[1] Joan Greenblatt and Mathew Greenblatt, *Pictorial Biography*, 9.

reading about the lives of the saints who were permeated with devotion for God, and his heart yearned to emulate them.

The Great Change

In July of 1896, Veṅkaṭarāman was sixteen years old. The spiritual experience that he was longing for was about to happen, quite suddenly, quite unexpectedly and, one must admit, rather uniquely in the annals of spiritual lore. Years later, he narrated what his state of mind was, immediately preceding the experience:

> At that time I had no idea of the identity of that current of my personality with a personal God or "Iśvara" as I used to term him. I had not even heard of the *Bhagavad Gītā* or other religious works. Except the *Periya-purāṇam* and the *Bible* class texts, the *Gospels* and *Psalms*, I had not read any other religious book. I had just seen, with my uncle, a copy of Vivekananda's Chicago address but had not read it. I could not even correctly pronounce the Swami's name but pronounced it Vyvekananda the 'I' the 'y' sound. I had no notions of religious philosophy, except the current notion of God that he is an infinitely powerful person, present everywhere, though worshipped in special places in images representing him and other ideas which are contained in the *Bible* text or *Periya-purāṇam* which I had read.

On July 17th, 1896 we know that Veṅkaṭarāman was in good health. We know that he had almost no scriptural or philosophical knowledge. We know that he had not performed any systematic spiritual discipline (*sādhana*). For all intents and purposes, he was an average village boy. On the day in question he was sitting alone on the first floor of his uncle's house in Madurai. In his own words:

> It was about six weeks before I left Madurai for good that the great change in my life took place. It was so sudden. One day I sat up alone on the first floor of my

uncle's house. I was in my usual state of health. A sudden and unmistakable fear of death seized me. I felt I was going to die. Why I should have felt so cannot now be explained by anything felt in the body. I did not however trouble myself to discover if the fear was well grounded. I did not care to consult doctors or elders or even friends. I felt I had to solve the problem myself then and there. The shock of fear of death made me at once introspective, introverted. I said to myself mentally, 'Now, death has come. What does it mean? What is it that is dying? This body dies.' I at once dramatized the scene of death. I extended my limbs and held them rigid as though *rigor-mortis* had set in. I imitated a corpse to lend an air of reality to my further investigation. I held my breath and kept my mouth closed, pressing the lips tightly together so that no sound might escape. Let not the word 'I' or any other word be uttered. 'Well then,' I said to myself, 'this body is dead. I will be carried stiff to the burning ground and there burnt and reduced to ashes. But with the death of this body, am "I" dead? Is the body "I"? This body is silent and inert. But I felt the full force of my personality and even the sound "I" within myself, apart from the body. So "I" am a spirit, a thing transcending the body. The material body dies, but the spirit transcending it cannot be touched by death. I am therefore the deathless spirit.' All this was not a mere intellectual process, but flashed before me vividly as living truth, something which I perceived immediately, without any argument almost. 'I' was something very real, the only real thing in that state and all the conscious activity that was connected with my body was centered on that. The 'I' or my 'self' was holding the focus of attention by a powerful fascination from that time forwards. Fear of death had vanished at once and forever. Absorption in the self has continued from that moment right up to this time. Other thoughts may come and go like the various notes of a musician, but the 'I' continues like the basic or fundamental *śruti* note which accompanies and blends with all other notes. Whether the body was engaged in talking, reading, or

> anything else, I was still centered on 'I'. Previous to that crisis I had no clear perception of myself and was not consciously attracted to it. I had felt no direct perceptible interest in it, much less any permanent disposition to dwell upon it. The consequences of this new habit were soon noticed in my life.[1]

Because we have Ramaṇa's own version of the experience, we can date the event with credible precision and trust in its veracity. Because of all he said and did after this experience, we can credibly declare that the experience was complete and unending. However, the factors responsible for this great awakening are not so obvious. It is a commonly accepted Hindu tradition that unless one is worthy and ready, that one is a qualified aspirant *(adhikārin),* the body and mind of a person will be shattered by the force of a full descent of divine grace. If a trillion volts of electricity suddenly illumine a hundred watt bulb, the bulb will shatter. If a small cup attempted to contain the entire ocean, it would drown in the attempt.

It is because of this anomaly, this seeming lack of preparation, that biographers, scholars, and devotees meticulously search for clues in Veṅkaṭarāman's *samādhi*-like sleep wherein he would be totally oblivious to the existence of his body for hours on end; to his deep introspection upon the death of his father wherein he concluded that it was his father's 'I' which had left his body while his 'I' was in his body making the difference between life and death; to his statements that from his "unthinking infancy the immensity of Aruṇācala had shone in his awareness;"[2] to his reading about the inspiring lives of the Nāyanmārs.

It should also be noted that the account of Ramaṇa's great experience, recounted years later, is usually cited in English and comes across as a first-person account. As well, when a reader reads of the account, the reader understands it by employing their intellect. But one should be careful not to take it too literally for, as B.V. Narasimha Swami explained:

---

[1] B.V. Narasimha Swami, *Self-Realization: The Life and Teachings of Sri Ramana Maharshi.,* 20-2.

[2] Ramana Maharshi, *Aṣṭakam* in *Five-Hymns*, Vol.1, 124.

> The exact words have not been recorded. The Swami as a rule talks quite impersonally. There is seldom any clear or pronounced reference to 'I' or 'you' in what he says. The genius of Tamil is specially suited for such impersonal utterances, and he generally talks Tamil. However, one studying his words and ways discovers personal references, mostly veiled. His actual words may be found too colorless and hazy to suit or appeal to many readers, especially of the Western type. Hence, the use here of the customary phraseology, with its distinct personal reference.[1]

Secondly, the Great Event looks to a casual reader as though it was arrived at through a process of reasoning. But Ramaṇa, when he recounted the experience, took great care to explain that it was not reasoned out. "All this was not a mere intellectual process, but flashed before me vividly as living Truth, something which I perceived immediately." The realization came to him in a flash, and the Truth was perceived immediately and directly. Fear of death vanished never to return. From that moment on, the "I" or Pure Consciousness was experienced as the only Reality; and this experience never ceased. Years later, when Ramaṇa was speaking of this event, he said: "Absorption in the Self has continued from that moment right up to this time." Whether his body was engaged in talking, walking, sitting, eating, or anything else, it would forever more be centered on the Imperishable.

Incredibly, Ramaṇa's experience was unmotivated. He recalled: "I knew nothing of life and had no idea that it was full of sorrow; and I had no desire to avoid rebirth or seek release, to obtain detachment or liberation." True, his awakening was set in motion by a "sudden fear of death", but it should be noted that this fear appeared suddenly, spontaneously. The boy was not consciously seeking to avoid death or seek a solution to life's problems.

The reader should take a moment to pause and reflect on this. Normally, this awareness is generated only after a long and

---

[1] Narasimha Swami, *Self-Realization*, 20.

difficult period of spiritual discipline. Ramaṇa narrated years later: "I have never done any *sādhana.* I did not even know what *sādhana* was. Only long afterwards I came to know what *sādhana* was and how many different kinds of it there were."[1] In Ramaṇa's case, his awakening happened spontaneously, without either prior effort or, more remarkably, desire. Further, Ramaṇa described his experience as permanent and irreversible. Throughout history there are individuals who have reported having seemingly similar experiences, but invariably such experiences are almost always temporary. As well, those who recount such experiences invariably also have been performing spiritual disciplines; and even if their experience did happen spontaneously and did not involve prior spiritual disciplines, they all involved a desire for an experience.

Another feature regarding this event that deserves notice is that it occurred spontaneously. The *Kaṭha Upaniśad* states: "The Self is not to be attained by conscious effort. The Self is known by him to whom it chooses to disclose itself."[2] Self-realization is an uncovering, an unveiling, and not something that is obtained in the way things are ordinarily obtained in the physical world. Self-knowledge is not a goal or an object that can be achieved through one's own efforts. Finite efforts cannot produce an infinite Reality. All one can do *vis-a-vis* the Self is to remove the obstacles which are blocking its revelation. One cannot create the realization itself. If a person is in a house and has all the doors and windows closed, one cannot see the sun. One can open the doors and windows, but one cannot create the sun.

Imagine, at this time Ramaṇa was just a boy of sixteen years. He was a village boy and all that took place in the late 1800's in Southern India. A child-Sage, ancient of the ancients, emerged and demonstrated to humanity once again what the behavior of such a one is like. In physical appearance he appeared to the world like an eccentric vagrant, with a wire-thin body, yet glowing and healthy. He would forever wear only a loincloth and live a life of utter simplicity. He could be found

---

[1] Mudaliar, *Day by Day with Bhagavan,* 168.

[2] KU 1.2.23.

sitting silent among trees, rocks, and in caves. To all intents and purposes it was as if Dakṣiṇāmūrti had reappeared.

From this time on, everyone noticed a change in the young boy. Things he had once valued before no longer interested him. He became utterly indifferent to friends, food, studies, everything around him. He could be found either sitting alone, absorbed in the Self, or else standing in front of the images of the deities or Nāyanmārs in the Mīnākśi temple with tears flowing from his eyes. As Ramaṇa said:

> In the first place I lost what little interest I had in my outward relationship with friends, kinsmen or studies. I went through my studies mechanically. I would take up a book and keep the page open before me to satisfy my elders that I was reading. As for my attention, that was far away, gone far indeed from such superficial matters. In my dealings with relatives, friends, etc., I developed humility, meekness, and indifference. Formerly, when among other boys I was given some burdensome task, I would occasionally complain of unjust distribution of work. If boys chaffed me, I might retort and sometimes threaten them, and assert myself. If someone dared to poke fun at me or take other liberties he would be made quickly to realize his mistake. The old personality that resented and asserted itself had disappeared. I stopped going out with friends for sports, etc., and preferred to be left to myself. Oftentimes I would sit alone by myself, especially in a posture suitable for meditation, close my eyes, and lose myself in the all-absorbing concentration on myself, on the spirit, current or force which constituted myself. I would continue it despite the constant jeers of my elder brother, who would mock me, address me by the titles, *Jñāni* (Sage), Yogiśvara (Lord of Yogis), and advise me jocularly to go away to a dense primeval forest like the *ṛṣis* of yore. All preference and avoidance in the matter of food had gone. All food given to me, tasty or tasteless, good or rotten, I would swallow with indifference to its taste,

smell or quality.[1]

One of the new features related to the Mīnākṣi temple. Formerly I would go there rarely with friends, see the images, put on sacred ashes and sacred vermillion on the forehead and return home without any perceptible emotion. After the awakening into the new life, I would go almost every evening to the temple. I would go alone and stand before Śiva, or Mīnākṣi, or Naṭarāja, or the sixty-three saints for long periods. I would feel waves of emotion overcoming me. The former hold on the body had been given up by my spirit, since it ceased to cherish the idea "I-am-the-body" . . . Mostly I would let the deep within flow on and into the deep without. Tears would mark this overflow of the soul and not betoken any particular feeling of pleasure or pain.[2]

The Call to Arunacala

All that is left to tell of Veṅkaṭarāman's early life is the denouement, the unraveling, the outcome of this profound experience. It began on August 29th, 1896, about six weeks after his enlightenment. His neglect of his studies did not go unnoticed by his brother, his brother-in-law, and his schoolmaster. He had performed poorly in English grammar, and as a punishment for his indifference had been instructed by his teacher to copy certain portions from *Bain's Grammar* three times. After writing the assignment twice, the futility of what he was doing forcefully struck him and he closed his eyes and turned inwards. Observing this, his brother scornfully remarked: "Why should one, who behaves thus, retain all this?" Veṅkaṭ arāman had been hearing such remarks fairly often, but this time the truth of the remark hit home. The main point of his brother's remark is that one should not live in another person's house and partake of all the facilities and amenities therein if one is going

---

[1] Narasimha Swami, *Self-Realization*, 22-3.

[2] Ibid., 23-4.

to act like a homeless mendicant. This is common knowledge oft given lip service among the Hindus, and yet it is seldom heeded. If one chooses to live in the empirical world and benefit from its perks, then one has certain duties to perform. If one wants to be a renunciate, then leave the empirical world and get on with one's renunciation. A person should not try to have it both ways.

Realizing the truth of his brother's remark, Veṅkaṭarāman decided then and there to leave home. There was no point in pretending to study and act as his old self. But where was he to go? Spontaneously, there arose the memory of the word "Aruṇācala." He knew that if he told his elders of his intention to go to Tiruvannamalai, they would not let him go. Thus, he got up and informed his brother that he had to attend a special class at school. His brother remarked: "Well then, do not fail to take five rupees from the box and pay my college fees in the college near your school." Destiny had provided him with the money necessary for his trip.

Veṅkaṭarāman went downstairs, quickly ate a meal served by his aunt, and received from her the five rupees. He then looked in an old outdated atlas that informed him that the nearest railroad station to Tiruvannamalai was Tindivanam. Actually there was a new branch line opened from Villupuram to Tiruvannamalai, but he remained unaware of this because of the outdated atlas. He calculated that three rupees would be sufficient for the fare. He left the balance of two rupees in the box along with a farewell note informing the family of what he had done and not to be unduly worried about him. The note said:

> I have, in search of my Father and in accordance with His command, started from here. This is only embarking on a virtuous enterprise. Therefore none need grieve over this act. No money need be spent looking for this. Your fee has not yet been paid. Two rupees are kept herewith. Thus, ______.[1]

The letter was not signed. Later he was to say of this note,

---

[1] Ibid., 20-2.

"You can observe in the letter at home at the time of starting, I first wrote 'in accordance to his command' and interposed above it 'in search of my father' and because it is he who drew me. I wrote that and started. The finding of funds was not my act. My brother of his own accord did it."[1] As well, the "search" was not his own volitional act, but in accord with the dictates of destiny and a sudden internal inspiration. His brother was the vehicle that served as the initial catalyst. Aruṇācala called, and he merely accepted that call. His brother provided the financial means. The entire scene was not preplanned but spontaneously occurred from an inner impulse and a willingness to accept.

There is a theory, to some a truth, that when one has three-fold purity of thought, word, and deed (*trikaraṇa śuddhi*), that whenever, whatever one thinks, says, and performs are in perfect accordance, then the world becomes a wonderful, wonder filled place. Having decided to leave home, food and financial means quickly and spontaneously manifested. After writing the letter, Veṅkaṭarāman went to the railway station. He was late but the train was also late! The ticket he purchased to Tindivanam was two *rupees* and thirteen *annas*. If only he had known that the exact price of a ticket, all the way to Tiruvannamalai, was exactly three *rupees*. Because of the presence of an old, out of date atlas and a lack of desire to enquire further, his body would have to undergo certain hardships and adventures on the way even if his mind was always immersed in bliss. Everything lined up perfectly, yet fate also had its part to play, apparently due to negligence or a lack of inner inspiration.

Veṅkaṭarāman's choice of Aruṇācala was not entirely by chance. Even as a little boy he was continually aware of something supremely holy whose name was Aruṇācala. In his later years he would say that it was the spiritual power of Aruṇācala that had brought about his Self-realization. His love for the mountain was so great that from the day he arrived in 1896 until he left his body in 1950, he was never more than two miles away from its base.

On the morning of September 1st, 1896, three days after

---

[1] Narasimha Swami, *Papers*, 'Scenes from Ramana's Life'.

leaving home, Veṅkaṭarāman arrived in Tiruvannamalai. Upon arrival, he made his way to the great temple of Arunācaleśvara. If one checks government and temple records, one will discover that every 30 to 40 years the temple totally closes its doors and gates so that it may clean the jewelry used in adorning the *mūrtis.* September 1st, 1896, is recorded as one such day. This "coincidence" would appear to give new significance to the young Sage's delays and apparent "missteps" on his journey to Tiruvannamalai. Inexplicably, Veṅkaṭarāman, upon arriving at the temple, appears to have found the doors and gates wide open. He noted that the temple was empty of devotees. He made his way to the innermost shrine, and presented himself before his Lord. This was his first and only visit to the *sanctum sanctorum.*

This is one approach to a biography, the familiar empirical way, the worldly view *(laukika dṛṣṭi)* to tell chronologically the early-life story of the Sage. There is a second approach known as the scriptural approach *(śāstra-dṛṣṭi)* which hints at, which talks about the Reality. The average person knows little, if anything, about true spirituality and cares even less. A seeker of spirituality finds clues and hints in the scriptures and lives of the Sages. Finally, there is a third approach, another story, the never-beginning, never-ending story that cannot be told except through silence. In this approach, what cannot be said cannot be said; the inexpressible cannot be expressed.

It is an incredible tale, and one not easily understood. How to establish the plausibility of this apparently astonishing claim that one's experience of multiplicity is false, an illusion, similar to a dream, a cinema show, or a snake superimposed upon a rope, or silver superimposed upon a shell? Certainly, it is easier to accept virtually everyone's *normal* experience of life than to accept that all that is, is only the one undifferentiated Consciousness.

How can one speak of Ramaṇa's "Great Change" as an "experience" when all experiences demand the presence of an experiencer and something to be experienced? Yet, according to Ramaṇa, neither actually is. There is no before and no after, because what happened is not dependent on time. This is the dilemma. How to speak of the eternal non-dual Sage? There is an indivisible and universal Consciousness wherein there is no question of birth nor death nor body; and from this perspective, what can one say and whom to say it to? "Who is it that speaks of an experience? The speaker is (but) the ignorant self, and he speaks of the pure Self. How can that hold?"

There is an unexamined premise in believing that any person in general, or Ramaṇa in particular, was born, experienced all life has to offer, became enlightened or not, and then died. The hidden premise is that there exists a distinct separate individual person. This is an unexamined assumption, a mere mental construct.

Life at Tiruvannamalai

Driven by an inner compulsion, this sixteen-year-old schoolboy left home, threw away all his money and possessions, made his way to Aruṇācala, and immersed himself in his real nature—the great inner Self, formless and forever. His initial absorption in this awareness was so deep and intense that he would live for almost three years completely oblivious of his body and the world around him. Insects chewed away portions of his flesh. He seldom ate, and his body wasted away.

His first couple of years were spent in and around the great temple. It was during this period that Veṅkaṭarāman began to be known as the Brāhmaṇa Swami. For the first few weeks, he took refuge in the thousand-pillared hall, a large, square, raised stone platform with one thous—and sculptured pillars supporting a flat roof, open on all sides, which was used only once or twice a year on festival days. There he sat, stone-like, oblivious to his surroundings, rarely moving, immersed in the bliss of the Self. One would have imagined that this place would be a perfect dwelling for a contemplative ascetic. However, the young Sage's presence soon attracted the attention of young urchin-boys who, having nothing else to do, used to amuse themselves by throwing stones at his motionless body. So, though undisturbed himself, the young Sage shifted to a vault under the hall known as the *Pātāla-liṅgam.*

The vault was pitch dark, damp, dusky, humid, and extremely dirty, for it was seldom cleaned. There, at the back of the vault, leaning against the wall, the young boy sat immersed in the Self. Besides him, the only other inhabitants were ants, mosquitoes, and vermin that feasted upon his body, causing sores and abrasions from which blood and pus would ooze. Nevertheless, the young Sage was oblivious to his body and what was happening to it, oblivious to whether it was day or night. Venkatachala Mundali recounts:

> Proceeding inside (the vault), I could make out nothing for a while, as I was coming from the glare into the darkness. In a few minutes, the faint outlines of a young face became discernible in that pit. Somewhat frightened, I went out to the adjoining flower-garden, where a *sādhu* was working with his disciples. Mentioning the facts to them I took some of them with me. Even then the youthful figure sat motionless and with closed eyes, despite the noise of our footsteps. Then we lifted the Swami from the pit, carried him from the hall up a flight of steps and deposited him in front of a shrine of Subrahmanya. The Swami still remained unconscious, his eyes closed; evidently, he was in deep *samādhi*. We noted the large number of sores on the nether side of his thighs and legs, with blood and pus flowing from some of them, and wondered how any one could remain unconscious of his body amidst such torture. Regarding it as irreverence, nay impertinence, to make any further noise in such presence, we bowed and came away.[1]

Thus, providentially—and as was about to happen a number of times in rather quick succession—the young Sage was deposited at a new location, this time near the shrine of Subrahmaṇya. He resided there for about two months before being moved to an adjoining flower garden, then to a banana grove, and then the foot of an *iluppai* tree. From the time of the Subrahmaṇya shrine on, someone or other appeared to take care

---

[1] Arthur Osborne, *Ramana Maharshi and the Path of Self-knowledge*, 31.

of the food needs of the Sage. His seat of residence changed frequently. Gardens, groves, shrines—all were provided to give shelter to the Sage. The boy-Sage himself never spoke during this period. Not that he took any vow of silence; he simply had no inclination to speak.

During this period, the young boy remained deeply absorbed in the inner Self and thus, like a variation on a theme from his childhood, was moved about without his knowledge. If you remember, he was such a heavy sleeper as a child that his schoolmates would beat him without him being any the wiser. Thus it was that, during the first few years at Tiruvannamalai, the young urchin-boys sought him out and played the same type of game with his body. The only difference was that, this time, he was sunk in a deep state of bliss rather than sleep. Outwardly, it made no difference to him, but the pranks of these urchins sometimes reached the heights of stupidity and malice.

One day, as he sat deep in *samādhi* at the foot of the *iluppai* tree, a mischievous urchin, perhaps in order to test the intensity of the Sage's absorption, urinated all over the Sage, who, being deeply absorbed, was quite unaware of what had happened until sometime later when his consciousness surfaced and he wondered how he came to be all wet. Then, upon perceiving the smell, he understood what had happened. Wonderfully, there was not a trace of anger in the Sage; he thought to himself that perhaps he had performed a similar prank during his infancy and the whirling of time had brought its revenge.

As the *iluppai* tree was a place of much disturbance for the Sage, one day, in February 1897, a *sādhu,* Annamalai Tambiran, who belonged to an order of Saiva ascetics in charge of a small shrine known as Gurumūrtam, located in a suburb of Tiruvannamalai, suggested that the boy move there and live in quiet seclusion. The change of place made no difference to the boy-Sage, and so he agreed to the proposal. At Gurumūrtam, where he would remain for eighteen months, his life continued as before, and he could be found sitting on the ground for hours on end, neither opening his eyes nor being aware of what was happening around him. As in the *Pātāla Liṅgam*, ants, mosquitoes, and other insects attacked him, his hair became matted, and his finger-nails grew long and curly:

> The hair had got matted and woven like a basket. Small stones and dust had settled in it, and the head used to feel heavy. I had long nails and a frightful appearance. So people pressed me to have a shave, and I yielded. When my head was shaven clean, I began to wonder whether I had a head or not, it felt so light. I shook my head this way and that to assure myself that it was there.[1]

The boy's fame spread spontaneously because of his extreme asceticism. Increasing numbers of pilgrims and sightseers came to visit him, though he was averse to any show of pretentious pomp or ostentation. Human nature being what it is, even Annamalai Tambiram developed a desire to worship the Sage in the way he would worship the sacred image in the temple. Coming to know of this, a new chapter in the life of the Sage was about to unfold. He wrote in Tamil upon the wall with a piece of charcoal, "This (food) alone is service for this (body)." When Annamalai saw the writing, he understood at once two things: what it was that the boy wanted and did not want him to do; and that the boy could read and write Tamil.

After this incident, upon hearing that the young Sage could write, the head accountant in Tiruvannamalai approached him with a desire to discover who he was and where he was from. Continuous entreaties fell on deaf ears until the accountant finally, in desperation, produced a pen and paper and demanded that, unless and until he was told the name and native place of the boy, he would fast and not return to his office. Out of compassion, the young Sage yielded to the accountant's demands and wrote in English, "Veṅkaṭarāman, Tiruchuzhi." Now it was known that the boy could read and write both Tamil and English. But a puzzle remained. What did the name, "Tiruchuzhi", spelled with a "zhi", refer to? The young Sage noticed that the book that the accountant had given him upon which to write was a copy of the *Periya-purānam.* The boy opened it and turned to the page where Tiruchuzhi is mentioned as a sacred place, whose praise has been sung by one of the

---

[1] K. Swaminathan, *Ramana Maharshi,* 14.

Śaiva saints. Thus it was that the world came to learn of the identity of the young Sage and his native place.

While at Gurumūrtam, both Annamalai Tambiran and then, a few days later, Uddandi Nayanar, the two *sādhu* attendants, who were looking after the boy, were called back to the headquarters of their ascetic order. There was now no one to look after the boy. That was not a problem as the pilgrims and devotees who flocked to see the Sage vied with one another to provide him food. The problem was how to keep the crowds away and maintain some semblance of order. It so happened that there was a young spiritual aspirant from Kerala, Palaniswami, who was living nearby in a Gaṇeśa temple and performing daily worship of the deity therein. Several people advised him to stop serving this non-living image and go to serve the living God in the form of the boy-Sage. He paid a visit to the Sage and, upon seeing him, instantly gave his heart to him and lived with the Sage for the next twenty-one years, serving him with total and utter devotion and faith.

After a year and a half at Gurumūrtam, by which time the growing reputation of the young Sage was providing fuel for frenzied distractions, the young Sage and Palaniswami moved to a neighboring mango orchard. In May of 1898, the owner of the orchard offered them protected shelter from the large number of daily visitors. It was during this period that the young Sage acquired his first familiarity with some of the basic texts of Advaita Vedānta, such as the *Ribhu Gītā*, *Kaivalya-navanītam*, *Vedānta-cintāmaṇi* and the *Vāśiṣṭam*. Palaniswami was keen on studying such texts and used to go to the town and borrow them from the library there. They were written in Sanskrit, Telegu, and Malayalam and, as Palaniswami struggled with them only knowing Malayalam, he would often read them aloud to the young Sage for help in understanding them. It was through these texts that the young Sage discovered corroboration of his own experience and that they had been experienced and expounded by sages before him. Ramaṇa later told of his surprise upon hearing an exact description of his own exalted state described in the *Ribhu Gītā*. Until then, he had no idea that what had happened to him had been experienced by others and was greatly sought after by seekers of the truth from time immemorial. Remember, before his great change, Ramaṇa neither knew anything of the great Self nor practiced spiritual disciplines.

From the mango orchard the young Sage moved in quick succession, first to a small temple, next to the large temple for a week, then to a garden, and finally, in late 1898 he made his first move onto the mountain, Aruṇācala, at a spur called Pavazhakkunru. It was here that the Sage's mother, having been informed of her son's whereabouts, visited him in hopes of persuading him to return to Madurai. His mother pleaded, cried, beseeched, and begged, but received no response from her son. Then, upon being asked to at least write her a reply, he was given a pencil and piece of paper. He took the pencil and paper and wrote:

> The ordainer controls the fate of souls in accordance with their past deeds—their *prārabdha-karma.* Whatever is destined not to happen will not happen, try how hard you may. Whatever is destined to happen will happen, do what you may to stop it. This is certain. The best course, therefore, is for one to be silent.[1]

It was obvious her son was not going to return with her and so she returned to Madurai with a heavy heart.

What is remarkable about the Sage's reply to his mother is his unequivocal presentation upholding the doctrine of predetermination. Throughout history, both East and West, philosophers, religionists, and even ordinary people have grappled with the thorny question of predetermination and free will. Here was a modern Sage advocating emphatically a clear and definite doctrine of predestination. Many years later he was asked by Arthur Osborne, "Are only important events in a man's life, such as his main occupation or profession, predetermined, or are trifling acts also, such as taking a cup of water or moving from one part of the room to another?" The Sage replied: "Everything is predetermined."[2]

---

[1] Narasimha Swami, *Self-Realization,* 66.

[2] Osborne, *Ramana Maharshi and the Path of Self-knowledge,* 78.

This doctrine is so counter-intuitive and produces such extreme reactions in individuals who hear of it that we will take up the issue in more depth in a subsequent chapter. Nevertheless, there exists the possibility that either one is free to choose whatever one decides at any and every moment or else what is to be will be and all the choice that exists, if one does, is only the choice of accepting or rejecting, that is, to happily accept what happens or sadly reject what happens. We know, if we coolly and logically look at the situation, there do exist a plethora of factors that are definitely not in our control at any given moment. The way and what we see is determined by the particular rods and cones in the eyes; the heart beating and the blood circulating; the strength in the arms or legs or brain; gravity; H_2O; on and on. If this is so, if many factors are definitely not in our control, then how can one know that, in actuality, none of it is really in one's control (other than one's attitude towards what happens at any given moment). Thus, perhaps Ramaṇa's remarks are not as incredible or hard to digest as they might have at first glance appeared.

Life on Arunacala

The young Sage would now spend the next twenty-three years living in caves up the Arunācala hill. In India, caves have always had a mystic aura associated with Sages. There are references in the Upaniṣads to "the thumb-sized cave of the heart",[1] "the secret cave located in the body", and "the celestial cave." Caves are considered ideal places to reside and meditate, physically, symbolically, and mystically.

Having climbed the hill, the young Sage began to reside in the Virupākṣa cave, a place he would live in for the next seventeen years. This cave was associated with the 13th-century Sage, Virupākṣa, who allegedly lived and was buried there. The shape of the cave resembled the mystic syllable "*Om*" which lent it added sanctity.

---

[1] On the cave of the heart, see: SU 3.11; 3.13; 3.20; 5.8; MU 6.38; BU 4.4.2; 5.3.1; CU 3.1.4.3; 8.1.1-3; 8.3.3; TU 1.6.1; TU 2.1.1; KU 1.2.12; 1.3.1; 2.1.7; 2.1.12-13.

Life in the caves, so far as the young Sage was concerned, continued much as before. Most of the time he could be found sitting in a deep, inner absorption. However, it was from this time that his life became more public. Slowly, a select band of dedicated and earnest seekers formed around him and put questions regarding spiritual matters to him and brought him sacred books so that he might explain the contents to them. Sometimes, the young Sage would remain quiet, at other times he would answer verbally or write out his answers to their questions.

The first photograph of the Brāhmana Swami dates from the early Virupākṣa cave period. As well, it was during this period that the Brāhmana Swami acquired the title of Ramaṇa Maharshi, the name by which he would be forever known.

In 1903, a great Sanskrit scholar came to Tiruvannamalai, T. Ganapati Sastri, who became famous as Ganapati Muni, because of the severe austerities he had been observing. He had the title Kāvya-kaṇṭha (one who had poetry at his throat), and his disciples addressed him as *nāyana* (father). On a visit to the Brāhmaṇa Swami in December 1907, Ganapati Muni enquired as to the nature of austerity *(tapas):*

> Śāstri quivered with emotion as he walked up to the Virupākṣa cave. Luckily for him the Swami was seated alone on the outer raised platform. Śāstri fell flat on his face and held the Swami's feet with both hands and his voice trembled with emotion as he cried: "All that has to be read, I have read. Even *Vedānta Śāstra* I have fully understood. I have performed *japa* to my heart's content. Yet, I have not up to this time understood what *tapas* is. Hence, have I sought refuge at thy feet. Pray enlighten me about the nature of *tapas.*"[1]

For fifteen minutes, the Sage gazed silently at Ganapati Muni as he sat at his feet in anxious expectation. No one came to interrupt them at that time. Then the Sage spoke in short, broken Tamil sentences:

---

[1] Narasimha Swami, *Self-Realization,* 89-90.

> If one watches whence this notion of 'I' springs, the mind will be absorbed in that. That is *tapas.* If a *mantra* is repeated and attention directed to the source whence the *mantra*-sound is produced, the mind will be absorbed in that. That is *tapas.*[1]

Ganapati Muni was elated with this teaching and the next day declared to his disciples that the Brāhmaṇa Swami should henceforth be known as the 'Maharshi' (great Sage), since his teachings were original, just as the teachings of the ancient seers *(ṛṣi)* were original. Since that day, the name has stuck and it has resounded around the world as the name of the Sage of Aruṇācala.

To give someone a name is an important rite. In Sanskrit texts, name-giving is one of the sacred rituals or rites of passage (*samskāra*). As a sacrament, giving a name signifies the outward expression of an inner refinement and grace. It is intended to give one a distinct aura. It stands guard against undesirable influences. It may inspire and/or motivate one to live up to the name's meaning. It may also invoke grace through the propitiation of the deity, *nāma japa*, for the repetition of a deity's name (*mantra*) invokes the divine power. Bestowing a name is a defining mark.

One's name is the means whereby one is able to approach the named. It is a means to reach the goal, for the goal is contained in the means. Consciousness of the name leads to consciousness of the named. As one thinks, so one becomes, like a piece of wood that has been placed in a fire, sooner or later, turns into fire. Likewise, a mind that is immersed in God's name will eventually become Divine. The individual *(jīva)* becomes the Divine *(Śiva)* through the Name. The *Chāndogya Upaniṣad* says, "Meditate on the Name as Brahman".[2]

Can you think of the word 'tree' without also thinking of its form? There is an intimate connection between the name and the form it represents. Further, it is said that the name is even sweeter than the form. If one thinks of a mango, one

---

[1] Ibid, 90.

[2] CU 7.1.5.

immediately becomes happy, and one's mouth begins to water. The word "mango" conjures up an image of a large, sweet, perfect mango. But if one sees a physical mango, all sorts of doubts may arise: "Is it sweet? Will it be stringy? Will it taste oily? How much will it cost?"

A name hints at its physical appearance; some hint at its attributes; some hint at its function or personality, or temperament or life-history. They are his or her calling cards, so to speak. They invoke the salient features of the named. Names are adorations. The name leads to the form (all of creation is but name and form, *nāma* and *rūpa*). The manifest universe is but name and form; the Unmanifest Truth manifests itself cyclically so that one may relate to it. A Sage is said to give three gifts to the world: his name, his form, and his life's example. We will speak of these three gifts in chapter eight.

Ramaṇa's mother had come to Tiruvannamalai in 1898 in a failed attempt to bring him back to Madurai. After Ramaṇa's elder brother died and her domestic situation was far from satisfactory, she again visited Ramaṇa in 1912 and 1914 during pilgrimages she undertook. Finally, in early 1916, with a desire to spend her last days with her son, Alagammāḷ came to the Virupākṣa cave, and this time Ramaṇa accepted her as a member of the small *āśrama* family. She began to cook for the inmates, and in 1922 she died in a quite significant manner.

As her end was nearing, Ramaṇa laid his right hand upon her heart and his left hand on her head. As he explained:

> Innate tendencies and the subtle memory of past experiences leading to future possibilities became very active. Scene after scene rolled before her in the subtle consciousness, the outer senses having already gone. The soul was passing through a series of experiences, thus avoiding the need for rebirth and making possible union with the Spirit. The soul was at last disrobed of the subtle sheaths before it reached the final Destination, the Supreme Peace of Liberation from which there is no return to ignorance.[1]

---

[1] Arthur Osborne, *The Teachings of Bhagavan Sri Ramana Maharshi in His Own Words*, 78.

When he was asked whether the procedure he performed was a success, he said: "Yes, in her case it was a success; on a previous occasion I did the same to Palaniswami when the end was approaching, but it was a failure. He opened his eyes and passed away."

Since no burials are allowed on the sacred Aruṇācala hill, it was decided to bury her body at the foot of the southern slope of Aruṇācala, near Pāli Tīrtham. A thatched roof was erected over her *samādhi* and a hut was constructed with mud walls. For six months, Ramaṇa used to visit the site daily, and then in December 1922, he shifted permanently to the proximity of his mother's shrine. When asked why he had shifted from Skandāśramam, Ramaṇa replied: "The same power which brought me from Madurai to Aruṇācala brought me here." What is also noteworthy is that this became the starting point of Śrī Ramaṇāśramam, which grew around Ramaṇa and the mother's *samādhi*.

In 1947, Ramaṇa's health began to fail, and towards the end of 1948, a small nodule appeared below the elbow of his left arm. As it grew in size, the doctor in charge of the *āśrama* dispensary cut it out, though in a month's time it reappeared. Surgeons from Madras were called and they operated. The wound did not heal, and the tumor came again. On further examination, it was diagnosed that the affliction was a case of sarcoma. The doctors suggested amputating the arm above the affected part. Ramaṇa replied with a smile: "There is no need for alarm. The body is itself a disease. Let it have its natural end. Why mutilate it? Simple dressing of the affected part will do." Two more operations had to be performed, but the tumor appeared again. Indigenous systems of medicine were tried as well as homeopathy. The disease did not yield itself to treatment. The sage was quite unconcerned and was supremely indifferent to suffering. He sat as a spectator watching the disease waste the body. However, his eyes shone as bright as ever, and his grace flowed towards all beings. Crowds came in large numbers. Ramaṇa insisted that they should be allowed to have his *darśana*.

Once it so happened that the operating surgeon had to prod the raw wound thoroughly. Declining an anesthetic, Ramaṇa stretched out his arm. The doctor caught his breath. The Maharshi's face remained calm and serene, not a single groan issued from his lips. Duraiswami, who was there, could not bear the sight. The arm was bleeding so profusely, and he went away shedding tears. The Maharshi smiled and addressed a disciple who stood before him: "Duraiswami is crying because he thinks I am suffering agonies! It is true that my body is suffering. But oh, when will he realize that I am not this body?"

Mahasamadhi

The end came on April 14th, 1950. That evening, Ramaṇa gave *darśan* to the devotees who came. Everyone present in the *āśrama* knew that the end was nearing. They sat singing Ramaṇa's hymn to Aruṇācala with the refrain *Aruṇācala-Śiva.* The Sage asked his attendants to make him sit up. He opened his luminous and gracious eyes for a brief while. He smiled. A tear of bliss trickled from the outer corner of his eye. At 8:47p.m. the breathing stopped. There was no struggle, no spasm, none of the signs of death. At that very moment, a shooting star moved slowly across the sky, reached the summit of the holy hill, Aruṇācala, and disappeared behind it.

The Sage laughs with the laughing, weeps with the weeping, plays with the playful, sings with those who sing, keeping time to the song. Among children he is a child. Among humans he is a human. What does he lose? His presence is like a pure, transparent mirror. It reflects the image exactly as it is. But the Sage, who is only a mirror, is unaffected by actions. How can a mirror be affected by the reflections? On the other hand, the actors in the world, the doers of all acts, ordinary individuals, must decide for themselves what song and what action is for their own good, is for the welfare of the world, what is in accordance with the scriptures, and what is practicable.

In his life, Ramaṇa experienced, demonstrated, and expounded the astonishing idea that the inner Self, and not the external universe, was all there was. Incredibly, the mystery of everything could be explained by this simple idea. Once again, a revolutionary Sage revealed in his life and teachings how different a universe from the one most people believe they inhabit actually exists. The profound mystical philosophy of the *Upaniṣads* had once again taken a physical embodiment and revealed to the world the living Truth of its teachings.

II

A Bird's Eye View of Advaita

Where knowledge is of the Self, how can there be various kinds or grades? Knowledge of the Self is one. Proceeding step by step refers to the stage where one has turned away from the pursuit of sense objects and one's gaze is entirely directed toward the Eternal. The Self has not yet been realized, but the treading of this path has become attractive.

Introduction to Indian Philosophy

It is useful to begin an investigation into the Indian philosophical schools by stating the fundamental categories. There are eight fundamental categories common to all the Indian philosophical systems: valid means of knowledge *(pramāṇa);* truth and validity *(prāmāṇyam)*; error and invalidity *(aprāmāṇyam);* God/Reality *(Īśvara/Brahman);* individuals *(jīva);* physical universe *(jagat);* liberation *(mokṣa);* and the means to liberation *(mokṣa-sādhana).* The first three categories deal with epistemology and theories of knowledge. They ask and answer the question, "*How* does one know what is known?" Collectively, they are called an enquiry into knowledge *(pramāṇa-vicāra).* The next three categories deal with metaphysics, i.e. an enquiry into Reality. They ask and answer: "*What* is capable of being known?" They are known as an enquiry into reality or "thatness" *(tattva-vicāra).* The last two categories deal with liberation and the practical teachings thereto. They concern the application of metaphysics to life itself, as it is lived in daily experience. They ask and answer the question, "*Why* should a person enquire?" So they pertain to the purpose of enquiry *(prayojana-vicāra).* Thus, all the Indian philosophical systems, being school-oriented, concern themselves with the fundamental questions of *how, what,* and *why.*

Depending upon how one views philosophy, one can either found metaphysics upon epistemological grounds or epistemology on metaphysical grounds. Method and material are interdependent. Any theory of knowledge presupposes certain declared and undeclared metaphysical assumptions, and any metaphysical theory is blind without a sound epistemological methodology. Method is barren without material, and material is blind without methodology. In Indian philosophy, the general trend has been to base epistemology upon metaphysics, for the simple reason that revealed wisdom embodies a direct experience of Reality. Thus, the nature of Reality, as well as the possibility of knowledge, is revealed in revelation. The task left to epistemology is to identify the various sources of knowledge, the validity and truth of knowledge, and the problem of invalidity and error. With this ascertainment, epistemology could then declare the proper method, if any, by which Reality may be known.

Epistemological theories appear to have originally developed so as to intellectually establish, and safeguard the validity of the revealed texts and the sayings and experiences of Sages from the onslaught of skeptical attacks leveled against them. However, notwithstanding their original impetus, once this endeavor was commenced, it seems to have taken on a life of its own. Epistemological doctrines gradually separated from the religious context and questions were raised about the nature, origins, and instruments of knowledge. Theories arose to explore the possibility of knowing perceptual, non-perceptual, and transcendental entities.

What is Vedanta?

The earliest known occurrence of the word *"Vedānta"* refer to that part of the *Vedas* known as the *Upaniṣads.*[1] The term

---

[1]The word Vedānta first makes its appearance as a synonym for the *Upaniṣads* in two places: MuU 3.2.6-8 and SU 6.22.

"Vedānta" = *veda* (wisdom) + *anta* (end/essence), was used as a synonym for the *Upaniṣads* for two reasons, one literal/physical, the other conceptual/ philosophical: (1) Because the *Upaniṣads* are literally, physically, found at the back of the *Vedas* (i.e., at the end of the book), they are said to form the concluding portion or end of the *Vedas.* (2) Besides literally expressing the fact that the *Upaniṣads* form the concluding part of the *Vedas,* the term also expresses the idea that the *Upaniṣads* represent the *essence* of the *Vedas.* As such, the *Upaniṣads* as Vedānta, are spoken of as the crown or summit of the Vedic wisdom. Thus, the term "Vedānta" is the most apt synonym for the *Upaniṣads.* Like most Sanskrit terms, there is a *śleṣa* or multivalent element involved. The Sanskrit *"anta"*, like the English word "end", means both "end" and "essence", (e.g., "the end/essence of practice is proficiency"). This transparent multiplicity of meanings permeates the philosophy of Vedānta. Multiple meanings from multiple standpoints coexist, and each possesses both a truth and a use from a given perspective.

The word *"veda"* (wisdom) traditionally has three different referents (which need not necessarily be exclusive).[1] One meaning refers to a "direct inner intuitive knowledge." This is most dramatically reflected in the great sayings *(mahāvākya)* of the *Upaniṣads.* It is testimony to the experience of the oneness of the Self with the Absolute. Ramaṇa remarked: "The essential aim of the *Vedas* is to teach us the nature of the imperishable *Ātman* and show us that we are That." Latent within it is the insight that one is what one always is. One is the Self, here and now. To attain the unattained, action is necessary. But to attain the already attained, no action is required. To bring out the full implication of this particular usage, for the seer, the Vedic statement declares, "*Veda* is no longer *Veda.*" The *Upaniṣad* itself claims that *Veda*-as-a-direct-inner-intuitive-wisdom is merely a contextual expression:

> Where verily there is, as it were, a duality, there one smells, sees, thinks, knows another. But when to the Knower of the Self, where everything has become the

---

[1]The *Vedas* declare that three levels of scriptural interpretation happen simultaneously: the transcendent or spiritual (*ādhyātmika*); the intrinsic or cosmic (*ādhidaivika*); and the extrinsic or physical (*ādhibhautika*).

> Self, then by what and whom should one smell, see, think, and know? Through what should one know That owing to which all this is known? Through what, O Maitreyi, should one know the Knower?[1]

Secondly, the word *"Veda"* refers to revealed knowledge which has been divided into four collections: *Rgveda, Yajurveda, Sāmaveda*, and *Atharvaveda* (along with their numerous recensions) and divisions into *mantra, brāhmana, āranyaka*, and *upaniṣad.* Thirdly, the word *Veda* refers to "the entire body of Vedic revelation". This usage refers not only to the content or subject-matter of the *mantras*, but also the form of expression that they assume. The later schools of Vedānta will draw upon this usage to present a body of teachings, which will be used as external and internal aids for self-realization. This standpoint represents "practice based upon theory".

Therefore, depending upon one's point of view, this three-fold schema permeates the *Vedas.* We shall see that the Advaita tradition employs this insight as it speaks of: (1) the "thunderous silence" which "speaks" about the Unspeakable; (2) "words to live by" for the spiritual aspirant who is seeking personal experience; and (3) a "philosophy" for the seeker/scholar who desires a theory with conceptual consistency. In other words, there are seemingly different perspectives, viz. (i) one could say that Ramaṇa may be approached from a position of radical non-duality; (ii) a position of qualified non-duality; or (iii) a position of multiplicity. For instance: A man may be viewed from the perspective of himself; from the perspective of father and child; and from the perspective of an employee. In other words, one person is viewed from three perspectives, with each succeeding perspective involving a greater degree of separation from oneself: At first, one feels one is in the light (the world is external to you); secondly, the light is in you (the world is within you); thirdly, you are the light. Ramaṇa often adopted these three different standpoints (sometimes known as *ajati-vāda, dṛṣṭi-sṛṣṭi-vāda*, and *sṛṣṭi-dṛṣṭi-vāda,* and sometimes as *pāramārthika, vyāvahārika,* and *prātibhāsika*) when he spoke

---

[1]BU 2.4.14. The sage Yājñavalkya to Maitreyī.

about the nature of the physical world; one should note that one or the other of them is applicable to whatever he spoke about. It cannot be stressed enough that it behooves the reader to be consciously aware of from what/whose perspective he is speaking to.

Indeed, Ramaṇa never got tired nor wearied of asserting that, from the viewpoint of a Sage, there is only the one indivisible Self; there is neither a knower, nor known, nor any process of knowing; neither a *guru,* nor disciples, nor teachings; neither a liberated individual, nor any bound individual. The essence of his teachings is that there is a single, immanent, partless, indivisible Reality, directly experienced by everyone, that is simultaneously the source, the substance, and real nature of all that is. In an attempt to speak of this non-relational, ineffable, indivisible Reality, Ramaṇa referred to it by various names: the Self, true Knowledge *(svarūpa-jñāna),* the Fourth (*turīya*), the Heart, Existence, Consciousness, Bliss *(sat-cit-ānanda),* That *(Tat),* the Self *(Ātman),* the Absolute *(Brahman), Śiva,* to name but a few. One should not misunderstand this and think that Reality has attributes, names, or forms, but only that each name signifies the one non-dual Reality. "Truth (ultimate Reality) is One; Sages call it by different names."[1]

What is Advaita Vedanta?

Though there exists a plethora of source material, as well as thousands of secondary works on Advaita Vedānta, it is extremely difficult to convey exactly what "absolute non-duality" *(advaita vedānta)* is, apart from an intellectual understanding of it. This is because Advaita is described in three different, interrelated ways. First and foremost, it primarily points to a direct inner intuitive experience. At this level, silence is the only adequate "description" of pure non-duality; and silence is a woefully inadequate communicator for most people. Historically, when Gautama the Buddha was asked, "What is the Truth?" he remained silent. When Pilate asked Jesus, "What is the Truth?" he remained silent. An Upaniṣadic Sage, Vāskalin

---

[1] *Rg Veda.*

when asked by a seeker Bhava, "What is the Truth?" the former remained silent. Interestingly, when I am asked, "What is the Truth", I, too, remain silent. On the surface, all the four answers appear similar, and yet the first three persons remained silent out of wisdom, while I remain silent out of ignorance. Such is the difficulty before us.

At another level, Advaita Vedānta connotes a body of words to live by. At this level, it is a system of spiritual instructions or indicators for "obtaining the already obtained", i.e. Self-realization. Śaṅkara said: "When the knowledge of *Brahman* is firmly grasped, it is conducive to one's own beatitude and to the continuity of the knowledge of *Brahman*. And the continuity of knowledge of *Brahman* is helpful to people as a boat is helpful to one wishing to get across a river."[1]

Finally, and what is by far the most commonly used designation, Advaita Vedānta is a system of philosophy, a conceptual theory, one among many, and for many individuals, a rather distasteful, dry, and absurd theory at that. Philosophy is for the scholar who desires conceptual consistency. In other words, there are seemingly several Advaitas; however, it would be more accurate to say that Advaita has often been approached from three perspectives, though it should never be forgotten that the final word in Advaita is always the one, non-dual Self or *Brahman/Ātman*.

Advaita Vedānta, as a philosophical system, derives its name *"Vedānta"* from the fact that it is based on the teachings found in the *Upaniṣads*. The *Upaniṣads* constitute the foundation for the all Vedānta (philosophical) systems, and the qualifier "Advaita" was later applied to this original school in order to distinguish it from other Vedāntic systems which subsequently arose.[2] The source books foundational to all Vedāntic systems alike are: the *Upaniṣads*, the *Bhagavad-gītā*, and the *Brahmasūtra*. Together these three are known as the *prasthāna-traya*, (triple canon of Vedānta). *"Prasthāna"* means

---

[1] *Upadeśasāhasrī* 2.1.3.

[2] Vedānta is a commonly used name by many schools of philosophy that have all based their teachings upon the *Upaniṣads*. Because Advaita was the first philosophical school to do so, it is very often referred to as *"the* Vedānta".

"foundation" and thus, these three constitute the three foundations. They are known as: Primary Scripture, the *Śruti-prasthāna* (i.e., *Upaniṣads*); Remembered Tradition, the *Smṛti-prasthāna* (i.e., *Bhagavad-gītā*); and Reason, the *Nyāya-prasthāna* (i.e., *Brahmasūtra*).

The *Vedas* are known as *śruti* (that which is "heard"). Since the *Upaniṣads* form part of the *Vedas*, their name *śruti-prasthāna* is apt. The *Bhagavad-gītā* stands next to the *Upaniṣ ads* in authoritativeness and importance. As the *Bhagavad-gītā* forms part of the Indian epic, the *Mahābhārata*[1], which is a remembered text (*smṛti*), it is called *smṛti-prasthāna*. The *Brahma-sūtra* represents the standpoint of reason, because therein the Upaniṣadic ideas are set forth in a logical order. Thus, we see that the basic sourcebooks of Advaita, and therefore its basic doctrines, are based upon scripture supported by tradition and reason. Ramaṇa, through the efforts and enquiries of others, became acquainted with all these sourcebooks and would refer to them and even quote them when the need of the occasion presented itself. However, it may be noted that he himself wrote no commentaries on the *prasthāna-traya*, though due to circumstance he did translate a few Advaitic works for the benefit of his devotees. He had absolutely no aspirations to establish a philosophical school, or be a traditional (or any other type of) philosopher. He said, "I have no school."[2]

The central question for Vedānta concerns the nature of *Brahman*. Thus, the *Brahmasūtra*, which philosophically strings together the central concepts of the *Upaniṣads* in an orderly manner begins: "Now, therefore, the enquiry into *Brahman*."[3] And this enquiry is not only intellectual, but also practical. Advaitic thought circles around the theme, *"Ātman* is

---

[1] *Mahābhārata, Bhīṣma pārva*, chapters 25-42.

[2] Osborne, *The Teachings of Bhagavan Sri Ramana Maharshi in His Own Words*, 123.

[3] *Athāto brahma jijñāsā.* BS I.1.1. Every *sūtra* of the BS is based upon an Upaniṣadic passage. The verse upon which BS 1.1.1 is based comes from the BU wherein Yājñavalkya tells Maitreyī, "The Self ought to be known".

Brahman".[1] Ramaṇa's thought centered around this theme as well, though with a new emphasis as we will see.

Advaita's approach is Self-enquiry. Ramaṇa's approach also is Self-enquiry, though with a new approach and emphasis. Advaita's concern is for individuals, here and now. Ramaṇa's concern is for individuals, here and now. Advaita's goal is that which is eternally present, immediate, and accessible. So was Ramaṇa's. Therefore, one should note that Advaita and Ramaṇa are concerned about *Brahman*, about the Self, not because *Brahman* is great, but because the Self is *Brahman*. Ramaṇa was insistent that the spiritual quest begins with enquiry, an enquiry into the Self, into who one really is. He did this, not because the *Upaniṣads*, the *Brahmasūtra* or the Advaita tradition advocate such a view, but because it was the fruit of his direct experience of the Self. Why should Self-enquiry alone be the direct means to liberation? "Because every kind of spiritual discipline except that of Self-enquiry presupposes the retention of the mind as the instrument for carrying on the spiritual discipline, and without the mind it cannot be practiced."

Is it not a fact that every individual, in some way or other, must partake of the Reality? If this is granted, and it does appear to be a logical necessity, then each individual, in the final analysis, must investigate to find out who it is that does so. When push comes to shove, it is just not good enough that an ancient Sage or the Buddha or whatever God or great individual is enlightened, peaceful, blissful, and so on. Each individual wants a "piece of the action" too. Thus, one should begin an enquiry into who one really is. "Who am I" is where the quest begins, as well as ends.

Scholars have observed that Ramaṇa's teachings are, in essence, in accord with the Upaniṣadic and Advaita doctrines, and the remarkable thing is that he *first* had the experience and only *subsequently* heard and read about it. A person once remarked about this: "Theory he learnt later and recognized it, just as a woman who had borne a child might read afterwards about child-birth."[2]

---

[1]MaU 2.7. *Ayam ātma brahma.*

[2] Osborne, *The Teachings of Bhagavan Sri Ramana Maharshi in His Own Words*, 11.

To reveal the Self is the be-all and end-all of Advaita. This experience, Advaita further claims, is within the reach of all. The same method of approach may not suit everyone. The average person can have no knowledge of the particular combination of factors that is necessary to bring to completion the hitherto neglected factors of one's being. Thus, it is not really theory that Advaita advocates, so much as experience. "Philosophy is not his (Śaṅkara's) aim, but is rather a vital weapon with which to fulfill this aim, which is to rescue people out of transmigratory existence."[1]

Advaita means "non-duality". The prefix "non" applies not only to duality, but also to "isms" and "systems of thought". The goal of Advaita is not so much to "know about" the Self, as it is to "personally experience" the Self. If "knowing about" is helpful, or conducive to this goal, so much the better. But Advaita never loses sight of the fact that "I am the Absolute" is an experiential statement, not a theory. Gauḍapāda explained: "This view (that there is duality) is only for the sake of instruction. When the truth is known, all duality disappears."[2]

Literally, Advaita Vedānta means: "Non-duality *(a-dvaita)* (is the) end/essence *(anta)* (of) wisdom (*veda*)". The essence of Advaita, succinctly put, is contained in the following oft-quoted verse: "The Absolute is Real; the world is non-real; the individual human being and the Absolute are not different."[3] This insight is simple to state, but devastating in its implications, and requires a precise understanding. What-is is, "I am That" or, to change the phrase, "There is nothing which truly exists which is not That".

The "Absolute alone is real" for the simple reason that Advaita defines the Real as that which is always real, which never changes. Anything that comes and goes is, in the ultimate scheme of things, not worth pursuing or obtaining. Anything that changes is declared to be "other than the Real". The world is defined as non-real (not un-real), as illusory (in a particular

---

[1] *A Thousand Teachings: Upadeśasāhasrī*, 11-12.

[2] MK 1.80

[3] *Brahma satyam, jagan mithyā, jīvo brahmaiva nā 'paraḥ* .

definition of illusoriness), *in relation to* the Absolute. Everything in the universe changes, and thus it can't be ultimately Real. But the world is not totally unreal, i.e., like a square-circle or a married-bachelor, because it *does* appear. Thus it has a strange status known as "neither real nor unreal", as illusory. Finally, the Self is not other than the Absolute. This does not mean that the finite individual human being as comprised of name and form is the Absolute, but that the true nature of an individual is not other than the Absolute. Let us see how M. Hiriyanna explains the subtle meaning of this oft-quoted verse:

> Śaṅkara regards all diversity as being an illusion. But it is very important to grasp correctly the significance of so describing it. Śaṅkara's conception of the real *(Sat)* is that of the eternal Being, and *Brahman* is the sole reality of that type. Similarly, his conception of the unreal *(asat)* is that of absolute nothing. The world, in all its variety, is neither of the one type nor of the other. It is not real in this sense, for it is anything but eternal. Nor is it unreal in the sense defined, for it clearly appears to us as no non-entity can. Nobody, as it is stated in Advaitic works, has ever seen or is ever going to see a hare's horn or a barren woman's son. They are totally non-existent. Further, it possesses, unlike non-entities, practical efficiency or has value, being serviceable in life. This is the reason why the world is described in Advaita as other than the real and the unreal *(sadasad-vilakṣaṇa)* or as an illusory appearance. The serpent that appears where there was only a rope is neither existent nor non-existent. It is psychologically given, but cannot be logically established. In other words, the things of the world, though not ultimately real, are yet of a certain order of reality. They are appearances in the sense that they depend for their being upon some higher reality. The "serpent", for example, points to the existence of the rope, and the dependence is one-sided, for while the disappearance of

the rope necessarily means the disappearance of the serpent, the reverse does not hold good.[1]

Synopsis of Advaita Vedanta

The central question for Vedānta concerns the nature of *Brahman*. The *Brahma-sūtra*, which philosophically strings together the central concepts of the *Upaniṣads* in an ordered manner, begins with: "*Athāto brahma-jijñāsā* (Now, therefore, the enquiry into *Brahman*)." Thus, Advaita begins its philosophical enquiry, here and now. Its metaphysics is immanent and not transcendent. *Brahman* is involved in, and is the basis of, all one's experiences. This is a key point because it has several far-reaching consequences. Advaita is primarily and foremost an enquiry into *Brahman*—the reality that is intimately and immediately involved in the individual's experiences. However, though *Brahman* is seemingly enmeshed in one's experiences, It is not consciously present to one's consciousness, at least not as the things of the empirical world are. The individual must make an earnest enquiry and divine *Brahman* through discrimination. Though *Brahman* is not something to be gained afresh, it does need to be discriminated from the not-Self. This search is not divorced from experience, nor is it outside one's daily experience. It comes through an analysis of one's day-to-day experience, at all levels.

The most distinguishing features of Advaita Vedānta are: (1) The non-difference of the individual human being *(jīva)* from the Absolute *(Brahman);* (2) the distinction between the absolute *(pāramārthika)* and relative *(vyāvahārika)* standpoints; (3) the doctrine of illusion/ignorance *(māyā/avidyā);* and (4) the conception of liberation here and now *(jīvan-mukti).* These features are also found, in some form or other, in Ramaṇa's thought, though one is tempted to say that the greatest distinguishing element of Ramaṇa's thought is his "Who am I?" methodology.

---

[1] *The Essentials of Indian Philosophy*, 155-58.

Absolute Non-Duality

I

The quintessence of Advaita is its doctrine that the individual human being is non-different from the Absolute. This essential identity is most directly and eloquently expressed in the four "Great Sayings" *(mahāvākya)* of the *Upaniṣads:* "The Absolute is Consciousness,"[1] "The Self is the Absolute,"[2] "That thou art,"[3] and "I am the Absolute,"[4] The inner meaning of these great sayings directly reveals, "All this is only One" *(ekam eva advitīyam).* In other words, That (Absolute) alone am I in which there is no form or formlessness, it is beyond name and form, transcending even the beyond. It does not imply, as some interpreters seem to think, that *Ātman/Brahman* is a "bare nothing". Śaṅkara foresaw this possible misinterpretation, for he said, "*Brahman,* free from space, attributes, motion, fruition, and difference, being in the highest sense and without a second, seems to the *slow of mind* no more than non-being."[5] In the *Vivekacūḍāmaṇi,* he says:

> What is the use of dilating on this subject? The individual is no other than the Absolute; this whole extended universe is *Brahman* Itself; the scripture persistently urges only *Brahman,* one without a second. It is an indubitable fact that people of enlightened minds who know their identity with *Brahman* and have given up their connection with the objective world, live palpably unified with *Brahman* as eternal knowledge and bliss.[6]

---

1 *Aitareya Upaniṣad* III.1.3 of *Rgveda, "prajñānam brahma".*

2 MaU 2.7 of *Atharvaveda, "ayam ātma brahma".*

3 CU VI.8.7 of *Sāmaveda, "tat tvam asi".*

4 BU I.4.10 of *Yajurveda, "aham brahmāsmi".*

5 CU *Bhāṣya* 8.1.1 and BSB 2.2.22.

6 V 394.

This identity of an individual with *Brahman* needs clarification. It is the individual in its true essential nature, *as Ātman,* which is identical with *Brahman* and not the individual as is empirically encountered. In the ordinary world, an individual thinks of oneself as an egotistic mind-body complex. This is an illusion, a delusion, an expression of ignorance caused by ignorance.

The essence of Advaita is persistently declared again and again, "You are That, here and now." To the person who objects, "But is not my search proof of my having become lost?" the reply comes, "No, it only shows that you *believe* you are lost." For, what are you in search of? How can you find that which you already are? A Sage once said, "Let me tell you a simple fact. If you set aside your ego for a moment, you will realize that you, the traveler, are that which you are seeking. Everything is within you. The supreme inner stillness is your destination."

Or, to word it another way, "Any seeking is a denial of the presence of the sought". To paraphrase Śaṅkara, "Why are you looking for the Self or God in city after city, temple after temple? God dwells in the heart within. Why look in the East and in the West? Don't look for God, look for the *Guru.* God dwells within you; in truth, you are God. You don't need to find God, you need to find a *Guru* who will guide you to yourself." How much similar is he to Ramaṇa, "The word 'liberation' *(mukti)* is so provoking. Why should one seek it? One believes that there is bondage and therefore seeks liberation. But the fact is that there is no bondage, but only liberation. Why call it by a name and seek it?" The questioner adds, "True, but we are ignorant." Ramaṇa replied: "Only remove ignorance. That is all there is to be done. All questions relating to *mukti* are inadmissible. *Mukti* means release from bondage that implies the present existence of bondage. There is no bondage and therefore no *mukti* either."[1]

Throughout history, individuals have found themselves tossed between the twin banks of pleasure and pain, gain and loss. They are seemingly alienated from themselves, alienated

---

[1] M. Venkataramiah, *Talks with Sri Ramana Maharshi*, 193.

from others, and alienated from the Absolute. From such a perspective it makes sense to ask, "How is it possible for a finite, relative, mortal individual human being to be identical with an infinite, immortal Absolute?"[1] Each of the Great Sayings *(mahāvākya)* of the *Upaniṣads* imparts a threefold knowledge that Advaita seizes upon to provide an answer to this question. First of all, the *mahāvākyas* remove the deep-seated misconception that the individuals are finite, bound, imperfect, and mortal beings; and conversely, they reveal that the true Self of each individual is infinite, ever-free, ever-perfect, immortal. Secondly, they remove the wrong notion that the supreme Reality is remote, hidden, unattainable, and declare that It is immediate, direct, the innermost Self of all. Thirdly, they reveal that there are not separate individuals *and* an Absolute. Instead, they declare unequivocally, "You are That," without an iota of difference. In other words, Advaita rejects all the three types of difference: "There is nothing similar to *Brahman*; there is nothing dissimilar to *Brahman*; and there is no internal variety."[2] Ramaṇa often quoted this verse about the three types of difference and their inapplicability to the Self. "The Self alone is and nothing else. However, it is differentiated owing to ignorance. Differentiation is threefold: of the same kind; of a different kind; and as parts in itself. The world is not another Self similar to the Self. It is not different from the Self; nor is it part of the Self."[3]

When individuals mistakenly superimpose various qualities (e.g. mortality, imperfection, gender distinction, and so on) upon themselves and the opposite qualities (e.g. immortality, perfection, omniscience, distance) upon the Absolute, Advaita resorts to a series of negations *(neti-neti)* to correct this misunderstanding.[4] Śaṅkara, commenting on this says, "The

---

[1] This is a frequently asked question in independent Advaita manuals.

[2] PD II.20. *Sajātīya vijātīya svagata bhedara hitam.*

[3] Venkataramiah, *Talks with Sri Ramana Maharshi*, 131. Quotes like this from Ramana are prolific throughout his talks.

[4] See BU 2.3.6; III.8.8; KU 1.3.15; *Upadesasāhasri* 17.70.

Absolute can never be properly denoted by any words, including the word 'Absolute' *(Ātman/Brahman)*."[1]

Hence, in the Advaita tradition, though there are passages like "Everything is *Brahman*",[2] "*Brahman* is Existence, Knowledge, Infinitude,"[3] "the Self is all this,"[4] "the world is an unbroken series of perceptions of *Brahman* and hence nothing else but *Brahman*,"[5] until one's ignorance is destroyed, such statements will neither be correctly understood nor experienced as true. Ramaṇa remarked: "The bonds of birth and death will not cease merely by doing many repetitions of the great sayings. Instead of wandering about repeating 'I am the Absolute,' you abide as the supreme Self yourself." The spiritual aspirants aspire towards a goal (the Self). Their viewpoint is conditioned by, "my body, my practices, my goal". From such a perspective, it is not possible to realize that nothing whatsoever is apart from the Self.

Any personal effort necessarily comes from the very same illusory separate individual from which one is seeking escape. It should seem obvious that the ego cannot understand that which it is not. The Self is not an "object" to be seen, felt, or obtained. Though there is nothing that It is not, to look for It is to lose it. The seeker is the sought. One cannot "hold" It, but then one cannot get rid of It. An individual person can only be concerned with the process of "becoming". Yet the Self is, and therefore cannot be attained or achieved.

Thus, for spiritual aspirants, Advaita speaks of "not-this, not-this", which is given, not so much as to say that appearances are not applicable to the Absolute, as to indicate the impossibility of attributing any conceptualization to It. The Self is beyond description, beyond what the finite mind can fathom. The Self is called *"a-dvaita"* to point to the fact that there is nothing that it may be compared.

---

[1] BU *Bhāṣya* 2.3.6. "There is no other and more appropriate description than this "not-this."

[2] CU 3.14.1, *Sarvam khalvidam Brahman.*

[3] TU 2.1, *Satyam, jñānam anantam Brahman.*

[4] CU 7.25.2.

[5] V 521.

It is the thesis of Advaita that the Self is ever-present and yet, one does not realize it. The entire problem for each individual can be reduced to the simple question of "knowing" or "not-knowing". With Vedānta there is actually nothing to be done; it is only a matter of understanding, but that understanding has to be *very accurate and refined.* Though the Self's nature is inexpressible, it cannot be denied. "A man may doubt of many things, of anything else; but he can never doubt his own being."[1]

The purpose of Advaita, of Ramaṇa, of the *Guru*, and of spiritual disciplines, is to kindle an awakening to this ever-present, already established Self. This it does by drawing one's attention to the fact that appearances cannot appear independent of a reality that upholds them. But we are getting ahead of ourselves. To realize that one is the Self, one must make an enquiry into the nature of the Self, the content of the notion "I". Advaita declares that the Self is not a hypothetical postulate. It is the most immediate, direct, and certain perception of all. Because one believes in oneself, the thinker, seer, hearer, and so forth, one has faith that what one thinks, sees, and hears is "real". Instead, why not doubt the things which come and go, for example, thoughts, sights, and sounds, and hold onto that which is always there and is foundational to it all, one's Self. The "I am" can never be changed into an "I am not." To say "I do not exist" is to affirm the "I" who will do the doubting.[2] *What* is experienced, as well as its meaning, is always open to doubt. But that *someone* experienced is certain.

Advaita asks one to enquire into exactly who this "I" is. It is seeking the ultimate unity that pervades the universe of multiplicity. To discover this essence, Advaita employs numerous methods. It employs the "time-honoured" method of prior superimposition and subsequent denial.[3] Because individuals find themselves superimposing qualities upon themselves, and upon the Absolute, one is led from the familiar to the unknown. Gradually, attributes are negated as a deeper

---

[1] BSB 2.3.7.

[2] V 240; *Upadeśasāhasrī* 1.2.1.

[3] BG *Bhāṣya* 8.12.

and deeper analysis is performed. One's attachment becomes detachment, and the Self finally stands revealed. Hand in hand with this method is "not-this, not-this". Or, to mention but one other method, Advaita employs *mantras* for conveying the Self. According to Advaita, the well-known final discipline for Self-realization is to hear the liberating word *(śravaṇa)*, reflect upon it *(manana)*, and digest and experience its purport *(nididhyāsana).*[1]

Advaita traditionally commences with an enquiry into the Self. How does one refer to oneself? Only as "I". It is one single syllable. Every person says "I", but who is making an effort to know what this "I" exactly is? One usually refers to the physical body when one speaks of "I", but a little reflection will reveal that the "I" cannot be the physical body. The body itself cannot say "I", for it is inert.[2] One says, "this is *my* coat, this is *my* hair, this is *my* body." What is "mine" belongs to me. "My" is a personal possessive pronoun implying ownership. What belongs to me is not me. I am separate from it; I possess it. Whatever I possess, I can dispense with, and still remain who I am. On a deeper level, when one says "I", one is referring to the faculties of thinking, feeling, and willing. Yet the same analysis applies. These are *my* thoughts, *my* feelings, *my* emotions—they come and go. I know them. I am the knower, and they are the known. No one says, "I am this shirt" or "I am this house". Likewise, it is a mistake to superimpose one's body, one's thoughts, and one's feelings, upon the "I".[3]

What is this "I"? In the body arises a sense of awareness. As a collection this is usually called the mind. What is the mind but a collection of thoughts. And this collection is where the "I" functions as their basis. Every thought relates to you, the "I", either directly about you or connected with you as individuals, objects, things, events, opinions. In other words, every thought is rooted in your "I". So what is this "I"—where is it rooted? Track it to its source. This process Ramaṇa called *ātma vicāra* or an enquiry into the Self.

---

[1] BU 4.4.22.

[2] V 87-92; *Ātmabodha* 10-11.

[3] V 93-96; *Ātmabodha* 12.

Advaitins propose that the "I" *(jīva)* performs two searches: one outwards and empirical and the other inwards and spiritual. When the *jīva* identifies itself with the mind-body complex, there arise the notions of "I" and "mine". This association is the result of an interaction among the Self, ignorance, the internal organ, and external objects. The Self which is one and non-dual is non-relational. When the Self associates with ignorance, it develops numerous relations with objects.

There is a pseudo "I", the empirical "I", and there is the real "I", the *Ātman* or Self. Between the ever-luminous Self (which neither rises nor sets) and the non-real, not-Self, the insentient body (which cannot of its own accord say, "I"), arises a false "I" which is limited to the body, the ego, and this meeting place is known as *cit-acit-granthi,* the knot between the sentient Self and the insentient body. The term "I", when used by the not-Self is but a convenient label.

Then, what is the "I"? Advaita avers that a little reflection will reveal that upon awakening from sleep, the first thought that arises is the "I"-thought. One thinks, *"I* slept well last night" or *"I* am still tired" or *"I* am going to the bathroom". First, the "I", and then the drama of one's life. Further, there is not a single thought anytime, which does not first invoke this "I". One has never, and will never have, a thought or experience without this "I" being present. It is the pillar around which each and every thought clings. Every thought relates to the "I", either directly or in connection with other individuals, objects, things, events, opinions, and so on. The "I" is the basis for everything else—the entire myriad universe of second and third persons, the universe of he, she, and it. Everything, inclusive, is rooted in one's "I".

Before anything can come into existence, there must be someone to whom it comes. All appearance and disappearance presuppose a change against some changeless background. The "I" is that support. One is not "what happens" to oneself, but to whom things happen. Who am I? Advaita avers that it is enough to know what you are not. The "I" is not an object to be known. Truly, all one can say is that "I am not this, not that". The "this" and "that" of the world come and go. But the "I" persists. If one can point to something, one cannot meaningfully say, "I am (only) that." If one can point to something, one is obviously more than that. One is not "something else" and yet, without you, nothing can be perceived, nor imagined either.

II

To understand, let alone appreciate, any philosophical system demands that one comprehend its particular perspective. In Advaita Vedānta, it is crucial that one understand the distinction made between the absolute *(pāramārtika)* and the relative *(vyāvahārika)* points of view.[1] This distinction pervades the entire system, and what is true from one point of view is not so from another. Without being absolutely clear regarding this distinction, it is likely that one will not only misinterpret Advaita's doctrine, but further accuse the Advaitin of inconsistencies, contradictions, and absurdities. One must be absolutely clear that these two "levels", two "truths" distinction is but a pragmatic device and does not mean, that there are *really* two truths or levels.

To illustrate the Advaita doctrine of perspectives with a simple analogy: From the sun's perspective, the sun neither rises nor sets; there is neither darkness nor concealment nor varying shades of light. By definition, darkness cannot be where light is. However, from the perspective of an individual upon the earth, the sun rises and sets; there are both light and darkness and varying shades in between, and it is valid to label the sun's light an enemy of darkness. Two seemingly contradictory propositions, both equally valid, and true, once their particular perspectives are correctly understood. Nevertheless, note that what is valid from one perspective *is not* from another. From the sun's perspective, "all is light". From darkness' perspective, there is relative light and relative darkness, and every shade in between. The question is, "Which do you identify with; are you the physical body, or are you the Self?"

While Advaita acknowledges that distinctions *appear* unique and individual at the empirical level, all distinctions lose their distinct individuality from the Absolute point of view. That

---

[1]MK 4.25; BSB 1.1.11.

is, "All this is *Brahman*" is absolutely true while "all this is individually separate and distinct" is relatively true. What is true from one point of view or level of reality is not from another. However, this does *not* mean that there are two realities, two truths. There is one Reality, as seen from two different perspectives. Śaṅkara avers that one perspective is from the point of view of ignorance; it is relatively true, (the sun seemingly rises and sets), while the other point of view is from the perspective of wisdom (I am the Light). The sun is *seen* to traverse across the sky, and yet everyone knows that it does not move! Water is *seen* in a mirage, and yet there never has been water there, nor will there be, nor is there now. I see my body and yours, and a myriad others, and yet I may be mistaken as to the validity of what I see. *That* I see something is not in question; *what* that something is, is the question.

The Advaita position is that there are not two types of being, nor two truths, but one reality, one truth, as seen from two different perspectives. This is the entire crux of the matter and precisely the point that is most easily misunderstood.

> *Brahman* is known in two forms as qualified by limiting conditions owing to the distinction of name and form, and also as the opposite of this, i.e. as what is free from all limiting conditions whatever . . . thus many texts show *Brahman* in two forms according as it is known from the standpoint of knowledge or from that of ignorance.[1]

Compare Ramaṇa's statement when a questioner enquired: "Some people say that *Brahman* is real; that the world is illusion is a stock phrase of Śrī Śaṅkarācārya. Yet others say the world is reality. Which is true?" Ramaṇa replied:

> Both statements are true, but at different levels of understanding and experience. The absolute truth is the Reality is non-dual. There is only Being in Self-realization, and nothing but Being. But the term "reality" is used also in a different sense and is applied

[1] BSB 1.1.11.

> loosely by some thinkers to objects. It is as a concession to them that degrees of reality are recognized. When one has recognized the absolute Truth, there is no sense in talking about degrees of truth or of reality.[1]

From the point of view of ignorance of the Self, Advaita admits of numerous distinctions, while from the absolute perspective of wisdom, of a Sage, there is only *Brahman/Ātman*, one and non-dual. Because it acknowledges these two perspectives, it is able to address and make sense of the metaphysical riddle of the One and the many; of how individuals are seemingly different from one another, and of the existence of a seeming plurality of things. Epistemologically, there is the problem of the subject-object dichotomy, as well as the problem of truth and error. Ethically, there is the problem of bondage, freedom, and the means thereto. Without these two perspectives, all such problems are philosophical enigmas.

Either a person is bewitched by multiplicity (and thus said to be under the sway of ignorance) or one experiences the all-pervading Consciousness. The pluralism that is experienced at the empirical level, and with which philosophical enquiry, and spiritual disciplines commence, is what is in question. Merely because one imagines that one is a distinct, limited physical being, a finite entity in a universe of infinite entities, does not make it so. Advaita avers that there is the Self, one and non-dual, not "my self", "his self", "her self". Because an individual is misled by the seeming diversity of names and forms, minds and bodies, one imagines multiple selves. However, that does not mean that multiplicity is the only vision possible.

All the great Advaitins throughout the ages not only realized the Self and emphatically declared that the Self alone is real, but then spent their lives in making clear what the duties of people are, compassionately assisting everyone to the goal of life. From the absolute perspective, the goal is emphasized. From the relative perspective, the means are emphasized. The aim is to know one's Self. But in order to know, one must *be able* to know.

---

[1] Venkataramiah, *Talks with Sri Ramana Maharshi*, 28.

Three Approaches to Creation Theories

Ramaṇa explained to a devotee that there are three modes of approach, or standpoints, to the metaphysical problem of creation. He spoke about all of them at different times, but it is clear from his comments that only the first one is always true and that the second mode is useful for spiritual aspirants:

> I do not teach only the *ajāta-vāda* doctrine. I approve of all schools. The same truth has to be expressed in different ways to suit the capacity of the hearer. The *ajāta* doctrine says, "Nothing exists except the one reality. There is no birth or death, no projection or drawing in, no seeker, no bondage, no liberation. The one unity alone exists." To those who find it difficult to grasp this truth and who ask, "How can we ignore this solid world we see all around us?" the dream experience is pointed out and they are told, "All that you see depends on the seer. Apart from the seer, there is no seen." This is called the *dṛṣṭi-sṛṣṭi-vāda* or the argument that one first creates out of one's mind and then sees what one's mind itself has created. Some people cannot grasp even this, and they continue to argue in the following terms: "The dream experience is so short, while the world always exists. The dream experience was limited to me. But the world is felt and seen not only by me, but by so many others. We cannot call such a world non-existent." When people argue in this way, they can be given a *sṛṣṭi-dṛṣṭi-vāda* theory, for example, "God first created such and such a thing, out of such and such an element, and then something else was created, and so on." That alone will satisfy this class. Their minds are otherwise not satisfied and they ask themselves, "How can all geography, all maps, all sciences, stars, planets, and the rules governing or relating to them and all knowledge be totally untrue?" To such it is best to say, 'Yes, God created all this and

so you see it. All these theories are only to suit the capacity of the learner. The absolute can only be one."[1]

The highest and supreme mode is the theory of non-origination *(ajāta-vāda)* as expounded by Gauḍapāda.[2] (However, even this perspective is but an approximation to the truth, a teaching with which Ramaṇa is in complete agreement. Gauḍapāda said, "*Ajāti* is meaningful only so long as *jāti* (birth) carries meaning. The absolute truth is that no word can designate or describe the Self."[3] From this level there is no creation, no birth, no death, no dissolution, no bondage, no liberation, and no one striving for liberation. It is a Sage's experience that nothing has ever happened, because the Self alone exists as the sole unchanging reality. From this perspective, the (relative) reality of the world is not denied. A Sage perceives appearances like anyone else. However, the Sage does not perceive the world as comprised of separate objects. An appearance is not unreal merely because it is an appearance. The real nature of an appearance is inseparable from the Self and partakes of its reality. What is not real is to mentally construct an illusory world of separate, interacting objects. Ramaṇa said, "The world is unreal if it is perceived by the mind as a collection of discrete objects, and real when it is directly experienced as an appearance in the Self."

The next mode, which is a middling concession to the absolute truth for seekers who find the *ajāta-vāda* impossible to digest, posits that creation is simultaneous with perception *(sṛṣṭ i-dṛṣṭi-vāda)*. According to this perspective, the world arises like a dream on account of a person's own thoughts induced by the defect of not knowing oneself as the non-dual Self. With the arising of the "I"-thought, the world simultaneously comes into existence and ceases to exist when the "I"-thought ceases. The world only exists when it is perceived. Upon awakening from sleep, the first thought a person has is the "I"-thought and upon

---

[1] Mudaliar, *Day by Day with Bhagavan*, 132.

[2] See MK; also KU 1.2.18 "The knowing Self is never born; nor does it die at any time"; BU 4.4.20; *BG* 2.20 "The Self is neither born nor does it die"; V 111 "It is not born; it does not die; it does not grow; it does not decline; it does not change. It is eternal."

[3] MK 4, 74.

its emergence, the entire universe consisting of objects other than oneself springs into existence. Once the "I"-thought, mistakenly taken as meaning "me" (male, father, professor, thin, healthy, etc.) arises as the subject, then everything other than me becomes an object. In deep sleep, when the "I"-thought is absent, so is the universe. This is everyone's personal experience, though they refuse to admit so. Ramaṇa would encourage his followers to accept this theory as a working hypothesis because, if one is constantly regarding the world as an unreal creation of one's mind, then it will lose its attraction, its seductiveness, and it will be easier for that person to then maintain an undistracted awareness of the "I"-thought. Thus, this theory is "true" in so far as the mind of an unenlightened person does create an imaginary world for itself. At the same time, from the standpoint of the Self, an imaginary "I" creating an imaginary world is no creation at all and thus does not contradict *ajāta-vāda.*

Finally, there is the "what has been created is perceived theory" *(sṛṣṭi-dṛṣṭi-vāda)* which is the ordinary common sense view that believes that the world is an objective reality governed by laws of cause and effect which can be traced back to a single act of creation by a creator. This theory states that the world exists prior to anyone's perception of it and that it is external to oneself. Ramaṇa only invoked this theory when the person he was speaking with was unwilling to accept either of the other two theories. Invariably, Ramaṇa would tell such a questioner that the theory of "what is created is seen" should not be taken too seriously, as all it does is to satisfy one's intellectual curiosity.

> There may be any number of theories of creation. All of them extend outwardly. There will be no limit to them because time and space are unlimited. They are, however, only in the mind . . . creation is explained scientifically or logically to one's own satisfaction. But is there any finality about it? Such explanations are called gradual creation. On the other hand, simultaneous creation is instantaneous creation. Without the seer, no objects are seen. Find the seer and

the creation is comprised in him. Why look outward and go on explaining the phenomena that are endless?[1]

The Key Concept of Advaita

The cornerstone of any philosophical system is that "key concept" upon which the system revolves; and such a key concept is *avidyā/māyā.*[2] This calls for a little explanation in order that a possible misunderstanding does not result. Critics sometimes label Advaita Vedānta as "illusion-theory" *(māyā-vāda),* and Advaitins are called "illusionists" *(māyā-vādins).* These terms are used disparagingly, and yet there is a grain of truth in the matter. *Avidyā/māyā* cannot exist, or function, independent of *Brahman,* and it ceases to bewitch a person once *Brahman* is realized. However, strictly speaking, *Brahman* is the be-all and end-all of Advaita, and if anything, Advaita should be called *"Brahma-vāda"* This is so because Advaita never loses sight of its central doctrine that *Brahman* is real, the world is non-real, and the individual is non-different from *Brahman.* Ramaṇa remarked:

> Śaṅkara was criticized for his views on *māyā* without being understood. He said that: *Brahman* is real, the universe is unreal, and the universe is *Brahman.* He did not stop at the second, because the third explains the other two. It signifies that the universe is real if perceived as the Self, and unreal if perceived apart from the Self. Hence *māyā* and reality are one and the same. At the level of the spiritual seeker, you have got to say that the world is an illusion. There is no other way. When a man forgets that he is *Brahman,* who is real, permanent, and omnipresent, and deludes himself into thinking that he is a body in the universe which is

---

[1] Venkataramiah, *Talks with Sri Ramana Maharshi,* 209.

[2] BSB 1.1 Preamble; See Radhakrishnan, *Indian Philosophy,* Vol. II, 565. Also See R. Balasubramanian in *Perspectives of Theism and Absolutism in Indian Philosophy,* 48. The extensive scholarship over the philosophical differences between *"avidyā"* and *"māyā"* arose only after Śaṅkara's time. Post-Śaṅkara *avidyā* or ignorance was said to pertain to the individual while *māyā* or illusion pertains to God who wields it.

> filled with bodies that are transitory, and labors under that delusion, you have got to remind him that the world is unreal and a delusion. Why? Because his vision, that has forgotten its own Self, is dwelling in the external, material universe. It will not turn inwards into introspection unless you impress upon him that all this external, material universe is unreal. When once he realizes his own Self he will know that there is nothing other than his own Self and he will come to look upon the whole universe as *Brahman.*

It would appear that for Ramaṇa, ignorance *(avidyā)* is a term that is fundamentally and basically a description of an affliction of the psyche, an existential description of a state of being, an experiential realm of ignorance. It is not a metaphysical entity, a full-blown philosophical concept, so much as it is a useful tool and a description. If this is so, and it should be, as it would be in keeping with the feeling that Ramaṇa was first and foremost concerned with an individual's liberation and not with philosophy *per se,* then I believe that a case may be made that the Advaita teachings of Ramaṇa, are first and foremost meta-philosophies.

Śaṅkara defined ignorance *(avidyā)* as: "the mutual superimposition of subject and object, the mutual transposing of the Self and the non-Self, the unacceptable combining of true and false."[1] In the same place, he also said that "learned men regard this superimposition *(adhyāsa)* thus defined as *avidyā*"[2] and that superimposition is the imposition of a thing on what is not that thing *(atasmims-tad-buddhiḥ*). As well, he said: *"Avidyā* is *parameśvarāsraya,* that is, ignorance depends upon *Brahman.* And in it *(avidyā*) individuals, having lost their identity with *Brahman,* rest."[3] Ramaṇa defined *māyā* as: *"Māyā* is that which makes us regard as non-existent the Self, the Reality, which is always and everywhere present, all-pervasive and self-luminous, and as existent the individual soul *(jīva),* the

---

[1] BSB 1.1.1.

[2] Ibid.

[3] Ibid. Also see *Upadeśasāhasrī* 2.2.51.

world *(jagat*), and God *(para*) which have been conclusively proved to be non-existent at all times and places."[1]

As a philosophical term, *avidyā/māyā* is crucial to the understanding of Advaita. Since Śaṅkara did not differentiate between *avidyā* and *māyā*, as post-Śaṅkarite Advaitins did, I present the two terms as one key concept here.

Avidyā/māyā is the means, not the end. It is an explanatory concept. Within Advaita, any "means" exists only at the relative level. From the absolute perspective, one is the Self, one does not become the Self. When the rope is seen, there is no question about a snake. When the Self is realized, there are no questions about *māyā*. Thus, *māyā* is a provisional explanation as to how the eternally all-pervasive Self appears otherwise to deluded individuals. Though *avidyā/māyā* is not ultimately real, its importance cannot be exaggerated for the role that it plays. No one can deny that individuals seemingly *perceive* multiplicity and distinctions. How does this happen?

> *Ātman,* the self-luminous, through the power of one's own *māyā*, imagines in oneself, by oneself (all the objects that the subject experiences within or without). This unborn, changeless, non-dual *Brahman appears* to undergo modification only on account of *māyā* and not otherwise.[2]

According to Advaita, the real is that which is eternal, which suffers no sublation, while the unreal is that which never is. Advaita contends the unreal can *never* appear, not even in one's wildest dreams, e.g. a square-circle or the child of a barren woman. Because appearances are *perceived,* they cannot be said to be unreal *(asat).* Similarly, because the real *(Sat)* never changes, appearances, which change, cannot be called real *(Sat).* Therefore, appearances are indeterminable. How miraculous, mysterious, inscrutable! All that is perceived as "other than you" is neither real nor unreal! There never has been, nor is, nor will be, water in a mirage and yet, somehow, it

---

[1] S. Natanananda, *Spiritual Instructions*, 2.6.

[2] MaU with Gauḍapāda's *Kārikā* and Śaṅkara's *Commentary,* 2.12; 3.19.

is perceived. Thus, Advaita calls all appearances, *sadasad-vilakṣ aṇa*, “what is other than the real or the unreal”. It is only in this sense that the seeming plurality of the universe is called “illusory” *(māyā).* Any enquiry into *māyā* is not to make the concept intelligible, but to enable one to go beyond it. Once one has destroyed ignorance, there remains no problem to be solved, no questioner to enquire whether appearances are real or not.

By the criterion of completeness, the Self alone is absolutely real. All else will be called “real” only by courtesy. The distinction between one individual and another, the existence of a plurality of things, the superimposition of attributes on the Absolute are all concessions to the Truth made from the relative point of view. By this criterion, *avidyā/māyā* is not a second entity. Only a person under the spell of ignorance perceives its effects. The sun does not ask, “Where is this darkness you speak about?” Because one denies what one is, the Self, and superimposes upon the Self what It is not, the not-Self, does not therefore make the not-Self real.

Liberation-While-Living

Finally, since Advaita is primarily an enquiry into the Self, the reality that is involved in, and is the basis of, an individual’s every experience, the Self is everyone’s birthright. The Self is here and now; not something to be obtained from outside, at a later time. The Absolute is not a God, above and beyond. That thou art declares the *Upaniṣad.* Thus, according to Advaita, *Ātman* and liberation *(mokṣa)* have the same meaning. This leads us to the nature of spiritual disciplines, and ultimately to the concept of liberation-while-living *(jīvan-mukti*).

In the Advaita tradition, all manifestations are considered but name *(nāma)* and form *(rūpa).* This is a subtle point. According to Advaita, so long as the seeker regards him/herself as a separate individual human being, then spiritual disciplines are absolutely essential. The final position *(siddhānta)* of Advaita is that there is no teacher, no taught, no teachings. “All this is *Brahman* only.” But until that vision becomes an experienced realization, Advaita advocates a series of preliminary disciplines, i.e. righteous behavior consisting of external remote aids which help purify the mind *(nitya-naimittika karmas),* the four fold proximate aids to spiritual discipline *(sādhana-catuṣṭaya),*[1] and the principal proximate aids of hearing the truth, reflecting upon the truth, and digesting the truth *(śravaṇa, manana,* and *nididhyāsana).*[2] Obviously, all of these disciplines presuppose and demand the presence of a teacher, an aspirant, and teachings as well as a place in which to practice the teachings. Advaita is not averse to spiritual disciplines such as the various *yogas* and all the myriad *sādhanas,* but considers them as being but preliminaries to liberation.

Another way in which the "means to liberation" can be analyzed is to analyze the nature of the aspirant. When an individual's sense of duality is very strong and their practices are predominantly external, then their spiritual disciplines fall under the category of "remote aids". When an individual's sense of distinctness is middling and their practices are predominantly internal, then their spiritual disciplines may be subsumed under the category of "proximate aids". Finally, when an aspirant's direct awareness of reality is awakened within through the grace of the preceptor *(guru),* and only a subtle distinction exists between the goal and the path, then such a one's disciplines are called the "principal proximate aids".

Hence, Advaita envisions a series of spiritual disciplines ranging from the grossest, most external, remote disciplines, all the way to liberation itself, about which, at the highest level, nothing can be said. There is no disciple, nor is any discipline rejected. Whichever means is adopted depends upon the nature and understanding of the disciple. Developing in different ways,

---

[1] I.e. the ability to discriminate between the transient and the eternal; the absence of any desire for securing pleasures or avoiding pain, either here or elsewhere; the attainment of the virtues, calmness, temperance, spirit of renunciation, fortitude, power of concentration of the mind, faith; a burning desire for liberation (*mumukṣutva*).

[2] The principal proximate aids obviously involve a *guru* who conveys the sacred text, a student who listens to the text, and a place where this knowledge is conveyed. Hearing involves removing any doubts one may have as to what one should know (the Self). Reflection removes any doubts one may have as to what one should know as to what the Self is like. Digestion is for removing any remaining thoughts that one is not the Self. Of the principal proximate aids, there are two types: Those statements (*avāntara vākya*) which indirectly convey wisdom and those statements (*mahāvākya*) which directly illumine the disciple.

from differing initial states, each disciple's practice leads to greater states of awareness, eventually culminating in the Self. Indeed, Śaṅkarācārya said: "Until a person awakens to the knowledge of their identity with the Self, liberation can never be achieved . . ."

> Therefore, let the wise person give up craving for pleasure in external things, and struggle hard for liberation. Let such a one seek out a noble and high-souled teacher, and become absorbed wholeheartedly in the truth that is taught by him.[1]

Though the transcendental Self is radically personal, individuals are not consciously aware of it in the way that they are aware of sense-objects. Human beings, with their outward turning sense organs, have been fascinated with an external world consisting of innumerable persons, places, things, and events. But in dealing with something that is not an object, and is totally unrelated to space-time concepts, their attention has been inadequate. Instead of directing one's attention outwards to the world of "others", one should learn to direct one's attention inwards, towards the indwelling Self.

In other words, to seek the Self, an individual must make an earnest enquiry into the Self through discrimination. Though the Self is not something to be gained afresh, it does need to be discriminated from the not-Self. Such a search is not divorced from, nor outside of, one's personal experience. This means that, at any given time, an aspirant's qualifications and readiness determine how seriously, earnestly, and completely one seeks the Self.

Vedānta teaches that one is the Self, here and now. Why one does not realize this ever-present fact and suffers, is due to ignorance.[2] Individuals aver, "I am deficient, inadequate, incomplete, right now." The evidence for this appears overwhelming. "Isn't it a fact that I am a male or female, who is compulsively pursuing pleasure and security? I am full of

---

[1] V 6; 8.

[2] BSB 1.1. Preamble; V 55; 137; 192.

desires, wants, and needs." Further, the fulfillment of these desires is so incredibly important precisely because they are going to be the means of one's fulfillment. The logic of separation is easy to understand: "What one doesn't have, one must obtain to thereby become complete." However, what is usually overlooked is that sense enjoyment has a double sting: it takes off the edge of the sense organs by making them blunt, and it sets the mind afire by making the mind desire for more of the same enjoyment. The mind wants enjoyment, but the body can't take it. One burns the candle at both ends. One is roasted in one's own desires. Desires are the root of suffering.

But the Self is not another "object", even the greatest of objects, to be obtained. The Self is the seeker as well as the sought, even though the seeker does not know this due to ignorance. Since the individual, as the not-Self, is neither real nor unreal, the very question of an individual self seeking union with the Absolute is ludicrous. And yet, if one does not seek, one will not find. As the *Gītā* says:

> Though quite self-evident, easily knowable, quite near and forming the very Self, *Brahman* appears to the unenlightened, to those whose understanding is carried away by the differentiated phenomena of names and forms created by ignorance, as unknown, difficult to know, very remote, as though he were a separate thing.[1]

The idea that the individual, as individual, is a mere fiction, and its corollary, that the individual is really here and now, the Self, is the purest Advaita. Generally, this is too difficult a teaching for one to digest immediately and thus arises the need for a gradual awakening. One is led from the unreal to the real, from darkness to light, from death to immortality, step by step. This is the general teaching of Advaita philosophy. Any, and every "other", be it an experience or an object, is, by definition, going to be ultimately inadequate. Experiences and objects come and go. Since they have a beginning, and they will have an end. The "other" must ultimately disappoint one. Thus, if there is truly something called the Self, something called

---

[1] BG 18.50.

completeness, it must be present, here and now, or it cannot be at all.

> The real teaching of Vedanta is that the ignorance that is destroyed never really existed. To destroy ignorance and attain bliss is to destroy what never was and to attain what we have always had.[1]

The final teaching of Advaita, from the absolute perspective, is that there is not incompleteness during *sādhana* and completeness upon liberation; there is no duality during spiritual practices and non-duality during liberation.[2] There is only the ocean of the Self, before, during, and after. This leads us to Advaita's conception of the nature of achievement. There are said to be two types of attainment: attainment of the not-yet-attained and attainment of the already attained. What has not-yet-been-attained, the attainment of a new automobile, is achieved in space and time. It may be attained by a limited effort and will produce a limited result, i.e. a new car. This type of attainment always involves both gain and loss. One gains a new condition and loses one's old condition.

However, Vedānta also talks about another type of attainment, "obtaining the already obtained."[3] To obtain the already obtained, neither space nor time is involved. One can only obtain that which one does not already have. Since there never was a time when one was not the Self, the *Upaniṣads* say: "And being already released, he is released; Being already *Brahman*, he attains *Brahman*."[4]

Since Advaita declares that liberation can be "attained" here and now, provided a person makes oneself fit, one need not wait until death overtakes the physical body. Such a person is called a *jīvan-mukta*, liberated even while living in a body.[5] The continuance of the body is in no way incompatible with the state

---

[1] Swami Muktananda, *Secret of the Siddhas*, 169.

[2] V 569-572.

[3] *Ātmabodha* 44.

[4] KU V.1; BU IV.4.6.

[5] BS 3.4.51; BU *Bhāṣya* 4.4.6; V 425-442; 551-54.

of Self-realization. What happens is merely a change of perspective; ignorance has been destroyed. Right knowledge of the Self puts an end to ignorance. If the body were real, then liberation could come only after the destruction of the body. But since one is not the physical body, its continued appearance or disappearance is of no consequence. From the standpoint of the *jīvan-mukta*, there is only *Brahman/Ātman*. It is to the ignorant that the *jīvan-mukta* appears to tenant a body. Even to refer to such a one as "him" or "her" is due to one's ignorance. The Self alone exists.

Ramana as a Philosopher

Right from the start, let us be clear. From the absolute perspective or settled conclusion *(siddhānta)* of Ramaṇa, there is no teacher, no taught, no teachings; there is no birth, no death, no universe; no enlightened being, no unenlightened being, and no path to enlightenment; there is no knower, no known, and no means of knowledge. There is only the one, indivisible Self. This is the highest and only supreme Truth. The Self is Truth and Truth is the Self. When it manifests itself, it manifests as Love. But from the perspective of an ordinary person under the sway of ignorance of the Self, the so-called unenlightened person, the entire universe of multiplicity seemingly exists and shouts out for explanations and answers. Thus, any issue that arises may be approached from either of these two angles.

One can discuss Ramaṇa's life and teachings from either of these viewpoints and give appropriate references to illustrate such. For instance, Ramaṇa replied in varying ways to the question, "What should I do?" He has replied, (1) There is no one to do anything. Nothing has ever happened. Your life in this world has no more substance than experiences or objects occurring in an illusion, a mirage, a hallucination or a dream; or (2) Whatever is destined to happen will happen, and whatever is not destined to take place will not; or (3) Begin Self-enquiry, cultivate the virtues, meditate, perform spiritual practices, and so on. Take responsibility with confidence.

Time, place, circumstance, qualification all must be taken into consideration. If the reader does not keep this in mind nor is able to understand from what perspective a reply is given, then confusions, inconsistencies, and/or contradictions will arise.

It may seem to a non-philosopher that philosophy is a dry, difficult, and mysterious subject. But it is actually not that complicated. A philosopher has a lot less information to absorb than those in many other disciplines. The task of a philosopher primarily consists in learning to ask fundamental questions, and in mastering the paradigms that are exemplary in dealing with these questions concerning the three main categories of philosophy (the Absolute/God, the world, and individual human beings) and the three basic questions (how, what, and why). Understand and apply the paradigm, and everything else should fall into place logically, consistently and coherently.

Philosophy the world over concerns itself with three basic questions: *how* does one know what one knows? (epistemology); *what* is knowable? (metaphysics); and *why* one should know? (practical teachings). What distinguishes philosophy from a mystic Sage's experience is that philosophy involves a rational investigation and explanation that involves rigor, coherence, and consistency, and it advances reasons for the answers it provides, while mystical utterances are not systematic, well thought out intellectual statements, but expressions based solely on the mystic's personal experience. This is a traditionally held distinction.

Was Ramaṇa a philosopher? Virtually every author who has written about Ramaṇa emphatically states that the Maharshi was not a traditional philosopher and that his teachings were not philosophy in the strict sense of the term. This is an oft-voiced view, and it is certainly the case that he did not instruct others to think out problems or analyze the world from a theoretical point of view. Ramaṇa was definitely not a systematic thinker or professional philosopher presenting a logically thought-out system of principles. He continually emphasized that thought must be eliminated, for it is in the elimination of thought that one discovers the deeper awareness that is behind and beyond thought. Ramaṇa said:

> Holding the mind and investigating it is advised for a beginner. But what is mind after all? It is a projection of the Self. See for who it appears and from where it rises. The "I"-thought will be found to be the root-cause. Go deeper. The "I"-thought disappears, and there is an infinitely expanded "I"-consciousness.[1]

One should also note that Ramaṇa had very definite views on the value of philosophy and its usefulness. Examples of his words on the subject include:

> Some theoretical knowledge is needed for Yoga and may be found in books, but practical application is what is needed. Personal example and instruction are the most helpful aids. As for intuitive understanding, a person may laboriously convince himself of the truth to be grasped by intuition, of its function and nature, but the actual intuition is more like feeling, and requires practical and personal contact. Mere book learning is not of any great use. After realization all intellectual loads are useless burdens and are to be thrown overboard.[2]
>
> Pre-occupation with theory, doctrine, and philosophy can actually be harmful, insofar as it distracts a man from the really important work of spiritual effort, by offering an easier alternative which is merely mental, and which therefore cannot change his nature.
>
> The intricate maze of philosophy of the various schools is said to clarify matters and to reveal the Truth, but in fact it creates confusion where none need exist. To understand anything there must be the Self. The Self is obvious, so why not remain as the Self? What need to explain the non-self?

---

[1] Venkataramiah, *Talks with Sri Ramana Maharshi*, 273.

[2] Ibid, 28.

> I was indeed fortunate that I never took to it (i.e. philosophy). Had I taken to it, I would probably be nowhere; but my inherent tendencies led me directly to enquire "Who am I?" How fortunate!

This being noted, Ramaṇa lived, spoke, wrote, and taught a type of philosophy, if one concedes to this term, which is known as Advaita (if it may be so called). Ramaṇa was a master of non-duality. He did not expound a closed system of philosophy, nor did he tell what reality is. All he ever did was to point to the total and absolute experience of non-duality where there is no split between subject and object, where there are no distinctions at all. Let me explain. When asked if his teachings were the same as Śaṅkara's, who is universally considered to be one of India's premier philosophers, if not its greatest, Ramaṇa replied: "My teachings are only an expression of my own experience and realization. Others find that it tallies with Śrī Śaṅkara's."[1]

Thus, the question arises: in what way, if at all, may Ramaṇa's teachings be said to be philosophy, and did he make a contribution to it as one of its builders? One can always "read" philosophy into or out of someone's teachings. But what I am asking is whether it is insightful and meaningful, in some sense or other, to think of Ramaṇa as a proto-philosopher and investigate his proto-philosophy as philosophy? Shouldn't this be obvious? "Proto" means "prime; original" and in Ramaṇa's case, *before* he knew of philosophers and philosophy, he experienced what they speak about. One could compare it to a person "having a child and then only later getting married."

Ramaṇa is an Advaitin. Regarding theory, his statements are amazingly similar, especially with those made by *ajāti-vāda* Advaitins. Where there exists a fundamental difference philosophically is with regards to the traditional Advaita's doctrine and attitude towards practice. Generally speaking, Advaitin's proscribe a system of meditation that mentally affirms that the Self is the sole reality. The famous injunction quoted is *śravaṇa, manana, nididhyāsana.* Thus, the great sayings such as "I am the Absolute" or "That thou art" are

[1] Osborne, *The Teachings of Bhagavan Sri Ramana Maharshi in His Own Words*, 223.

generally used as *mantras* or *foci* of meditation. On the other hand, Ramaṇa advocated self-enquiry.

Though, it is rarely stated by scholars, Advaita Vedānta is not *just* one of the orthodox systems of Indian philosophy but is an exposition and revelation of the non-dual Reality. The philosophy of Advaita is not a system of thought, is not an "-ism", is not truly speaking a school among schools of philosophy. The "non" applies both to duality, as well as, any "isms," or a system among systems. Ramaṇa and Advaita are in total agreement about this. The implications of this mean that Advaita Vedānta is not merely, or only, a philosophical school of thought, but that it was founded and grounded in a deeper sphere; and though Ramaṇa is not a philosopher in the strict sense of the term, his teachings may be fruitfully analyzed from this radical philosophical perspective. Ramaṇa himself first called his own thought, "intuitive knowledge of the heart".[1] He spoke about doctrines only when doubts expressed by scholarly devotees had to be cleared, or questions had to be answered. He came to know of these doctrines only long after he had the experience of non-duality.

In order to form a correct understanding of Ramaṇa's teachings, one must be clear about why, when, and how he employs various concepts, categories, and arguments. His thought appears to be intellectually simple, because it revolves around just two categories, the Self and the not-Self, in terms of which they explain God/Absolute, human beings, and the world, or, everything that can be known, the means to know what can be known, and the purpose thereof.

I believe I am on safe ground to state that, like such ancient Sages as Uddālaka, Aṣṭāvakra, Dattātreya, Ribhu, and Gauḍapāda before him, Ramaṇa sometimes, on occasion when asked by ardent seekers, *did* present rational explanations and illustrate them with examples *vis-a-vis* the non-dual Self. Though he himself was not interested in philosophy, due to fortuitous (for us) circumstances he came into contact with philosophical writings mainly through the efforts of

---

[1] 'Self-enquiry' in *Collected Works*, 28.

Palaniswami.[1] To cite but a few instances, Ramaṇa often quoted or referred to various Advaita scriptural and philosophical works/passages; he often alluded to the three philosophical standpoints of *ajāta-vāda, dṛṣṭi-sṛṣṭi-vāda*, and *sṛṣṭi-dṛṣṭi-vāda* (the theories that: nothing ever happened at all; that perception is creation; and that creation is that which is perceived); he employed traditional philosophical analogies such as the rope-snake, shell-silver, red-crystal, reflection of the sun in pots of water, reflections in a mirror, movie screens, and dreams. The number of examples that could be cited is actually very, very large.

Further, like the Sages of old, he successfully demonstrated in his life and sayings that the non-dual Self is not a theological dogma and that it does not depend even upon the mystical experiences and sayings of Sages; it is the great Truth which forever has been, is, and will be and that Silence is eloquence *par excellence*. Even if there were no texts, or if the texts differed from Ramaṇa in their teachings (which actually is not the case), Ramaṇa's personal experience was, is, and forever will be self-validating, a wonder to behold.

It is often said that Ramaṇa communicated and transformed mainly through silence. He said: "Silence is never-ending speech. Vocal speech obstructs the other speech of silence. In silence one is in intimate contact with the surroundings. Silence is true exposition; it is the perfect teaching *(upadeśa)*." A teacher employing words necessarily implies the dualities of the teacher, teachings, and the taught, while Ramaṇa's truth, his silence, embodied the pure non-dual Essence. Ramaṇa himself said: "The *Guru's* silence is the loudest teaching *(upadeśa)*. It is also grace in its highest form. Silence is the most powerful form of teaching transmitted from master to adept."

While it is true that Ramaṇa said his silent teachings were more direct and more powerful, he used verbal expositions when asked. It is primarily from these verbal teachings that we explore Ramaṇa's philosophy. Silence has an ancient history of being the supreme mode of teaching in Advaita.[2] Further, this

---

[1] See chapter one.

[2] See the *Upaniṣads*.

reverence reaches its peak in the figure of the young, silent Sage, Daksināmūrti, whose name is universally depicted as the form of Lord Śiva, as the grace-bestowing *Guru*, the primordial *Guru* of *gurus*. On the same side of the road, down from the Ramaṇāśrama, stands a Dakṣiṇāmūrti Maṇḍapam, a temple Ramaṇa often referred to. Śaṅkara gave a famous, oft quoted hymn praising the young Sage and silence: "A young Sage is sitting with aged disciples under a banyan tree. The Sage teaches in silence and the doubts of the students are dispelled."[1] Ramaṇa would often cite this verse as approval to those who came for teachings.

Advaita employs a number of different methods by which to convey "Self-knowledge" linguistically. Human beings not only want to know the unknown; they also want to know the unknowable. One such method is described by Śaṅkara in his commentary on the *Bhagavad-gītā*. This method has been time-honored in the Advaita tradition as the traditional method for teaching the trans-phenomenal *Brahman*.[2] It employs the technique of prior superimposition and subsequent denial *(adhyāropa* and *apavāda)*. First, qualities and relations like perfection, infinitude, omniscience, omnipotence, omnipresence, causality, etc., are superimposed upon the Absolute so as to enable one to form some sort of understanding. Then, gradually these attributes are negated as a deeper and deeper analysis is performed. From the familiar, one is led to the unfamiliar. From the known, one is led to the unknown. As Śaṅkara put it: "Their aim (religious knowledge) is to be the means of detachment from the objects towards which one is naturally attracted."[3]

A second method, which goes hand-in-hand with the above technique, is the method of *via negativa*. The *Bṛhadāraṇyaka Upaniṣad* says: "Now therefore the description (of *Brahman*): 'Not this, not this'. Because there is no other and more appropriate description than this 'not this'."[4] Śaṅkara, commenting on

---

[1] See *Dakṣiṇāmūrti Stotra and Dakṣiṇāmūrti Upaniṣad.*

[2] BG 8.12.

[3] BSB 1.1.4.

[4] BU 2.3.6.

this passage, says that the Absolute can never be properly denoted by any words—including the word "Absolute". Thus, the only appropriate way to indicate the Self is to say, "not this, not this". Though no positive description of the Absolute is possible, Advaitins claim that a negative characterization may be comprehensible. Its import is not so much to say that there are no characteristics applicable to the Absolute as to indicate the impossibility of attributing any conceptualization to it. Thus "not this, not this" has been called a way or manner of expounding the Truth. Ramaṇa, when asked if "not this, not this" *(neti-neti)* was an appropriate meditation, replied, "There is now wrong identification of the Self with the body, senses, and so on. You proceed to discard these and this is *neti.* This can be done only by holding to the one that cannot be discarded. That is *iti* (that which is; the Self)."

An often, overlooked phenomenon occurred in the life of Ramaṇa connected with *via negativa.* As Ramaṇa's great awakening was taking place, he did not know of the theory or practice of "not-this, not-this", and yet he mentally said to himself, "Now, death has come. What does it mean? The body dies. I am not the body, I am not the mind . . . this was not a mere intellectual process, but flashed before me vividly as living truth." In rejecting his body, mind, and so on, Ramaṇa had undergone a comparable, though non-intellectual, process of *neti-neti.*

A third technique consists in the use of metaphor and analogy. Ramaṇa often alluded to metaphors, and those he employed usually involved superimposition.. The Self is said to be indicated, pointed to, through implication. Since the Self cannot be known by the express meaning of words, Sages often resort to analogies. An illusory silver is superimposed upon a shell; an illusory snake is superimposed on a rope; the Self is said to reside in the heart-cave; consciousness is described as an ocean; multiple suns are reflected in a pail of water; multiple colors are reflected in a crystal, and so on. It is easy to see why metaphors are often used by Advaitins to explain, show by example, how the One may appear as many. For instance, there is the analogy of the sun being reflected in water. The role of an illustration is to refer to some common feature(s). When two things are compared, they are compared only with reference to some particular point(s) they have in common. It is well known that no comparison is ever totally equal, for, if they were the case, there would not be a comparison but identity. The special feature of the sun that warrants comparison in this case is known as "participation in increase and decrease". The reflected image of the sun increases when the water expands, and contracts when the water shrinks. Further, the reflected image trembles when the water is agitated, and divides itself when the water is divided. Thus, the reflected image participates in all the conditions and attributes of the water even as the real sun remains unaffected all the while. Similarly, the Self, although changeless, participates as it were in the attributes and states of the body. It seemingly grows, shrinks, and so, as the body grows, shrinks, and so on.

When a person's attention is on the reflection, it ignores the real sun in the sky. In order to perceive the original, one must turn one's attention from the reflection to the prototype. The sun does not include the pot, the water, and the reflection. If anything, they are there only to turn one's attention to the original. One should not mistake the reflection for the original. Imagine a big building collapsing. Some rooms are in ruins, others intact. But can one speak of the space as ruined or intact? The structures suffer damage and change, not the space. A goldsmith melts down old ornaments to make new ones. Sometimes a good piece accidentally goes with the old. He is not worried. He knows that no gold has been lost. Transformation is only a verbal handle, a name. Gold is gold, no matter what shape it is in. Water is water, no matter as appearing as waves, whirlpools, bubbles, or drops. Clay is clay whether in the shape of a pot, a mug, or a plate.

There are two ways in which ineffability may be understood. There is the literal meaning implying that there is an utter impossibility of any description of the Self at all. Obviously, Ramaṇa did not accept this definition in that he did not shun language. He only stressed the inadequacy of language to capture reality. He did not preclude talking about the Self; otherwise he would have remained totally silent. The other way one may interpret ineffability means an inability of language to do justice to the Self, because language is conceptual and polarized. Neither thought nor language can escape these limitations, but that doesn't necessarily imply that it can't be a useful, almost indispensable approximation. All terms which Ramaṇa used for the Self such as *sat-cit-ānanda*, the Heart, *Brahman, svarupa-jnāna, turiya,* and so on, even though they are outdistanced by the Self, serve some sort of use at the rational level.

Another possible technique for conveying knowledge of the Self is silence as we have already noted—a technique that was Ramaṇa's favorite:

> Preaching is simple communication of knowledge; it can really be done in silence only. What do you think of a man who listens to a sermon for an hour and goes away without having been impressed by it so as to change his life? Compare him with another who sits in a holy presence and goes away after some time with his outlook on life totally changed. Which is the better, to preach loudly without effect or to sit silently sending out an inner force?

To know "That" is the end-all and be-all of life according to both the ancient Upanisadic wisdom and also to Ramaṇa. In some sense or other this is the purpose of philosophy. Yet, it must be noted that the Hindu culture does not have a univocal word for the term "philosophy." However, this being acknowledged, the term *"darśana"* is widely considered to be the most appropriate Hindu terminological analogue to "philosophy." *Darśana* is abundantly and profoundly rich with meaning. *Darśana,* from the Sanskrit root meaning "to see", implies not only "vision" (which includes insight, intuition, and vision of the truth), but also the instrument of vision (such as viewpoint, worldview, doctrine, philosophical system). In a word, *darśana* implies "sight" in all its myriad connotations and the term, like many of the Sanskrit terms, is pregnantly multi-significant, multivalent. Thus, besides expressing "viewpoints or perspectives", the term also suggests the idea of "right vision or (Self)realization" *(mokṣa).*

The former meaning customarily refers to the great Indian philosophical systems, one of which is Advaita Vedānta. Philosophically, from this perspective, Advaita is not so much a search for the truth as it is an exposition, elaboration, clarification, vindication and conceptual fixation of what has been experienced. From this view, it is always second-hand, indirect, and conceptual. The latter meaning, on the other hand, refers to the person experiencing a vision or insight. In this case, it is direct, personal and experiential. In other words, the "seeing" implied by the term *"darśana"* includes, both conceptual knowledge *and* perceptual observation, critical exposition *and* intuitional experience, logical enquiry *and* spiritual insight, concrete and abstract, gross and subtle. It is my contention that Ramaṇa's thought was a philosophy if one wants to use that term, primarily in this latter sense and only secondarily in the former.

The English expression "I see" contains a hint of this multivalence in that it denotes both a "direct vision" (I see the tree) as well as a "correct understanding" (a three year old child when told that two plus two equals four exclaims, "I see, I understand". In passing, it may be noted that this second "inner sight" is actually more reliable than one's external sight. As well, the term *darśana* is also used, in certain contexts, to refer to the "audience or auspicious sight of a revered, great, or holy person, a Sage, deity, or place." Regarding "sight", Śaṅkara said:

> Seeing is of two kinds, ordinary and real. Ordinary seeing is a function of the mind as connected with the visual sense; it is an act, and as such it has a beginning and an end. But the seeing that belongs to the Self is like the heat and light of fire; being the very essence of the Witness (Self), it has neither beginning nor end . . . The ordinary seeing, however, is related to objects seen through the eye and of course has a beginning . . . The eternal seeing of the Self is metaphorically spoken of as the Witness, and although eternally seeing, is spoken of as sometimes seeing and sometimes not seeing.[1]

Bhagavān asked: "Can the eye see itself?" Reply: "Of course not. It can see everything else, but not itself." Bhagavān:

---

[1] Śaṅkara on BU 3.4.2.

"But what if it wants to see itself? That is it! Creation is the mirror for the eye to see itself." Reply: "Do you mean e-y-e or I?" Bhagavān: "You can take it figuratively as e-y-e and literally as 'I'."

One should never lose sight of the fact that the word *"darśana"* is rich with meaning. The *darśanas*, as philosophical systems of thought, embody the cumulative reflection of Indian wisdom through the ages and include epistemology, metaphysics, ethics, social customs, aesthetics, psychology, cosmology, physics, grammar, logic, speculations about language, exegesis of scriptural texts, psycho-physical practices, dialectics, and even protests against orthodoxy. To study, understand, interpret, and continue the scholarship of the Indian *darśanas,* it is imperative that one realize that it holistically includes both thinking and living, theory and practice, an ancient, continuous, and seamless tradition. It has been able to combine, in an almost uncanny manner, conformity to tradition with an adventurous, enquiring mind.

Gauḍapāda (c. 5th century CE) was one of the most venerated Sages of Indian philosophy and the first historical person whose teachings on the Upaniṣadic wisdom of Advaita have survived. His place within the Advaita tradition is immense and commands the highest respect and homage. Ramaṇa was fond of quoting Gauḍapāda.

Employing scriptural statements, Gauḍapāda analyzed the three states of existence (waking, dream, and deep sleep) and showed that the Self (which is referred to as the "fourth" or "transcendent" *(turīya),* underlies and transcends these changing states.[1] The Self is constant, not subject to change, the ground of the other three, and the one reality of which the other three states are appearances. It alone is Real, being permanent, while the other states come and go. Then, employing reason, Gauḍapāda established logically this absolute non-duality (the Self alone is truly Real) and the illusory nature of the phenomenal world (though it appears, it is not Real inasmuch as it changes). His central doctrine was that "nothing has ever been

---

[1] See the MK.

born, nothing has ever happened".[1] Using impeccable and remarkable reasoning, Gauḍapāda advanced the doctrine which he is best known for, "nothing is ever born" or the theory of non-origination *(ajātivāda)*—nothing is ever born, not because "nothing" is the ultimate truth, but because the Self is the only unchanging reality. This is the pinnacle of Advaita thought. It is also the pinnacle of Ramaṇa's thought. Ramaṇa remarked: "There is no dissolution or creation, no one in bondage, nor anyone pursuing spiritual practices. There is no one desiring liberation nor anyone liberated. This is the absolute truth. This verse appears in the second chapter of Gauḍapāda's *Kārikā*. One who is established in the Self sees this by his knowledge of reality."[2]

Advaita, being based on the *Upaniṣads*, accepts the doctrine that knowledge has been divided into these two broad categories, the empirical and the trans-empirical. The body, the mind, the senses, and all the objects of the external world, are all subsumed under the empirical, the not-Self and are objects of knowledge. They can only be known through one of the valid means of knowledge. Wisdom or the Self is trans-empirical and not an object of knowledge. Ramaṇa said: "The Self alone exists and is real. The world, the individual and God are, like the illusory appearance of silver in the mother-of-pearl, imaginary creations in the Self, they are the not-Self."[3]

Ramana and Free Will

Finally, Ramaṇa's views on free will *vis-a-vis* predetermination are so astounding that it behooves us to explore the issue. According to Ramaṇa, at the level of an ordinary person *(ajñāni)*, individuals, from birth to death, will experience a series of preordained activities and experiences, all of which are the consequences of previous acts and thoughts. The only freedom which exists, if one does, is to realize that, in actuality, no one is acting and no one is experiencing. If, the

[1] MK 3, 48; 4, 71.

[2] Venkataramiah, *Talks with Ramana Maharshi*, 25.

[3] Devaraja Mudaliar, *Gems from Bhagavan*, 6.

Self is realized, then the words "freedom" and "predestination" lose all value, for, the Self neither acts nor experiences, is neither free nor bound. For the Self, "nothing has ever happened", and thus all words and concepts lose their meaning.

Are human beings victims of an inescapable fate, or do we really have the power to create our own destiny? That is the age-old question that has plagued philosophers, theologians, and even the common person on the street. Açcording to Ramaṇa, the question of free will or predetermination does not at all arise from the point of view of non-duality. Individuality itself is illusory. However, so long as one imagines that one has a separate individuality, so long does one imagine that one has or does not have free will.

To set the stage, look at two quotes from Arthur Osborne:

> Sri Bhagavān was uncompromising in his teaching that whatever is to happen will happen, while at the same time he taught that whatever happens is due to *prārabdha*, a man's balance-sheet of destiny acting according to so rigorous a law of cause and effect that even the word "justice" seems too sentimental to express it. He refused ever to be entangled in a discussion on free-will and predestination, for such theories, although contradictory on the mental plane, may both reflect aspects of truth. He would say, "Find out who it is who is predestined or has free will."[1]

> Actually, however, the question of free will or predestination does not arise at all from the point of view of non-duality. It is as though a group of people who had never heard of a radio were to stand around a wireless set arguing whether the man in the box has to sing what the transmitting station tells him to or whether he can change parts of the songs. The answer is that there is no man in the box and therefore the question does not arise. Similarly, the answer to the question whether the ego has free will or not is that there is no ego and therefore the question does not

[1] Osborne, *Ramana Maharshi and The Path of Self-knowledge.*

> arise. Therefore Bhagavān's usual response to the question would be to bid the questioner to find out who it is that has free will or predestination.[1]

Ok. But what about at the level of individuality—what happens there, where ordinary individuals live and experience? What are we to make of Ramaṇa's own words in the light of a person's everyday experience of cause and effect in the world?

Osborne himself asked Ramaṇa:

> "Are only important events in a man's life, such as his main occupation or profession, predetermined, or are trifling acts also, such as taking a cup of water or moving from one part of the room to another?" Ramaṇa replied: "Everything is predetermined." Osborne said, "Then what responsibility, what free will has man?" Ramaṇa replied, "Why does the body come into existence? It is designed for various things that are marked out for it in this life . . . As for freedom, a man is always free not to identify himself with the body and not to be affected by the pleasures and pains consequent on its activities."[2]

On another occasion, in a remarkably similar manner, Ramaṇa was asked:

> I can understand that the outstanding events in a man's life such as his country, nationality, family, career or profession, marriage, death, etc. are all predestined by his *karma*, but can it be that all the details of his life, down to the minutest, have already been predetermined? Now, for instance, I put this fan that is in my hand down on the floor here. Can it be that it was already decided that on such and such a day, at such and such an hour, I should move the fan like this and put it down here? Ramaṇa replied, "Certainly. Whatever this body is to do and whatever experiences it

---

[1] Osborne, *The Teachings of Bhagavan Sri Ramana Maharshi in His Own Words*, 66-67.

[2] Osborne, *The Teachings of Bhagavan Sri Ramana Maharshi in His Own Words*, 78-79.

> is to pass through was already decided when it came into existence."[1]

Finally, there is Ramaṇa's reply to his mother when she came to visit him in Tiruvannamalai for the first time. She had come in the hope of taking him back to Madurai. Ramaṇa remarked:

> The Creator, remaining everywhere makes each one play his role in life according to their past deeds *(prārabdha karma).* Whatever is not destined to happen will not happen, try how hard you may. Whatever is destined to happen will happen, do what you may to stop it. This is certain. Therefore, the best course is for one to remain silent.[2]

So what is one to make of this? Ramaṇa, in his own words, from the empirical perspective, seems to uphold a doctrine of predetermination that, on the face of it, seems almost shocking, so counter-intuitive, rather disconcerting and astounding in its total thoroughness. "All the activities that the body is to go through are *determined* when it first comes into existence. It does not rest with you to accept or reject them. The only freedom you have is to turn your mind inward and renounce activities there."[3]

The consequences of this are not lost on any intelligent person. One's next question becomes, if this is the case, then what responsibility does a person have? Where is the scope for bettering oneself, let alone for liberation? To this Ramaṇa replied: "Why does the body come into existence? It is designed for the various things that are marked out for it in this life."[4]

Then again, on a different occasion, to a questioner with perhaps different needs, Ramaṇa replied: "Free will exists together with the individuality. As long as the individuality last,

---

[1] Mudaliar, *Day by Day with Bhagavan,* 90-91.

[2] *Bhagavan Ramana and Mother,* 11-12.

[3] Mudaliar, *Day by Day with Bhagavan,* 32.

[4] *Ibid,* 99.

so long is there free will. All the scriptures are based on this fact and advise directing the free will in the right channel. Find out who it is who has free will or predestination and abide in that state. Then both are transcended. That is the only purpose in discussing these questions. To whom do such questions present themselves? Discover that and be at peace."[1]

There appears to be no contradiction here. According to Ramaṇa, individuality has only an illusory existence. However, as long as a person imagines that they have a separate individuality, so long do they also imagine they have free will. These two, individuality and free will, exist together inexorably and inevitably.

Stated differently, the problem of free will, according to theologians, places God, the Creator, between the horns of a dilemma. If God gave human beings free will, then God is neither omnipotent nor omniscient. If humans have free will, then God does not know what will happen because what happens will depend on the free will of what people decide. God will not have control of everything, because humans will have the power to change things. On the other hand, if God is omniscient and omnipotent and does control everything, while humans have no free will or possibility to do things other than as they happen, then such a God is unbelievably cruel and capricious. People are advised by Sages and scriptures to be good; yet, if they have no ability to change their fate, then that is just cruel.

For example, in a movie that has been filmed, each actor plays his or her part and that part is written out beforehand and cannot be changed after the film is made. Each actor plays a role and yet remains unaffected by their actions, because they know it is a role that they play. When an actor is born or dies on the screen, the person playing the role is neither born nor dies. When fire burns or water wets, the screen remains unaffected.

Or again for example: If one acts a part in a play, the whole part is written out beforehand, and one acts faithfully, whether one is Caesar who is stabbed or Brutus who stabs. The actor is unaffected by events on the stage because they are playing a

---

[1] Venkataramiah, *Talks with Sri Ramana Maharshi*, 426.

role and not "real". In the same way, that person who realizes his identity with the deathless Self acts his part on the human stage without fear or anxiety, hope or regret, not being touched by the part played. If one were to ask what reality one has when all one's actions are determined, it would lead only to the question: Who, then, am I? If the ego that thinks it and makes decisions is not real, and yet I know that I exist, what is the reality of me? This is but a preparatory, mental version of the quest that Ramaṇa prescribed, but it is an excellent preparation for the real quest. "Others are not responsible for what happens to us. They are only instruments of what would happen to us some way or other."

III

Ramana and Epistemology

Understand that there is a state "where" problems of knowledge are no longer settled in any particular way. No solution is ever conclusive. In other words, go beyond the level where there is certainty and uncertainty. The resolution of a problem arrived at by the mind must of necessity be from a particular point of view. Consequently, there will be room for contradiction, since any solution represents but one aspect.

Introduction

Indian philosophy in general and Ramaṇa in particular aim at discovering an ultimate unity that runs throughout the universe of multiplicity. Both advocate more than a mere theoretical construct. It is in pursuit or search for that which is eternally real and existent and common to all, and to which all of their epistemological conjectures should correspond. Ramaṇa called this unity the foundation of all, *Brahman/Ātman*. As the Being of all beings, it logically must be one and non-dual, eternal, immediate, and immutable. Such a unity cannot be a partial harmony or an aggregate. It cannot be established by fusing individual particulars together. Entities held together by a coherence or a *genus* that includes all species is but a temporal fusion. That which can be put together, can be broken apart. That which is born will necessarily die. Thus Ramaṇa's unity is a denial of duality from the very beginning itself.

Those who want to know the Reality must make an enquiry.[1] "For release from the bonds of empirical existence, the wise and learned person completely gives up all desire-motivated actions and commences an unceasing enquiry of the Self. Actions help to purify the mind; not to perceive reality. Reality is attained through enquiry and never in the slightest degree by even a hundred million actions."[2] "Without enquiry, the sacred teaching is incapable of generating *Brahman*-knowledge."[3] Ramaṇa said: "Self-enquiry is the one, infallible means, the only direct one, to realize the unconditioned, absolute Being that you really are."[4]

This being said, the question arises as to exactly how this knowledge of the Self is conveyed. Other than silence, religious instruction necessarily has recourse to ordinary words and their meanings to reveal the Reality. How are common words able to indicate this Reality when it is said to be free from all qualities, actions, class features, and relations? An established fact is said to be known through sources of knowledge like perception. Yet the nature of Reality defies any description in terms of the categories known to thought. The oft quoted verse in the *Pañcadaśī* says: "There is nothing similar to the Absolute, dissimilar to the Absolute, and there is no internal differentiation within the Absolute."[5] How can an ineffable, unconceivable to thought Reality be revealed by thought? Or, as Ramaṇa said: "People see the world. Their perception implies the existence of a seer and the seen. The objects are alien to the seer. The seer is intimate, being the Self. They do not, however, turn their attention to finding out the obvious seer, but run about analyzing the seen. The more the mind expands, the farther it goes and renders Self-Realization more difficult and complicated. Individuals must directly see the seer and realize the Self."[6]

---

[1] BSB 1.1.1. *Athāto brahma jijñāsā.*

[2] V 10-11.

[3] Mahadevan, *Invitation to Indian Philosophy*, 379.

[4] T. N. Venkataraman, *Maharshi's Gospel*, 19.

[5] PD 2.20-21. *"sajātīya vijātīya svagata bhedara hitam"*. See also BSB 2.1.14.

[6] Venkataramiah, *Talks with Sri Ramana Maharshi*, 231.

Ramaṇa remarked that the Self is an established fact and that an established fact need not be perceptible. He said:

> What is obvious, self-evident and most immediate to us, the Self, we say we are not able to see. On the other hand, we say that what we see with these eyes alone is *pratyakṣa* (direct perception). There must first be the seer before anything could be seen. You are yourself the eye that sees. Yet, you say you don't know the eye that sees, but know only the things seen. But for the Self, the Infinite Eye, what can be seen? You want direct experience, Self-realization *(sākṣātkāram).* You are now producing *(kāram)* all these things, *i.e.* realizing these things, regarding as real all these things, making real what is not real. If this "*kāram*" is given up out of your present *sākṣātkāram* of the unreal, then what will remain is that which is real or *sākṣāt.*[1]

Nor, for that matter, need it be inferential either: "To infer one's existence no other evidence is necessary. The *indriyas* (sense organs) and the mind arising from the ego cannot serve as evidence relating to the Self. The Self is their basis. They do not exist independently of the Self. One's own existence is self-evident."[2]

Perceptibility is not the criterion for an established fact existing prior to the sources of knowledge. If the imperceptible Self exists, this is learnt only from Sages and/or scriptures. Further, it is realized in one's direct personal experience as one's Self. Since the Self is non-dual and exceedingly subtle, there are no other means of discovering it. Ramaṇa never says that the Self is such-and-such, "this" or "that". His communication is only to reveal that the Self is not an object of any kind. There is not necessarily a contradiction in speaking about the Unspeakable because the Absolute transcends all empirical categories but logic does not forbid saying such. The Self's ineffability means that it is to be known differently than one knows empirical things. Once the distinctions of the

---

[1] Mudaliar, *Day by Day with Bhagavan,* 174.

[2] Venkataramiah, *Talks with Sri Ramana Maharshi,* 234.

knower, the known, and the resulting knowledge are rooted out, the Self will be revealed as an ever-existent, self-luminous fact.

Even if the Self escapes objectification, it does not escape certainty. Nothing is more certain than the fact of one's own existence. It is self-evident, immediate and direct. A man may doubt of many things, of anything else; but he can never doubt his own being. This is because the very act of doubting would be but an affirmation of one's very own existence. It cannot be proved since it is the basis of all proof and is established prior to all proofs. How can that, by which all the means of valid knowledge are established, be itself established by the means of valid knowledge? Ramaṇa remarked: "To infer one's existence no other evidence is necessary. The *indriyas* (sense organs) and the mind arising from the ego cannot serve as evidence relating to the Self. The Self is their basis. They do not exist independently of the Self. One's own existence is self-evident."[1]

Śaṅkara was fond of stating that the Self, which is the content of everyone's understanding of the "I", is the most immediately known entity possible. Perception of the Self is the most immediate, though it is not mediated by the senses. In fact, perception need not always be sense-mediated. The distinguishing character of perception is its immediacy. This immediacy is a oneness of Being. Thus, in this manner, knowing is, or becomes, identified with being. An individual knows the Self as the most certain perception of all because one is that Self. And not only is it that the Self of a sentient being is manifested immediately in one's indubitable experience, but even in the perception of an ordinary object the Self is revealed, for the Self is everything. As Ramaṇa said:

> Objects perceived by the senses are spoken of as immediate knowledge *(pratyakṣa).* Can anything be as direct as the Self—always experienced without the aid of the senses? Sense-perceptions can only be indirect knowledge, and not direct knowledge. Only one's own awareness is direct knowledge, as is the common

---

[1] Ibid.

experience of one and all. No aids are needed to know one's own Self, *i.e.* to be aware.[1]

From the perspective of epistemology, methods and means of valid knowledge are presented, discussed, and analyzed. Ramaṇa was not opposed to giving verbal teachings to anyone who asked for them. But it was his contention that his silent teachings were more direct and powerful than any verbal teaching could be. In his presence, he was continually emanating a spiritual force that silently, effortlessly, and automatically quieted the minds of those who were attuned to this force.

Fundamental to Ramaṇa is the message that ultimately there is no other shore, no bridge, and no path. The Reality is not to be attained for it is already attained, present, here and now. To realize this is to be liberated. Thus silence is the best conceivable means to convey this wisdom. All else will only increase one's illusion and delusion. Silence—not because there is no answer, but because there is no question. Silence is eloquent because it best characterizes the Reality.

Further, Ramaṇa's unique contribution to methodology was his focus on the Self through Self-enquiry, on directing the seeker to ask, "Who am I?" Still, seekers came to him with diverse backgrounds and with varying degrees of earnestness in their search for the Truth. No sincere enquiry was left unanswered. Because of this, Ramaṇa's teachings included a diversity of answers. It is in this sense that one finds "philosophy" in the classical sense of the term in his teachings.

Classical philosophy concerns itself with the categories of God, the world, and individuals and provides various answers according to a seeker's state of readiness and qualifications. Ramaṇa said: "All systems of thought postulate the three principles (i.e. the world, soul, and God)." He went on to say: "To say that the three principles ever remain as three principles is only so long as the ego lasts." Thus, Ramaṇa's prime focus was entirely on the individual, who each person thinks they are, and who they really are. He shifted one's attention to the

---

[1] Ibid, 55.

familiar, to the known and, as the Upaniṣad says: "When once That is known, all things are known."

Describing knowledge, the *Muṇḍaka Upaniṣad* says: "There are two kinds of knowledge, the higher and the lower."[1] Higher knowledge is knowledge of the Absolute, of Reality (*Brahman, Ātman*) and lower knowledge is knowledge of everything pertaining to the world, up to and inclusive of scriptural knowledge. These two types of knowledge are neither comparable, nor equal. Higher knowledge can neither be reached through a progressive accumulation of lower knowledge nor through any mode of lower knowledge. Higher knowledge is not the final or ultimate aspect of lower knowledge but is declared to be immediate, intuitive, and beyond any relation of subject and object. Higher knowledge is not one form of knowledge among others. It is unique and ultimate.

Advaita, being based on the Upaniṣads, accepts the doctrine that knowledge has been divided into these two broad categories: the empirical (knowledge, information, the not-Self) and the trans-empirical (wisdom, the Self). The body, the mind, the senses, all the objects of the external world, are all subsumed under the empirical, the not-Self and are objects of knowledge. They can only be known through one of the valid means of knowledge. Wisdom or the Self is trans-empirical and not an object of knowledge. Ramaṇa said: "The Self alone exists and is real. The world, the individual and God are, like the illusory appearance of silver in the mother-of-pearl, imaginary creations in the Self, they are the not-Self."[2]

We shall observe later that Ramaṇa was critical of the way in which the Advaita tradition employs the Upaniṣadic sayings *vis-a-vis* a person's *sādhana*, but here let us note what he said about the authority of the *mahāvākya*:

> The one Infinite Unbroken Whole becomes aware of itself as "I". This is its original name. All other names, *e.g.*, *OM*, are later growths. Liberation is only to remain

---

[1] MuU 1.1.4.

[2] Mudaliar, *Gems from Bhagavan*, 6.

aware of the Self. The *mahāvākya* "I am *Brahman*" is its authority. Though the "I" is always experienced, yet one's attention has to be drawn to it. Only then does knowledge dawn. Thus, the need for the instruction of the *Upaniṣads*, and of wise Sages.[1]

Epistemological Issues

We know that like Śaṅkara, Ramaṇa did not specify how many means of valid cognition *(pramāṇa)* were accepted by him, though both indicated in numerous places the ways in which perception, inference, and scripture function as means of knowledge and also their limitations. Ramaṇa, like Śaṅkara, always emphasized, never missing an opportunity to indicate, the importance of the Self/Consciousness in any process of knowing whatsoever, for Consciousness is always a basic presupposition of all means of knowledge. Ramaṇa said: "You won't find any of the names and forms of the world separate from the substratum *(adhiṣṭhāna)*. When you try to get at name and form, you will find Consciousness only."

Advaita epistemology is not easy to expound, and Ramaṇa rarely ever, even indirectly, addressed the issue about "valid means of knowledge" as a distinct philosophical topic. Often, what he did say was that the empirical means of knowledge is inadequate to realize the Self. "All mistake mind-consciousness for Self-consciousness."[2] Thus, we will have to flush out his thoughts on epistemological topics from his metaphysical statements as they are inferred or interwoven therein.

A number of seemingly irreconcilable epistemological issues need to be addressed. How is it that the one, indivisible, non-dual Consciousness appears to divide itself into the constituent parts of the knower, the known, and the resultant knowledge? Can this be explained or is it a mystery? Ramaṇa declared that, from the highest level, epistemology is inexplicable and thus discuss it, even if just in passing, not to

---

[1] Vekataramiah, *Talks with Sri Ramana Maharshi,* 55.

[2] Ibid, 309.

explain the problem of empirical knowledge, but to transcend it. In this context, an exposition of the various means of knowledge has as its aim the demonstration of their relative nature and resulting insufficiency, thus opening up the way to pure or higher knowledge. Ramaṇa said:

> The essence of mind is only Awareness or Consciousness. When the ego, however, dominates it, it functions as the reasoning, thinking, or sensing faculty. The cosmic mind, being not limited by the ego, has nothing separate from itself and is therefore only aware. This is what the *Bible* means by "I am that I am".[1]

Ramaṇa was ever vigorous and never varied in asserting that the essence of his teachings is that there is a single, immanent, indivisible Reality, directly experienced by everyone, that is simultaneously the source, the substance, and the real nature of all that is. All that is, this Reality, he called by various names as we have already noted. One should not misunderstand this and think that the Reality has attributes or parts but only that each name signifies the same one, non-dual, partless Reality.

This indivisible, objectless, pure Consciousness is easily the most distinctive feature of Advaita Vedānta. Both Advaita and Ramaṇa are so committed to this position that they are reticent to even speak of it, let alone call their thought "monism." In this Ramaṇa and Advaita are in perfect accord. Advaita is often spoken of as a type of monism. However, Advaita or non-dualism is not a monism as this term is generally understood in Western philosophical parlance. Advaita emphasizes "non"; it negates *all* duality and difference. Advaitins say (and Ramaṇa occasionally quoted this verse) that "differences are of three kinds: between members of the same class, between different species, or, lastly, internal differences". A mere monism may not allow the first two types of difference, but it is compatible with the last type, i.e. one tree with internal differences like the trunk, branches, leaves, roots, etc. However, Advaita rejects all the three types of difference. For this very same reason,

---

[1] Venkataraman, *Maharshi's Gospel*, 154-55.

Advaitins reject a view of the ultimate Reality as a Person (as is advocated by theism). Thus, to call Advaita "monism", one should be aware that it is, if one wants to use such a term, really a "radical or absolute monism," (so as to distinguish it from all other types of monism). However, Advaitins prefer and employ the term, "non-duality".

This non-dualistic doctrine is obviously, strikingly, glaringly in apparent contradiction with a person's normal everyday experience of life, characterized as it is by a plethora of multiplicity. For both Ramaṇa and Advaita, all of their efforts (when viewed from the standpoint of effort, of philosophy, of description, analysis, and instruction) were directed only establishing the plausibility and soundness of this apparently astonishing claim. On this point, Ramaṇa said:

> Who asked you to think about all that? All those are also thoughts. What good will it do you to go on thinking about memory and perception? It will be endless, like the old dispute, which came first, the tree or the seed. Ask who has this perception and memory. From where does that "I" that has perception and memory arise? Find out that. All perception, memory or any other experience only appears to that "I". You don't have such experiences during sleep, and yet you say that you existed during sleep. And you exist now too. That shows that the "I" continues while other things come and go.[1]

Let us be clear here. Ramaṇa never sought, nor was his intention ever to provide a philosophical theory. Ramaṇa has remarked that he did not prefer one view or theory to another. In each and every instance, his principal concern was to enable an individual to experience an awareness of the Self. To this end, Ramaṇa always insisted that practice was more important than theory. He said:

> "I approve of all schools. The same truth has to be expressed in different ways to suit the capacity of the

---

[1] Mudaliar, *Day by Day with Bhagavan,* 143.

hearer. Different seers saw different aspects of truth at different times, each emphasizing one view. Why do you worry about their conflicting statements. The essential aim is to teach the nature of the imperishable Self and show us we are that."[1]

This pure Consciousness does not act in any way whatsoever. Action, on the other hand, always and necessarily, involves a fluctuation or modification *(vṛtti)* of the internal organ. In any and every act, an individual who is the agent, uses some instrument(s) to bring about a change in some object. Acting requires differentiation and pure Consciousness is forever undifferentiated. There are no instruments, nor are there any objects to contrast with the Self as knower. The implications of this are profound and deep. One must understand that pure Consciousness can never be an object of knowledge and that the entire presuppositions and understandings an individual normally accepts must be finally subsumed into the Self.

Knowing is an interesting phenomenon. Even ordinary knowing, let alone scriptural knowledge, is not exactly like ordinary actions. In acting one does something to get something else, whereas knowing is not necessarily a means to something else—in spite of one's beliefs to the contrary. Knowing resembles acting in that it involves something coming into a relation with something different from itself but whereas acting changes something in the object as a result; in knowing nothing happens to the object. As Ramaṇa said:

> The world is "sensed" in the waking and the dream states or is the object of perception and thought, both being mental activities. If there were no such activities as waking and dreaming thought, there would be no "perception" or inference of a "world". In sleep there is no such activity and "objects and world" do not exist for us in sleep. Hence "reality of the world" may be created by the ego by its act of emergence from sleep; and that reality may be swallowed up or disappear by

---

[1] Ibid, 93.

> the soul resuming its nature in sleep. The emergence and disappearance of the world are like the spider producing a gossamer web and then withdrawing it. The spider here underlies all the three states—waking, dreaming, and sleep; such a spider in the person is called *Ātman* (Self), whereas the same with reference to the world (which is considered to issue from the sun) is called *Brahman* (Supreme Spirit). He that is in man is the same as He that is in the sun. While Self or Spirit is unmanifest and inactive, there are no relative doubles; e.g., subject and object, seer and seen—*dṛk* and *dṛṣya.* If the enquiry into the ultimate cause of manifestation of mind itself is pushed on, mind will be found to be only the manifestation of the Real which is otherwise called Atman or Brahman. The mind is termed *sukṣma śarīra* or "subtle-body"; and *jīva* is the individual soul. The *jīva* is the essence of the growth of individuality; personality is referred to as *jīva.* Thought or mind is said to be its phase, or one of the ways in which the *jīva* manifests itself—the earlier stage or phase of such manifestation being vegetative life. This mind is always seen as being related to, or acting on, some non-mind or matter, and never by itself. Therefore mind and matter co-exist[1]

Almost the first question that every one of the Hindu systems of philosophy tries to settle is, *how* does one know? Before one asks, "*what* is it that is known," one should enquire into "*how* one knows whatever it is that one knows." Epistemology is an enquiry into knowledge. It asks such questions as: What is knowledge? Where does it come from and how does it arise? What are its instruments? How is the object related to the subject, the knower to the known? What is truth and what is error? What is the source and test of validity and invalidity? What is the ontological status of knowledge?

The reason why we are discussing epistemology at all is that from the perspective of Ramaṇa, all of a person's problems, suffering, and confusion derive from a misconceived way of

---

[1] Venkataramiah, *Talks with Sri Ramana Maharshi*, 19.

perceiving things. How interesting. Both the Sage and the ignorant person experience the world. But where an ordinary person perceives multiplicity, objects separate from one another as well as from the knowing subject, the Sage perceives only the Self. Ramaṇa said:

> Seeing the world, the Sage *(jñāni)* sees the Self which is the substratum of all that is seen; the ignorant person *(ajñāni)*, whether he perceives the world or not, is ignorant of his true being, the Self . . . the ordinary man lives in the brain unaware of himself in the Heart. The Sage lives in the Heart. When he moves about and deals with men and things, he knows that what he sees is not separate from the one Supreme Reality.[1]

How to know what the term "valid cognition" *(pramā)* means? If it is defined as "knowledge of the real", how does one know what that reality is apart from how it is known? Such a definition involves the self-contradictory idea of having knowledge of an object before even knowing it! To overcome this defect, some say that valid cognition is the experience of an object "as it is." However, what does one mean by "as it is?" Is it cognition of the reality itself or of something *like* the reality? It can't be the first, as it has already been shown to be defective in the first definition given above. It can't be the latter as even illusory objects have some similarity to real objects and, as such, even illusory objects would have to be called real.

Thus, the validity of perception cannot be determined and the idea becomes empty of meaning. Others attempt to overcome this distasteful conclusion by stating that perception is the cognition of an individual object that is different from all other objects of the same class and from all other objects of all the other classes. Yet, this too, is indefensible because other objects of the same class and of other classes are not the content of the cognition. If it were not so, then one could never validly say, "This is X" for it would merely be a cognition confined to a person's mind only. As Ramaṇa said:

---

[1] Venkataraman, *Maharshi's Gospel,* 60-61.

> People see the world. The perception implies the existence of a seer and the seen. The objects are alien to the seer. The seer is intimate, being the Self. They do not, however, turn their attention to finding out the obvious seer, but run about analyzing the seen. The more the mind expands, the farther it goes and renders Self-Realization more difficult and complicated. The man must directly see the seer and realize the Self.[1]

Traditionally, Advaita Vedānta philosophy accepts all the six sources of valid knowledge (perception, inference, verbal testimony, comparison, presumption, non-cognition), accepted by the Bhāṭṭa Mīmāmsakas. Why Advaitins did this is open to speculation. Perhaps they did it, as some suggest, because the final investigation (Uttara Mīmāmsā/Vedānta) logically follows the prior investigation (Pūrva Mīmāmsā) or, as I suspect, the Bhāṭṭa theory was, in the Advaitin's opinion, an adequate investigation into the means of valid *pragmatic empirical* knowledge.

A radical position, taken by some Advaitins like Śrī Harṣa who employed a dialectic to demonstrate the untenability of every valid means of knowledge,[2] is that none of the six valid means of knowledge are accepted – only the ultimate indeterminate intuition of the Self (*svarūpa jñāna*) is a "valid means of knowledge". This latter position is based on the conclusion that every one of the six means of pragmatic valid knowledge is self-contradictory. Furthermore, if one wants to act, to do anything—think, feel, experience, walk, talk—then one needs a means to do so; but if there is nowhere to go and nothing to do and no one to do it, then where is the necessity of positing a valid means of knowledge? So speaks the Sage. Ramaṇa remarked:

> Whatever state one is in, perceptions partake of that state. The explanation is that in the waking state the gross body perceives gross names and forms; in the dream state the mental body perceives the mental

---

[1] Venkataramiah, *Talks with Sri Ramana Maharshi*, 231.

[2] See Śrī Harsha's *Khaṇḍana-Khaṇḍa-khadya.*

creations in their manifold forms and names; in deep dreamless sleep the identification with the body being lost, there are no perceptions; similarly in the Transcendental state identity with *Brahman* places the individual in harmony with everything, and there is nothing apart from the Self.[1]

According to Advaita, perception is a function *(vṛtti)* of the internal organ *(antaḥkaraṇa)* called by four different names: mind *(manas),* ego *(ahaṁkāra),* reason *(buddhi),* and apperception *(citta).* The function of the mind is analysis and synthesis of whatever is perceived by the sense organs. When a tree is perceived, the mind receives impressions of color, shape, size, name, form, and so on. The mind then synthesizes them and separates the total unified object thus constructed from other objects. The function of the ego is to appropriate the object as *its* object as in "I see a tree". Until reason does its work, the object is an object of my experience and not an object of the everyday world. Reason functions to make this particular object an object of the objective world through an assertion or decision. "That is an apple" is the result of a decision of reason. Finally, after the perceived sensations are synthesized into a unified object, apperception brings in past experiences (memory) and relates the tree, the earth, seeds, wood, and so forth. Different ideas about the object are then collected and related.

(In this regards, Ramaṇa, in his characteristic way spoke of perception and memory and their use: "Who asked you to think about all that? All those are also thoughts. What good will it do you to go on thinking about memory and perception? It will be endless, like the old dispute, which came first, the tree or the seed. Ask who has this perception and memory. That "I" that has the perception and memory, whence does it arise? Find out that. Because perception, or memory, or any other experience, only comes to that "I". You don't have such experiences during sleep, and yet you say

[1] Venkataramiah, *Talks with Sri Ramana Maharshi*, 7.

> that you existed during sleep. And you exist now too. That shows that the "I" continues while other things come and go."[1])

To this analysis, Advaitins add another factor. Before the inner instrument functions, before the perceptual cognition of the tree arises, a person is ignorant of, unconscious of, the object's existence. The darkness of ignorance or unconsciousness must be lit up in order for a perception to arise. This light comes from the light of Consciousness, either reflected or limited in the senses and mind, when coming into contact with an object. The light of a person's consciousness, reflected in one's mind and senses, lights up an area, thereby disclosing any object therein. The disclosure takes place in one's mind. The object has its own reality, its own place, in the universe. But one's mind also has the power to take on exactly the same form as the object and, if necessary, can abstract the mental form later as in memory. Ramaṇa said:

> The Self is the Heart. The Heart is self-luminous. Light arises from the Heart and reaches the brain, which is the seat of the mind. The world is seen with the mind, that is, by the reflected light of the Self. It is perceived with the aid of the mind. When the mind is illumined it is aware of the world. When it is not itself so illumined, it is not aware of the world. If the mind is turned in towards the source of light, objective knowledge ceases and Self alone shines forth as the Heart. The moon shines by the reflected light of the sun. When the sun has set, the moon is useful for revealing objects. When the sun has risen, no one needs the moon, although the pale disc of the moon is visible in the sky. So it is with the mind and the Heart. The mind is useful because of its reflected light. It is used for seeing objects. When it is turned inwards, the source of illumination shines forth by itself, and the mind remains dim and useless like the moon in day-time[2]

---

[1] Mudaliar, *Day by Day with Bhagavan,* 143.

[2] Venkataramiah, *Talks with Sri Ramana Maharshi*, 58.

Another doctrine of Advaita in regards to their position *vis-a-vis* perception is that a perceptual cognition reveals, along with objects, Being *(sattā)* that is common to every existent and without which the various forms cannot be real and cannot have objective status. When one says, "That is a tree," along with the form of the tree, Being is also revealed. All the things of the empirical world are said to be endowed with five characteristics: Existence *(asti),* cognizability *(bhāti),* attraction *(priyam),* name *(nāma),* and form *(rūpa).* The first three of these characteristics constitute the basis of everything whatsoever. What makes one thing appear different from another is its apparent name and form. The name is only a convention of speech, but there is actually no *essential* difference between one thing and another. The name exists only in one's mind, and thus the Upanisadic dictum, "All this is verily *Brahman."*

Ramana and Epistemological Issues

Countless are the number of individuals who have had an insatiable curiosity about the state of Self-realization *(mokṣa)* and especially about *how* a Sage experiences the world. A well-known example was Arjuna who enquired of Kṛṣṇa: "O Keśava, what is the description of a person of steady wisdom, whose being is Self-absorbed? How does he speak, sit, move?"[1] In the *Bhagavad-gītā,* Kṛṣṇa's replied: "With the elimination of attraction and aversion, *even though moving among the objects of the sense organs* (italics mine) he who is controlled by the Self, by self-control attains serenity."[2]

Questions about how a Sage experiences himself and the world around him are not the only epistemological issues we will look at, but without a doubt, they were more frequent and insatiable than perhaps any others.

In regards to Ramaṇa and epistemology, some of the major issues involve:

---

[1] BG 2.54.

[2] BG 2. 64.

1 – How does a Sage's awareness of pure Consciousness, one and indivisible, experience multiplicity when there is no individual awareness? Does the Sage's awareness go back and forth between non-duality and multiplicity and if so, how? In other words, *how* did Ramaṇa perceive the world?

2 – How does pure Consciousness function regarding one's mind, body, actions, and the alternating states of waking, dreaming, and deep sleep when all the while the Sage declares that he "does nothing?"

3 – What is the object of knowledge and given that object, in what sense may it be said to be illumined?

4 – Why doesn't consciousness have direct access to all the objects of mediate and immediate knowledge instead of being dependent upon a *vṛtti* that it illumines?

5 – How do the words of scripture/a Sage/or silence reveal the non-dual Self? (This issue we will take up in the section on Ramaṇa's silence, as well as in chapters 6 and 7).

Regarding the first two issues, there is an unacknowledged assumption made by people who ask such questions that there is a person (Ramaṇa/Sage/*jñāni/jīvan-mukta*) who experiences a state called the Self. One way to answer their queries is to point out that this assumption is nothing more than a mental construct, a delusion, invented by people who have not realized the Self, in an attempt to make sense of Ramaṇa's experience. Because they accept ignorance, and therefore multiplicity as real, they assume that there are Sages/*jñāni*, there is a state called liberation *(mokṣa)*, there is a state called bondage, and there is a realized person known as Ramaṇa. The Truth of the Self is that there are neither Sages nor bound individuals, neither liberation nor bondage – there is only the Self. This is one perspective, what Advaita and Ramaṇa call the highest perspective or the Truth. Ramaṇa remarked: "An *ajñāni* sees someone as a *jñāni* and identifies him with the body. Because the *ajñāni* does not know the Self and mistakes the body for the Self, he extends the same mistake to the state of the *jñāni.*"

Again and again, both directly and indirectly, Ramaṇa patiently and unmistakably denied these unspoken (even unknown to the questioners themselves) assumptions. What is noteworthy and a bit puzzling, is how few of his questioners were able to grasp, even intellectually, the purport of his replies. If you will recall, there are four perspectives from which Ramaṇa could reply to such questions. Either he could remain silent; he could reply from the non-origination *(ajāta-vāda)* perspective; he could reply from the "perception is creation" *(sṛṣṭi-dṛṣṭi-vāda)* perspective; or he could reply from the theory "creation is what is perceived" *(dṛṣṭi-sṛṣṭi-vāda)* perspective. Examples of each include:

> 1 – Either Ramaṇa remained silent or else he spoke of silence. "Silence is the language of the Self and it is the most perfect teaching. Language is like the glow of the filament in the electric lamp; but Silence is like the current in the wire."
>
> 2 – "The *ajāta* doctrine says, "Nothing exists except the one reality. There is no birth or death, no projection or drawing in, no seeker, no bondage, no liberation. The one unity alone exists."[1] "The Self alone exists, the pictures come and go. If you hold on to the Self, you will not be deceived by the appearance of the pictures. Nor does it matter at all if the pictures appear or disappear . . . The *jñāni* knows that the screen and the pictures are only the Self. With the pictures the Self is in its manifest form. To the *jñāni* it is quite immaterial if the Self is in the one form or the other. He is always the Self."[2]
>
> 3 – Yes, a *jñāni* does dream, but he knows it to be a dream, in the same way, as he knows the waking state

[1] Mudaliar, *Day by Day with Bhagavan,* 132.

[2] Venkataraman, *Maharshi's Gospel,* 85-86.

to be a dream. You may call them dreams no. 1 and dream no. 2. The *jñāni* being established in the fourth state—*turīya*, the supreme Reality – he detachedly witnesses the three other states, waking, dreaming, and dreamless sleep, as pictures superimposed on it."[1]

4 – "Seeing the world, the *jñāni* sees the Self which is the substratum of all this is seen; the *ajñāni*, whether he sees the world or not, is ignorant of his true being, the Self."[2] When bitten by an insect, the *jñāni* has a sensation and there is also the "I-am-the-body-idea". The latter is common to both *jñāni* and *ajñāni* with this difference, that the *ajñāni* thinks only the body is myself, whereas the *jñāni* knows all is of the Self, or all this is *Brahman*. If there be pain, let it be. It is also part of the Self. The Self is perfect. After transcending the "I-am-the-body-idea" one becomes a *jñāni*. In the absence of that idea there cannot be either doership or doer. So a *jñāni* has no *karma*, that is, a *jñāni* performs no actions. That is his experience. Otherwise he is not a *jñāni*. However, the *ajñāni* identifies the *jñāni* with his body, which the *jñāni* does not do."[3]

I will cite one further example and leave it to the reader to understand from what perspective Ramaṇa gave his reply. One morning Ramaṇa was speaking about the state of a *jīvan-mukta*, how he is the ever-aware Self, the Witness-Consciousness transcending space and time and causation, the fullness of Being; how he is the non-actor, non-enjoyer, and yet at the same time the greatest of actors, the greatest of enjoyers, and so forth. Mr. Noles, an Italian, who was well read in both Eastern and Western philosophy, finally could not contain himself and remarked, "Are you, or are you not, now talking to us?" Ramaṇa looked at Mr. Noles and said in a most emphatic tone of voice: "No, "I" am not talking to you."[4]

---

[1] S. S. Cohen, *Guru Ramana*, 100.

[2] Venkataraman, *Maharshi's Gospel*, 60.

[3] Ibid, 349-50.

[4] T.K. Sundaresa Iyer, *At the Feet of Bhagavan*, 47.

Ramaṇa sometimes referred to various illustrations that are given in spiritual books which attempt to enable ordinary individuals to understand how the *jñāni* can live and act without the mind, in spite of the notion that living and acting require the use of the mind. For instance, a potter's wheel continues to turn round and round for some time even after the potter has ceased to turn it. Or, in the same way, an electric fan continues to revolve for some time even after the current is switched off. In a similar manner, an individual's predestined *karma (prārabdha)* that created the body will continue to its destined conclusion performing whatever activities it was meant for. The *jñāni* thus experiences various activities, but without the idea that he is the doer of them. If this is too difficult to grasp, Ramaṇa would refer to the example that a *jñāni* performs actions much like the way a child that has just been aroused from sleep eats, but does not remember the next morning that he ate.

Another illustration that Ramaṇa gave to show the connection between the Self which is pure Knowledge and the triple factors of knower, known, and the resulting knowledge thereof was the "workings of a cinema." Just as the pictures appear on the screen as long as the film throws the shadows through the lens, so the phenomenal world will continue to appear to the individual in the waking and dream states as long as there are latent mental impressions. Just as the lens magnifies the tiny specks on the film to a huge size and as a number of pictures are shown in a second, so the mind enlarges the sprout-like tendencies into tree-like thoughts and shows in a second innumerable worlds. Again, just as there is only the light of the lamp visible when there is no film, so the Self alone shines without the triple factors when the mental concepts in the form of tendencies are absent in the states of deep sleep, swoon, and *samādhi.* Just as the lamp illumines the lens, etc., while remaining unaffected, the Self illumines the ego *(cidābhāsa),* etc., while remaining unaffected.

The philosopher may well respond: these illustrations are nice, but exactly *how* does the *jñāni* do this, that is, perceive the world and individuals? Ramaṇa said: "The existence of the ego in any form, either in the *jñāni* (where it subsists in its pure form) or the *ajñāni* (where it appears as something real), is itself an experience. But to the *ajñāni* who is deluded into thinking that the waking state and the world are real, the ego also appears to be real. Since he sees the *jñāni* act like other individuals, he feels constrained to posit some notions of individuality with reference to the *jñāni* also."

From the *jñāni's* perspective, there is no separate individuality, no one acting, no actions, no world of diversity separate from the Self. "The ordinary man lives in the brain unaware of himself in the Heart. The *jñāni* lives in the Heart. When a *jñāni* moves about and deals with men and things, he knows that what he sees is not separate from the one supreme Reality, *Brahman*, which he realized in the Heart as his own Self, the Real."[1] To explain how this is possible, a bit of a digression and explanation of Advaita epistemology is necessary. Please be patient until we pick up the thread again.

Advaita realistic epistemology demands that knowledge, all knowledge, must have an object, must involve multiplicity: a knower, the known, and the process thereby and that cognitions should have the form of that object. So the question arises, how does the *jñāni* know, cognize sense data? Even if one were to grant that Ramaṇa was the non-dual Self, how did he recognize that a monkey just entered the hall or that food was being wasted, or that his mother had come, or a million other examples? Further, if he is the one Consciousness, why doesn't that Consciousness illumine the entire universe even as it illumines the mental modifications of the internal organ (since both are superimposed upon the Consciousness alike)? Is a Sage omniscient or is it that a Sage doesn't perceive the world with all its multiplicity at all? How does the non-Self reside in the Self, how does ignorance reside in pure Consciousness?

What follows sets the perspective of Advaita so that the detailed discussion that is to come will be correctly understood.

Distinction Between Standpoints

It is absolutely crucial that one understands the distinction both Advaita and Ramaṇa make between the absolutely real

---

[1] Sastri, *Sat Darshana Bhāṣya*, xx.

(pāramārthika) and the empirically real *(vyāvahārika)* points of view. This distinction pervades everything they say and what is true from one point of view is not so from another. Without being entirely clear with regard to this distinction, it is likely that one will accuse them of inconsistencies and contradictions.

While Śaṅkara and Ramaṇa are prepared to admit a plethora of distinctions at the empirical level, all distinctions are denied from the Absolute point of view. What is true from one point of view or level of reality is not true from another. However, this does not mean that there are two realities, two truths. There is one Truth, one Reality, as seen from two different perspectives.[1] One perspective is from the point of ignorance and is relatively true (the sun seemingly rises and sets) and the other is the perspective of the Sage. The pluralism that is experienced at the empirical level, and with which philosophical enquiry commences, is not the final Truth. Though Ramaṇa often used the following quote in other contexts, it is worth presenting here; Ramaṇa said, "Can a man be possessed of two identities, two selves? To understand this matter it is first necessary for a man to analyze himself. Because it has long been his habit to think as others think, he has never faced his "I" in the true manner. He has not a correct picture of himself; he has too long identified himself with the body and the brain. You ask me to describe this true Self to you. What can be said? It is That out of which the sense of the personal "I" arises and into which it will have to disappear."[2]

From the empirical point of view, numerous distinctions are accepted. Epistemologically, there is the subject-object dichotomy, as well as the problem of truth and error. Metaphysically, the problem of the One and the many must be addressed. Individuals are different from one another and there exists a seeming plurality of things. Ethically, there is the problem of bondage and freedom, the teacher and the taught, right and wrong, auspicious and inauspicious. However, from

---

[1] BSB 1.1.11. "scripture speaks of Brahman in two forms according as it is known from the standpoint of knowledge or from that of ignorance."

[2] Osborne, *Ramana Maharshi and the Path of Self Knowledge*, 18-19.

Ramaṇa's absolute point of view, there is only the Self—One and non-dual *(ekam eva advitīyam).*[1]

Ramaṇa regarded all diversity, all multiplicity as being an illusion. However, it is extremely important to grasp correctly the significance of describing diversity as an illusion. His conception of the real *(Sat)* is eternal Being, that which never changes. As such, it is only the Absolute that merits the name "real". On the other end of the spectrum is the unreal *(asat)* or that which never appears, not even in one's wildest imagination, hallucination, or delusion. Examples of the unreal are: a child of a barren woman or a square circle. Such things will never ever appear or be perceived. The physical universe, in all its diversity, is obviously not real by this criterion, nor is it unreal. It is not real because everything in the universe changes. Nor is it unreal in the sense defined, for the universe clearly appears to individuals as no non-existent entity can. Further, the physical universe possesses a practical efficiency; it has value, being both durable and useful in everyday life.

The pluralism that is experienced at the empirical level is not the final truth. All Advaitins aver that anything that is experienced is real, in some sense or other.[2] Therefore, their epistemology is realistic and posits that every cognition points to an objective referent—whether veridical or erroneous. The question to be asked is: Exactly *how* real are the things that are experienced in the empirical world? Śaṅkara avers that the things of the world are real only so long as the empirical order lasts for a given individual. He said:

> The division of real and unreal depends upon knowledge or experience: That is real whose knowledge does not miscarry; the unreal on the contrary, is the object of a knowledge that fails or goes astray.[3]

---

[1] CU 6.2.1.

[2] VP 7.

[3] BG *Bhāṣya* of Śaṅkara 2.16. Also: BSB. 2.1.2 and 3.2.4.

As we alluded to earlier, Ramaṇa spoke of three different standpoints about the nature of the physical world *(ajāta-vāda, dṛṣṭi-sṛṣṭi-vāda,* and *sṛṣṭi-dṛṣṭi-vāda).* He often alluded to the perspectives of the Self and non-self. He would address or advocate them at different times, dues to various circumstances and it is clear his statements were geared to conform to the different levels of understanding of his questioners.

As a consequence of this line of thought, if the resulting knowledge is not later contradicted, it follows that the real is that which lasts or is eternal. Things of the world may be said to be real until they suffer sublation. This is the reason why the physical universe, with all its diversity, is described as other than the real and the unreal *(sadasadvilakṣaṇa)* or illusory *(mithyā).* It is an illusory appearance *(māyā)* that "is not" *(yā-mā).* A snake appears where there is only a rope. Silver appears where there is only a shell. The snake and silver are neither existent nor non-existent. They are psychologically given *(prasiddha),* but they cannot be logically established *(siddha).* In other words, all the myriad things of the physical universe, though not ultimately real, are yet (provisionally) of a certain order of reality. Since they are *cognized*, they are not unreal *(asat).* What a mystery! The sun is seen to traverse across the sky, and yet everyone knows that it does not move! Water is seen in a mirage, and yet there has never been water there, nor will there be, nor is now. Ropes are mistaken as snakes and shells are mistaken for silver. They are mere appearances in the sense that they depend for their being upon some higher reality. The snake points to the existence of the rope, and the silver points to the existence of the shell. Their dependence is one-sided, for, while the disappearance of the rope or the shell necessarily implies the disappearance of the snake or silver, the reverse does not hold good.

So long as an individual functions at the empirical level, one is under the spell of superimposition *(adhyāsa).* Superimposition pervades everything one knows and everything one does in one's empirical life. It is defined as the apparent presentation of the attributes of one thing in another thing.[1] Superimposition and the theories of illusory appearance, both of

---

[1] BSB 1.1.1.

which help to explain the problem of error, presupposes ignorance. An inert, material mind needs the help of Consciousness for knowledge to arise. Knowledge exists in and through a conscious experience of multiplicity. And it is ignorance that is the cause of all these empirical distinctions.

Epistemologically, the subject-object dichotomy is based upon superimposition. The Self is pure Consciousness though, identifying itself as the ego, it views itself as a knowing subject in relation to a known object. It wrongly imagines that it is a knowing subject because of its relation to the mind. Yet, the mind is insentient and can function only due to its relation with the Self that is Consciousness. Thus, one thing is superimposed upon another and the entire relation is false. The Self is real and the mind is non-real. How can there be a real relation between the real and the non-real? It is all a product of ignorance.

As we have said, knowledge may be viewed in two aspects: the empirical and the metaphysical.[1] Metaphysically, the fundamental essence of knowledge *(svarūpa jñāna)* is pure Consciousness beyond the relative duality of the knower and the known.[2] It is self-luminous and self-existent. It is the non-relational, non-dual Reality. It is not an aspect of, nor an attribute of pure Consciousness. Empirical or relative knowledge, on the other hand, is an expression of pure Consciousness through a mental mode *(antahkaraṇa vṛtti)* of a cognizer. This empirical knowledge takes various relational forms according to the nature of the object, i.e. internal cognitions that are psychological and external sense-perceptions which are psycho-physical.

The indivisible pure Consciousness appears divided in relational knowledge. Such knowledge is referred to as *vṛtti-jñāna.* Ramaṇa remarked: "There is a subject, object and perception which form the triad *(tripuṭī).* There is a reality beyond these three. These appear and disappear, whereas the Truth is eternal."[3] Or again: "It is true in the same degree as the seer (*drastā*), subject, object and perception form the triad *(tripuṭ*

---

[1] VP VII, 150.

[2] Ibid, I, 9.

[3] Venkataramiah, *Talks with Sri Ramana Maharshi*, 202.

ī). There is a reality beyond these three. These appear and disappear, whereas the truth is eternal."[1]

Vrtti-Jnana

Vṛtti-jñāna, or empirical knowledge, is a blend of the modification of the mind and the reflection of Consciousness therein. It is an expression of pure Consciousness through a mental mode corresponding to an object. Fundamentally and primarily, knowledge is pure Consciousness. When it is expressed through a mental mode it is called (secondarily) knowledge-by-courtesy.[2] Further, knowledge is said to be of two kinds: mediate and immediate.

Advaita philosophers posit that there are three senses of immediacy: (i) The self-luminosity of Consciousness which manifests as immediate knowledge of oneself as "I", (ii) immediate knowledge of one's own subjective internal states produced by the witness-self *(sākṣin);* of the modifications of the mind *(vṛtti)* such as pleasure and pain, and of ignorance *(avidyā)* itself, and (iii) perceptual knowledge of physical objects perceived through the sense organs.[3]

Knowledge, from an absolute sense as contrasted with an empirical sense,[4] is said to be immediate or mediate depending upon the nature of the object that is known, (though, it must be noted, that both types of knowledge necessarily require the functioning of the mind). The pure Consciousness that is the Self, given the necessary conditions, inspires the insentient material mind to reflect knowledge. In all knowledge situations, the mind as well as pure Consciousness must necessarily be present or no knowledge whatsoever is possible. In this context,

---

[1] Ibid.

[2] Ibid.

[3] Ibid, 1, 15.

[4] Empirically, Advaita epistemology subscribes to the doctrine that the same object can be known by different valid means of knowledge (*pramāṇa*). The point I wish to make here is that *Atman/Brahman* is the only immediate "object" of knowledge in the *pāramārthika* sense of the term.

only Self-knowledge can be classified as immediate and all else will be mediate.

Advaita defines the process of relative knowledge thus: Ignorance *(avidyā)* is the cause of all empirical distinctions. This ignorance obscures the pure Consciousness and transforms itself in the form of multiplicity. "Of these, that transformation of ignorance which resides in the body and is called the internal organ, being prompted by merit and demerit, goes out through the channel of the eyes, etc., pervades suitable objects like the pot, and becomes of their respective forms."[1] The distinctions of the knower, the known, and the resulting knowledge are the creations of ignorance with the help of Consciousness.

Epistemologically, an analysis made by the Advaitins will reveal two things. First, any source of knowledge only functions due to the part played by Consciousness. Without the help of Consciousness, no source of knowledge is a source of knowledge, while on the other hand, Consciousness does not need the help of any source of knowledge. And second, two conditions are necessary for anything to be an object of knowledge. There must be a pervasion by a mental modification *(vṛtti-vyāpyatva)* and there must be a pervasion by knowledge *(phala-vyāpyatva).* Yet in regards to the Absolute, there is no objectified knowledge since the Absolute is not subject to objectification.

What this analysis reveals is that the work of Ramaṇa's Self-enquiry method can be taken as negative, in that the mental modifications employed in enquiring into the source of the "I" remove the objects superimposed upon the Self by ignorance, but that the source of the enquiry, with its purport being the Self, is positive. That ignorance exists seems obvious. Generally, to remove ignorance knowledge is required. This removal takes the form of a fragmented mental cognition. Yet Self-enquiry exists in order to point to a type of mental cognition that is not fragmented *(akhaṇḍākāra vṛtti jñāna)* and in which the mind becomes "no-mind" to use Gauḍapāda's terminology. Once its work is done, it removes itself too, thus leaving the self-luminous Reality "revealed". It is similar to the

---

[1] *Vivaraṇaprameya-sangraha,* Vizianagaram Sanskrit Series, No. 7, 71.

act of using a thorn to remove a thorn and then discarding both. Thus the saying, "By the mind alone It is to be perceived" and "That which cannot be thought of by the mind".[1] The *vṛtti-vyāpyatva* brings the unknown Self into contact with the mind thus destroying one's ignorance concerning the Self. However, it may be noted that this does not help to reveal the Self. The Self is Self-luminous. It doesn't take another Consciousness to reveal itself and thus, though there is no *phala-vyāpyatva*, the individual self is identical with the Self.

Generally it is said that the Reality cannot be presented positively as "this" or "that". The Reality is not an object of Self-enquiry in this sense. However, the Self is "un-veiled" due to the enquiry. The apprehending consciousness *(phala)* cannot comprehend an inexpressible-to-words Self. But the process, "discover the source of "I", destroys all ignorance including the apprehending consciousness' attempt to reveal the Self. Thus all mentation ceases and the Self alone remains.

The Advaitin assumes the necessity of the internal organ *(antaḥkaraṇa)* for the sake of associating the Self with objects. Without this association, no knowledge is possible. So, what is this process by which Ramaṇa perceives objects? On the one hand, is the self-illuminating pure Consciousness and on the other is the contingent modification of the mind *(vṛtti)*. The question arises: Either the pure Consciousness associates itself with the *antaḥkaraṇa* and therefore ceases to be pure, or else, if association is possible with the *antaḥkaraṇa*, then why doesn't the pure Consciousness by-pass the *antaḥkaraṇa* and directly associate itself with objects? Why bring in the mind, the *antaḥkaraṇa*, the senses, and *vṛttis*, when the self-luminous omnipresent Self can directly cognize objects? Why is this unwarranted restriction of the Self necessary?

The relation between the knowing self and its object is determined by one's conception of the individual and of an object. Among Advaitins there are three general conceptions posited.[2] However, a detailed discussion of these positions is unnecessary for our purpose here. It is enough to note that the

---

[1] KeU 1.5.

[2] See Datta, *Six Ways of Knowing*, 73-80.

Advaitins are unanimous in saying that the omnipresent Self is obscured by ignorance. They all agree that the nature of the relation between the witness Self *(sākṣin)* and the object perceived is one of superimposition.

An individual's consciousness, by itself, is incapable of manifesting objects because it is obscured by ignorance. It is only through its association with the inner organ *(antaḥkaraṇa)* that the individual apprehends objects. A logical concept like "tableness", though universal, applies only to objects subsumed under it and not to all objects. Likewise, the individual, though intrinsically universally luminous, reveals only those objects that appear to it through the medium of the *antaḥkaraṇa.* One might as well ask why the light of a lamp, which is pervasive of color, etc., only manifests color.

Advaitins maintain that pure Consciousness (defined by egoity) has the omnipresent ignorance as its adjunct and thus it cannot be directly associated with objects since it is not the material cause of the objects. The *antaḥkaraṇa* is necessary for consciousness to contact external objects. The functions of mental modifications *(vṛtti)* are three-fold: For the sake of contact with objects by consciousness; for the manifestation of non-difference of the Consciousness-Self and the object-defined Consciousness; and for the removal of the obscuring ignorance with regard to the particular object.[1]

Thus, we observe that the *antaḥkaraṇa* is necessary for an association of consciousness with objects, and without any association no cognition is possible. As well, besides the *antaḥkaraṇa* being necessary, the *vṛtti* must reach and take the form of the object. Even in internal cognitions, it is the *antaḥkaraṇa* that has transformed itself into a *vṛtti* (i.e. happiness, etc.)[2] and is manifested by the inner witness-self *(sākṣin)* (because of the sameness of locus of the *vṛtti* and consciousness conditioned by the happiness).

According to the Advaitin, ignorance causes all empirical distinctions. It obscures the omnipresent, intelligent Self, and

---

[1] *Advaita-siddhi,* ch. L.

[2] There are some Advaitins who do not admit a *vṛtti* in the case of pleasure and pain; regarding them as *kevalasākṣ-ivedya.*

transforms itself into the world of multiplicity. It is the function of the *vṛtti* to manifest objects. The consciousness that is defined by these objects is called the object-defined intelligence. That which manifests this consciousness is a transformation of either the *antaḥkaraṇa* or of ignorance and is called a mental modification *(vṛtti).* The individual that is of the nature of consciousness, cannot manifest objects without the help of *vṛttis,* because consciousness as such does not destroy ignorance.

So, let us ask the question again, *how*, that is, by what valid means of knowledge did Ramaṇa perceive the various objects in the world? We are not asking about *the way* in which they are perceived—we know that already. Ramaṇa said: "The ordinary individual lives in the brain unaware of himself in the Heart. The Sage lives in the Heart. When a Sage moves about and deals with men and things, he knows that what he sees is not separate from the one supreme reality, *Brahman*, which he realized in the Heart, as his own Self, the Real."[1] Thus, Ramaṇa, on numerous occasions said that he "perceives the appearances", he sees monkeys and people, chairs and doorways, food and squirrels, all that ordinary people see, but he doesn't see them as separate, independent objects, that is the difference. (Note: on other occasions, to other individuals, Ramaṇa would say, replying from the *jñāni's* perspective: "You say that the *jñāni* sees the path, avoids them, etc. In whose eye-sight is all this, in the *jñāni's* or ours? He sees only the Self and all in the Self").[2]

The *Upaniṣad* gives an analogy as to how this might be possible. "The arrowhead of an arrow implanted deeply in the target will not come out even when pulled. The arrow shaft may come out, but not the tip. The shaft is then useless. When the mind is fixed upon Brahman it will never come out. The sense of sight, etc., may function towards external objects but they will serve no purpose whatsoever."[3] Thus, a Sage may have his sense-organs functioning, but he is not overwhelmed by them.

---

[1] *Sat-Darshana Bhāṣya,* xx.

[2] Mudaliar, *Day by Day with Bhagavan,* 144.

[3] MuU 2.2.4.

The Sage's mind is always centered on *Brahman*. There is also the Upaniṣadic analogy given to show how, even though the Sage is not the body, the body survives and functions. A trained horse yoked to a chariot will take it home without its charioteer. The vital airs are directed by God to maintain the body according to its fructified merits and demerits. Just so, a child in the womb is maintained naturally by the mother.[1]

Another way to explain how the *jñāni* perceives the world is to invoke the example of the self-luminous sun. When a room is dark, a lamp is necessary to provide light enabling the eyes to perceive objects in it. When the sun has risen, there is no need of a lamp to see the objects. To see the sun no lamp is necessary, it is enough that one turns one's eyes towards the self-luminous sun. In a similar way, to see objects, the reflected light of the mind is necessary. But to a *jñāni*, it is not the reflected light of the mind dominated by the ego that illumines objects. The essence of the mind is only Consciousness. When the mind is not dominated by the ego, or "I"-thought, then the pure self awareness shines through the mind illuminating whatever is presented to it.

> Bhagavān explained: The Self is the Heart. The Heart is self-luminous. Light arises from the Heart and reaches the brain, which is the seat of the mind. The world is seen with the mind, that is, by the reflected light of the Self. It is perceived with the aid of the mind. When the mind is illumined it is aware of the world. When it is not itself so illumined, it is not aware of the world. If the mind is turned in towards the source of light, objective knowledge ceases and Self alone shines forth as the Heart. The moon shines by the reflected light of the sun. When the sun has set, the moon is useful for revealing objects. When the sun has risen, no one needs the moon, although the pale disc of the moon is visible in the sky.[2]

---

[1] CU 8.12.6.

[2] Venkataramiah, *Talks with Sri Ramana Maharshi,* 58.

Ramaṇa compared the Heart to the sun, the brain to the moon, and objects to the earth.[1] The light from the sun is reflected on the moon and the earth is illumined. In a similar way, the brain acts by consciousness derived from the Heart and objects are thus projected. So it is with the mind and the Heart. The mind is useful because of its reflected light. It is used for seeing objects. When it is turned inwards, the source of illumination shines forth by itself, and the mind remains dim and useless like the moon in day time. Ramaṇa remarked, "See the moon and also the cloud in the sky. There is no difference in their brilliance. The moon looks only like a speck of cloud. The *jñāni's* mind is like this moon before sunlight. It is there, but not shining of itself."[2] The Heart is the center from which vitality and light radiate to the brain, thus enabling it to function. The latent tendencies of individuals are enclosed in the Heart in their subtlest form, and then flow to the brain that reflects them highly magnified, corresponding to what is then perceived. The latent tendencies originate in the Heart and not the brain that is only the place for their manifestation.

What is important to note is that in the *jñāni's* mind is like the moon before sunlight. In the sky one can see the moon and also clouds. There is no difference in their brilliance and both shine only by the reflected light of the sun. Like the moon or clouds, the *jñāni's* mind is there, but not shining of itself. This, the *jñāni* is aware of and so, even if "objects" are perceived by the *jñāni*, they are not seen as individual objects but only shining appearances of the one indivisible Self. The *jñāni's* mind is not beclouded by the "I"-thought, the ego, and thus, what obscures the Self in others, just as the clouds obscure the ever-present, ever-luminous sun, does not obscure *jñāni's* perceptions.

The *aham-vṛtti*, the "I"-thought, the sense of individuality, does not function in a *jñāni*. The ordinary mind is full of excitement/passion *(rajas)* and dullness/lethargy *(tamas),* which both conceal the reality and project the unreal. The mind of a *jñāni* is pure *(śuddha-sattva)* and formless, functioning in the

---

[1] See *Ramana Gita.*

[2] Venkataramiah, *Talks with Sri Ramana Maharshi,* 254.

subtle sheath of knowledge *(vijñāna-maya-kośa)*, and it is through this that he keeps contact with the world.[1] Though *perceiving* the world, the *jñāni* sees the Self. A *jñāni* has a body, sense-organs, and a mind – from the perspective of ordinary reality. These continue to function, though they do so through the lens of *śuddha-sattva* and not through the three basic qualities of nature *(sattva, rajas,* and *tamas).* Quoting from the *Kaivalya*, Ramaṇa remarked:

> The modes of mind take shape as external objects and the light reflected on the modes illumines the objects. Now neglecting the modes of mind, look for the light illumining them. The mind becomes still and the light remains self-shining. The undulating mind (*i.e.* the mind associated with *rajas* = activity and *tamas* = darkness) is commonly known as the mind. Devoid of *rajas* and *tamas*, it is pure and self-shining. This is Self-Realization. Therefore the mind is said to be the means for it.[2]
>
> Bhagavan further explained: The Self is the Heart. The Heart is self-luminous. Light and it arises from the Heart and reaches the brain, which is the seat of the mind. The world is seen with the mind, that is, by the reflected light of the Self. It is perceived with the aid of the mind. When the mind is illumined it is aware of the world. When it is not itself so illumined, it is not aware of the world. If the mind is turned in towards the source of light, objective knowledge ceases and Self alone shines forth as the Heart.

On another occasion, Ramaṇa said in regards to how a *jñāni* perceives the world:

> Knowledge *(jñāna)* is not incompatible with ignorance *(ajñāna)* because the Self in purity is found to remain along with ignorance-seed *(ajñāna bīja)* in sleep. But

---

[1] See Cohen, *Guru Ramana*, 101-02.

[2] Venkataramiah, *Talks with Sri Ramana Maharshi*, 59-60.

> the incompatibility arises only in the waking and dream states. *Ajñāna* has two aspects: *āvaraṇa* (veiling) and *vikṣepa* (projection). Of these, *āvaraṇa* (veiling) signifies the veil hiding the Truth. That prevails in sleep. Projection *(vikṣepa)* is activity in different times. This gives rise to diversity and prevails in waking and dream states *(jagrat* and *svapna).* If the veil, *i.e.*, *āvaraṇa* is lifted, the Truth is perceived. It is lifted for a *Jñāni* and so his *kārana śarīra* (causal body) ceases to exist. *Vikṣepa* alone continues for him. Even so, it is not the same for a *Jñāni* as it is for an *ajñāni.* The *ajñāni* has all kinds of *vāsanas*, i.e.. *kartrtva* (doership) and *bhoktrtva* (enjoyership), whereas the *Jñāni* has ceased to be a doer *(kartā).* Thus, only one kind of *vasana* obtains for him. That too is very weak and does not overpower him, because he is always aware of the *sat-cit-ānanda* nature of the Self. The tenuous *bhoktrtva vāsanā* is the only remnant of the mind left in the *Jñāni* and he therefore appears to be living in the body.[1]

Thus, pure Consciousness shining through the inner organ, plus the reflected light of consciousness is known as the *jīva* or knower and the subsequent modes of the mind, together with the light are said to be the known, i.e. objects. Ramaṇa said: "The radio sings and speaks, but if you open it you will find no one inside. Similarly, my existence is like the space; though this body speaks like the radio, there is no one inside as a doer."[2]

How Can Duality Reside in Consciousness?

Ramaṇa maintained that the Self is pure Consciousness. As well, he maintained that the Self is One and non-dual. Knowledge *(jñāna)* is of the nature of light and ignorance is of the nature of darkness. The question arises: how can light and darkness, which are opposed to each other, co-exist in the same place at the same time? If they do co-exist in the same place,

[1] Ibid, 288-89.

[2] Sadhu Om, *Guru Vachaka Kovai Urai*, 360.

then they are not mutually exclusive and ignorance *(avidyā)* cannot be said to be destroyed by knowledge. Yet, if *avidyā* does not reside in Consciousness (either of the *jīva* or of Brahman[1]), then it would have to be admitted that omniscience would be a fact the moment that the Self is manifested. Further, if *avidyā* is located in Consciousness, is it located in the whole of Consciousness or only in part? It cannot be in the whole of Consciousness because an individual's Self-realization is defined as "the destruction of *avidyā*" *(avidyā-nāśa).* Nor can it be in a part, for Consciousness, by definition, is partless.

Advaitins accept that the Self, which is of the nature of Consciousness, is different from insentient objects. Advaita also declares that knowledge is opposed to ignorance. However, Advaita makes a distinction between *Brahman*-knowledge *(svarūpa-jñāna)* and empirical knowledge *(vṛtti-jñāna).* The former is pure Consciousness or *Brahman* while the latter is knowledge through a mental mode. When Advaita says that knowledge is opposed to ignorance, they mean *vṛtti-jñāna* and not *svarūpa-jñāna.* Brahman is not opposed to *avidyā*—but in fact reveals it. They are related as revealer and revealed. Thus, it is said that *Brahman* is not known. When *avidyā* is removed, it is said that *Brahman* is known. Being known or not known, both presuppose *avidyā* and are the work of the inner organ *(antaḥkaraṇa).* However, whether one has the cognition that *Brahman* is known or unknown, it does not follow that there is no *Brahman* or that *Brahman* is affected thereby.

The Self is of the nature of knowledge and reveals everything including ignorance *(avidyā).* How does one know that there is *avidyā?* It is not known through a valid means of knowledge *(pramāṇa)*, for, anything known through a *pramāṇa* must be valid.[2] If *avidyā* was admitted to be known through a *pramāṇa*, it too would be real and if real, it could not be sublated (i.e. the real never ceases and the unreal never is). If it could never be sublated, liberation would become an impossibility and, as well, the non-duality of *Brahman* would fall.

---

[1] Generally it may be said that the Bhāmati School says that the locus of *avidyā* is the *jīva* while the Vivaraṇa School places it in Brahman.

[2] *Pramā karaṇam pramāṇam*

Then how is *avidyā* revealed? If ignorance is revealed by the inner Witness-self *(sākṣin),* that raises a question. If ignorance is revealed by the Self on which it is dependent, how can it destroy that Self? According to Advaita, all things are revealed by the Witness-self as assisted by the external and/or internal sense organs. There are three things, however, which are revealed by the Witness-self alone *(kevala-sākṣi-bhāṣya):* Illusory *(prātibhāsika)* objects, subjective states of the mind (pleasure, pain, etc.), and ignorance. Valid cognitions come only through the mind *(vṛtti-jñāna)* while the *sākṣin* reveals both valid and invalid cognitions. Thus, the Self is not opposed to *avidyā*; it merely witnesses both knowledge and ignorance.

So, "how can *vṛtti-jñāna* be removed"? Advaita replies to this enquiry by stating that *vṛtti-jñāna* is of two types: partite knowledge *(khandākāra-vṛtti-jñāna)* and impartite knowledge *(akhaṇḍākāra-vṛtti-jñāna).* The former removes ignorance when both of them have the same content. But, to obtain knowledge of *Brahman*, the *vṛtti* that is required is no ordinary *vṛtti.* Ordinary *vṛttis* have the form of an object and are thus fragmented, but *Brahman* has no form. Thus the modal cognition through which *Brahman* is apprehended is called indivisible modal knowledge. It alone is able to remove the ignorance which conceals the nature of *Brahman.*

The *akhaṇḍākāra-vṛtti-jñāna* is the indivisible knowledge of the Self through which *Brahman* is apprehended. It is the knowledge that arises through a mental mode, the object of which is the indivisible *Brahman.* It destroys every other *vṛtti,* giving rise to the direct perception of *Brahman,* and then perishes itself, as well, leaving only the ever-existent Reality. Ramaṇa said:

> O mind, other than meditation which takes the form of the *akhaṇḍākāra-vṛtti* [unbroken experience] that shines as the Self, have you discovered any means to burn to ashes the evil "I am the doer" belief that propels and plunges the *jīva* into the bottom of the ocean of *karma*? If you have, let me know.

The Advaitin says that *avidyā* is not permanent, but can be removed by knowledge. Further, the Advaitin says that ignorance is inexplicable *(anirvacanīya)*. If knowledge is its antidote, knowledge must be *nirvacanīya*. As "definable" *(nirvacanīya)*, is knowledge real or unreal, both, or neither? It cannot be neither, for we have already eliminated the possibility of its being *anirvacanīya*. It cannot be both for that violates the law of contradiction. If it is real, is it identical with *Brahman* or different? It cannot be identical for it would then be *svarūpa-jñāna* and *svarūpa-jñāna* is not opposed to *avidyā*. If it is real and different *(vṛtti-jñāna)*, then dualism arises which is against the fundamental tenet of Advaita.

The Advaitin accepts that knowledge is real—for it comes from a *pramāna*, i.e. either scripture or the words *(sabda)* of Sages, and what comes from a *pramāna* is real, according to Advaita. *Vṛtti-jñāna* is empirically real and *akhaṇḍākāra-vṛtti-jñāna* is uniquely real as it holds a special status. *Akhaṇḍākāra-vṛtti-jñāna* removes *avidyā* as well as all of *avidyā's* effects and then perishes because its material cause *(avidyā)* is destroyed. The traditional example given is: "poison being taken as an antidote for poison and once it has done its work, it vanishes along with the original effects".

This "removal" is called, *"avidyā nivṛtti upalakṣita"*. It seems as though *avidyā* is present and obscuring *Brahman*. It also appears as though *avidyā* gets removed. But, truly, the final position of the Advaitin is that nothing is happening, ever happened, or will happen. *Brahman/Atman* alone is, was, and will be.

Note that *akhaṇḍākāra-vṛtti-jñāna* is no ordinary *vṛtti*. Generally, to remove ignorance requires knowledge. This removal takes the form of a fragmented mental cognition. Yet, impartite knowledge is unique. In the words of Gauḍapāda, "The mind becomes no-mind". Once its work is finished, it removes itself too, thus leaving the ever-existent, self-luminous Reality "revealed". It is similar to the act of using a thorn to remove a thorn and then discarding both once the job is finished. Thus, there is the saying, "By the mind alone It is to be perceived" and "That which cannot be thought of by the mind".[1] In such an impartite cognition, the *vṛtti* brings the unknown

---

[1] KeU I.5.

Brahman into contact with the mind—thus destroying one's ignorance concerning *Brahman.* However, it doesn't take another consciousness to reveal *Brahman*, for, *Brahman* is self-luminous.

Perception

Perception (*pratyakṣa*) is the foundation stone, without which no epistemological or metaphysical structure can be built. It is the most fundamental, and therefore the most important, of the *pramāṇas.* Philosophy commences with the common, everyday view of the world and that view is built upon perception. All subsequent theories, therefore, either start from perception or else must offer a satisfactory account of perception. It is a basic fact that the world is perceived. Any philosophical account of the world must acknowledge this fact.

The distinguishing feature of perception is its immediacy or directness. As well, perception is possible only of things present and capable of being perceived. For example, yesterday's experiences are not currently present and the mind, though present, is not capable of being an object of perception. Finally, knowledge derived from perception is valid only when it is not sublated by other knowledge.

The sublatability of knowledge test means that knowledge of *Brahman* is the only (true) *pramana.* Empirical knowledge remains unsublated up to the cognition of *Brahman* and it is only in this sense that it is regarded as valid. Empirical validity belongs to the knowledge of the world.

Perception is defined as "that which is the distinctive cause of valid perceptual knowledge." Perception's immediacy follows from the fact that in perceptual knowledge the non-difference of the cognitive consciousness from the content-defined consciousness is brought about through a mental modification *(vṛtti).* We noted earlier that knowledge arises when there is a modification of the mind in the form of an object. Truly speaking, this is but an expression of Pure Consciousness appearing as knowledge through a mental mode.

Thus, the rationale behind perceptual knowledge is that the indivisible Pure Consciousness appears as a divided trio of knower, known, and knowledge. Perceptual knowledge is immediate because the subject and the object are one. The known object is consciousness limited and the knowing subject is the same consciousness-limited by a modification of the internal organ. Perception's immediacy and directness is possible because it partakes of the metaphysical nature of Reality.

Perception is special because it gives immediate knowledge. No other *pramāṇa* does this. Inference is dependent upon perception and verbal testimony is dependent upon perception and inference. Perception alone is the primary source of knowledge, and all the other *pramāṇas* (excepting that which relates to the supersensible) are dependent upon it in one way or another.

According to Ramaṇa, perception *(pratyakṣa)* is special, immediate, and direct, but he redefines exactly what true perception is:

> Direct perception is ever-present Experience. God Himself is known as directly perceived. It does not mean that He appears before the devotee with four-arms, etc. Unless the Realization be eternal it cannot serve any useful purpose. Can the appearance with four hands be eternal realization? It is phenomenal and illusory. There must be a seer. The seer alone is real and eternal. Let God appear as the light of a million suns: Is it *pratyakṣa?* To see it, the eyes, the mind, etc. are necessary. It is indirect knowledge, whereas the seer is direct experience. The seer alone is *pratyakṣa.* All other perceptions are only secondary knowledge. The present super-imposition of the body as "I" is so deep-rooted, that the vision before the eyes is considered *pratyakṣa* but not the seer himself.[1]
>
> What is *pratyakṣa?* Do you call perception of a mango *pratyakṣa?* It involves the play of *karma, kartā,* and

[1] Venkataramiah, *Talks with Sri Ramana Maharshi,* 258.

kārya (action, doer and deed). So it is relative and not absolute. Because you see a thing now, you say there is nothing afterwards (*i.e.*, when you no longer see it). Both are functions of the mind. What lies behind both these assertions is *pratyakṣa.* There is *indriya pratyakṣa* (directly perceived by senses), *manasa pratyakṣa* (directly perceived by the mind) and *sākṣat pratyakṣa* (realized as the very Being). The last alone is true. The others are relative and untrue.

Pratyakṣa is very being and it is not feeling, etc. See if you are the seeker. The Self is often mistaken for the knower. Is there not the Self in deep sleep, *i.e.*, nescience? Therefore the Self is beyond knower and knowledge. These doubts are in the realm of mind. To speak from this point of view, the advice is to keep the mind clear, and when *rajas* and *tamas* are wiped off, then the *sattva* mind alone exists. So the "I" vanishes in the *sattva. Jñāna cakṣus* does not mean that it is an organ of perception like the other sense-organs. So long as there is a subject and also an object it is only relative knowledge. *Jñāna* lies beyond relative knowledge. It is absolute. The Self is the source of subject and object. When ignorance is prevailing, the subject is taken to be the source. The subject is the knower and forms one of the triads whose components cannot exist independent of one another. So the subject or the knower cannot be the ultimate Reality. Reality lies beyond subject and object. When realized there will be no room for doubt. The heart knot is snapped; doubts are set at rest. That is called *pratyakṣa* and not what you are thinking of. *Avidyā nāśa* (destruction of ignorance) alone is Self-Realization. Self-Realization is only a euphemism for the elimination of ignorance.[1]

---

[1] Ibid, 280.

The Process in Knowing

When an object is manifest to the subject-consciousness, there is external perception. The object must exist at the time of perception; it must be able to be directly known; an intimate relation must exist between the subject and the object; and the object must not be contradicted.

In any external perception, four distinct factors are operative: the knowing self, the mind, the sense-organ, and the object. If any one of these is missing, no perception is possible. However, of these four, the knowing Self alone is conscious and intrinsically luminous. Without its light, no object will be manifest. "This light is reflected in all. That shining, everything shines."[1] Not only must the mind be joined with the sense-organ, but the self must be related to the object. It is obvious that the mind is distinct from the sense-organ and both again are distinct from the object. Further, these three are distinct from the self. The mind, along with the sense-organs and objects is inert, non-conscious. "It (mind) is not self-luminous, because it is observable."

The mind, in conjunction with the sense-organs, perceives sense-objects. It is impelled by its outgoing tendencies as induced by the impressions of previous actions. Both the mind and a sense-organ are necessary to complete the connection between the subject and the object in external perception. This is obvious from examples where the connection is lacking, i.e. where the sense-organ is defective or where the object is too near or far away and thus no perception is possible.

Though both the mind and the sense-organs are necessary in external perception, it is the mind which is the decidedly instrumental factor. "The other organs are but channels of the mind." This is obvious from such examples as, "though I was looking in that direction, I did not see it, for my mind was somewhere else."

The process of external perception of an object is that the mind goes out to an object through a sense-organ. On reaching the object, the mind becomes identified with it and assumes its

---

[1] MuU 2.2.10-11.

form. This modification of the mind *(vṛtti)* is then illuminated by the *Atman* or consciousness which is present as the observer *(sākṣin)* in all acts of knowledge. This process may be broken into the following parts: the knower *(pramātā),* the object known *(prameya),* the resulting knowledge *(pramiti),* and the means of knowledge *(pramāṇa).* All of these parts are manifestations of the same underlying Consciousness.

The process may be summarized: (1) The mind of the knower in conjunction with a sense-organ reaches out to an object, identifies with it and assumes its form. (2) The modification of the mind removes the veil of ignorance that was hiding the object from the knower. (3) The consciousness underlying the object, which is being manifest through the mental modification, illumines the object; (4) The mental modification associates the object-consciousness with the subject-consciousness; (5) The knower perceives the object.

Ramaṇa spoke of a similar process:

> Now you think that you are the body. You see things around you and you want to see the Self in a similar manner. Such is the force of habit. The senses are mere instruments of perception. *You* are the seer. Remain as the seer only. What else is there to see? *Āvaraṇa* (veiling) does not hide the *jīva* in entirety; he knows that he is; only he does not know who he is. He sees the world; but not that it is only *Brahman*. It is light in darkness (or knowledge in ignorance). In a cinema show the room is first darkened, artificial light is introduced; only in this light are the pictures projected. For differentiation a reflected light is thus necessary. A sleeper dreams, he is not out of sleep: only in the darkness or ignorance of sleep can he see the unreal dream objects. Similarly the darkness of ignorance gives rise to the knowledge of the perceptions of the world. This veiling is a characteristic of ignorance; it is not of the Self: it cannot affect the Self in any manner; it can veil only the *jīva.* The ego is insentient: united with the light from the Self, it is called *jīva.* But the ego and the light cannot be seen distinct from each other; they are always united together. The mixed product is

the *jīva*, the root of all differentiation. All these are spoken of to satisfy the questioners.[1]

[1] Ibid, 303, 309-10.

IV
Ramana and Metaphysics

> *Once there was a seeker by name Vāskalin who approached the Upaniṣadic Sage, Bahva, about the Absolute. Three times the question was asked by Vāskalin and three times Bahva remained silent. Finally, Vāskalin, in exasperation, pleaded: "Why don't you answer me?" Bahva replied: "I am teaching you, indeed, but you do not understand. Silent is the Self."*[1]

Ramaṇa Maharshi has often been praised as one of the greatest embodiments of Advaita Vedānta, as great as the greatest of that illustrious group. Such a wonder the world seldom sees. An Advaitin's Advaitin if you will. Frequently he is described as "an incarnation of Advaita". The description is an intriguing philosophical oxymoron as the truth of Advaita boldly declares that no one has ever been born, lived, or died, and yet it is without doubt an astonishingly powerful image in conveying the profound affinity that exists between the teachings of Advaita and Ramaṇa. As one passes the philosophically relevant portions of Ramaṇa's teachings through the lens of Advaita, they will be seen to be in perfect accordance with the philosophy of Advaita. What is all the more astonishing is that Ramaṇa's teachings emerged spontaneously as the fruit of his great awakening and only subsequently, almost by accident, did he learn of the ancient teachings. Paul Brunton said about this:

> The ancient lore, the Upaniṣads, has received a striking confirmation from the life and teachings of the Sage of

[1] BSB 3.3.17.

Aruṇācala, known as Bhagavān Śrī Ramaṇa. To his disciples, both eastern and western, the written and oral teachings of the Sage are the *primary* revelation, and the ancient lore is of value because it is found to be in full accord with those teachings. But even for those who look upon the ancient lore as of primary authority, the teachings of a living Sage must be profoundly interesting.[1]

Ramana and Reality

The central teaching around which all of Ramaṇa's teachings are centered is: "In the center of the heart-cave the pure *Brahman* alone shines directly in the form of the Self, as 'I'—'I'. Abide in the Self." Anything he said, he said not with an interest in building a system of thought, but as a spontaneous revelation of the Self. His sole function was in revealing the Self. Everyone and everything is a manifestation of the Self and, if one wants to attribute a purpose to Ramaṇa's teachings, it was in showing the direction in which everyone is this Truth.

Ramaṇa would sometimes, even if infrequently, give definitions of Reality when asked. Once, when an enquirer asked, "What is reality?" he replied:

> Reality must always be real. It is not with forms and names. That which underlies these is the Reality. It underlies limitations, being itself limitless. It is not bound. It underlies unrealities, itself being Real. Reality is that which is. It is as it is. It transcends speech. It is beyond the expressions "existence, non-existence", and so on.[2]

The Reality, according to Ramaṇa, is not a "He," a personal being, nor is it an "It", an impersonal concept. The Reality, Brahman, is a name for the experience of the timeless fullness of Being.

---

[1] See *Mahā Yoga*, foreword by Paul Brunton.

[2] Venkataramiah, *Talks with Sri Ramana Maharshi*, 123.

> The Reality, which is the pure Consciousness that remains when ignorance is destroyed along with knowledge of objects, alone is the Self *(Ātman)*. In that real form of the Absolute *(Brahma-svarūpa)*, which is limitless Self-awareness, there is not the least ignorance.[1]

The Absolute is Truth, Wisdom, Infinitude, says the *Upaniṣ ad*.[2] The Absolute is Existence, Consciousness, Bliss, says Ramaṇa.[3] What is the Reality? Silence is the answer for Reality is that whence all speech along with the mind retreat, being unable to reach, not attaining It."[4]

Reality is a tantalizer. It is the immense mystery which knowledge cannot contain. It is a pathless land. It is the song that calls to every philosopher who seeks to find the basic, intrinsically intelligible bedrock of it all from which everything arises and into which individual personal experience culminates. Is there a truth, anywhere, which is so certain that no reasonable individual could possibly doubt its veracity? The siren of certainty beckons. The thunderous silence roars.

What is what-is? Reality must be found in oneself—whatever that self is or may be. Bliss lies in the realization of what is. The search for that which "Is," in the most concrete and fundamental sense, is the motivating force and inspiration behind both Śaṅkara and Ramaṇa's thought. It is the song of the siren. The discovery of that which "is" constitutes the discovery or unveiling of the truth, as well as itself embodying freedom.

What is this aspiration for Reality? The quest is to find that which is not bounded, not limited. There are said to be big truths and little truths. There are useful truths and not so useful truths; objective truths and subjective truths; truths with a small "t" and Truth with a capital "T." Against the manifold

---

[1] Ibid.

[2] TU 2.1.1. *satyam jñānam anantam brahma.*

[3] Suri Nagamma, *Letters from Sri Ramanasramam,* 196.

[4] TU 2.4.1 *yato vāco nivartante aprāpya manasā saha.*

conventions of society, Ramaṇa experienced Reality where it could not escape into theory—in one's very heart. The *Upaniṣad* says: "Having known every branch of knowledge but the Self, one knows, verily, nothing, and one is miserable."[1] Ramaṇa said:

> What use is the learning of those who do not seek to wipe out the letters of destiny (from their brow) by enquiring: "Whence is the birth of us who know the letters?" They have sunk to the level of a gramophone. What else are they, O Aruṇācala?

The Being of being is the Reality. According to Śaṅkara, the individual human being is a conscious living being. The individual is singled out as the principal being because individuals uniquely have eligibility for action and knowledge.[2]

> The *Atman* is expanded only in humans. They, indeed, are most endowed with intelligence. They give expression to what is known. They see what is known. They know what is to come. They know the visible and the invisible. They perceive the immortal through the mortal. Thus are they endowed. But with other animals, eating and drinking alone constitute the sphere of their knowledge.[3]

According to both Śaṅkara and Ramaṇa, nothing is more certain than the fact of one's own existence. It is self-evident, immediate and direct. No one is able to disbelieve in one's own existence. "A person may doubt of many things, of anything else; but one can never doubt one's own being."[4] "Everyone knows "I am". No one can deny his own being."[5] This is because the very act of doubting would be but an affirmation of

---

[1]CU 7.1.1. The story of Nārada and Sanatkumāra

[2] TU *Bhāṣya* Also: KU *Bhāṣya* 2.2.35; BU *Bhāṣya* 1.4.19 'Of all creatures man *alone* has the power of discrimination and freedom of will.'

[3] *Aitareya-Āraṇyaka* III.11.3.

[4] BSB II.3.7.

[5] Mudaliar, *Day by Day with Bhagavan*, 244.

one's very existence. In the act of saying, "I don't exist", who is the "I" who is doing the doubting? The siren of certainty beckons.

One notices that Ramaṇa, in a manner similar to the Advaita tradition, would define Reality employing words in one of two ways: By stating its essential nature *(svarūpa-lakṣaṇa)* or, for the purpose of distinguishing it from other things, by stating its accidental attributes *(taṭastha-lakṣ-aṇa).*[1] For example, one may be defined in terms of one's essential nature as (Existence, Consciousness, Bliss) or by any of his/her accidental attributes, e.g., maleness, femaleness, height, weight, profession, and so on. While both definitions define a thing from all others, the essential nature of a thing is eternally present while accidental attributes remain in that thing only for a limited period of time. Which definition Ramaṇa used depended upon context and convenience.

While the Advaita tradition makes use of both definitions, it traditionally begins with the definition of accidental attributes first. It does this for two practical methodological reasons. First of all, a definition that is based on familiar modes of thinking is easily comprehensible to most people. The teacher leads a seeker "from the known to the unknown." First attributes, qualities and relations are superimposed on the Reality so as to enable a person to form some sort of rudimentary understanding. Then gradually these attributes are negated as a deeper and deeper analysis is performed. From the familiar, one is led to the unfamiliar. Secondly, there arises an unusual difficulty in the case of *Brahman/Atman* because it is not an empirical object. We have already noted that the non-dual Self cannot be defined using words since it is beyond, it transcends the reach of words and the mind.[2] This being noted, the *Upaniṣ ads* do attempt to define the Absolute from both the *svarūpa* and *taṭastha-lakṣaṇa* perspectives for teaching purposes. Since individuals are familiar with the world and the concept of causality, Brahman is first defined as the cause of the universe. This causality is an accidental attribute superimposed on

---

[1] VP 7.

[2] TU 2.4.1.Also see BU *Bhāṣya* 2.3.6 wherein Śaṅkara states, "The Absolute can never be properly denoted by any word(s), including the word 'Absolute' (Ātman)."

Brahman. Such a definition makes the Absolute appear subject to categories, attributes, and the causal scheme. Such definitions are always open to challenge. The concept of causality or the "proofs for the existence of God" are evidence enough to show the tentativeness and uncertainty that accompanies such a definition. Categories cannot transgress their logical limits. Either the unconditional Absolute is within the realm of the phenomena, and thus not unconditional, or else its existence and nature can only be dogmatically asserted. Acknowledging this, it is said that such a (provisional) definition is still useful in certain circumstances.

Then, having defined *Brahman* in this preliminary manner as the cause of the world, the *Upaniṣads* go on to define *Brahman* in terms of its essential nature. Such definitions include: *"Brahman* is the Truth of truth, the Real of the real"; *"Brahman* is Real *(Satyam),* Wisdom *(Jñānam),* Infinite *(Anantam);¿* "Being *(Sat),* Consciousness *(Cit),* Bliss *(Ānanda)."* It should be noted here that these terms are not separate or accidental attributes of *Brahman* but its essential nature; *Brahman* is Real, It is Being, It is Consciousness; Consciousness is Infinite, is Bliss and so on.

Perhaps the most common and oft-quoted essential definition of *Brahman* is *sat-cit-ānanda*. Śaṅkara said that these three words were employed merely for the purpose of differentiating Brahman from the name and form world that is unreal, non-intelligent, and finite.[1] Though these three words in the *Upaniṣad* are affirmative in form, their import is only negative because they are being used to indicate what *Brahman* is not, i.e. *Brahman* is not unreal, not non-conscious, and not finite. Ramaṇa remarked: "*Sat-cit-ānanda* is said to indicate that the Supreme is not different from Being *(asat),* not different from Consciousness *(acit)* and not different from Bliss *(anānanda).* Because we are in the phenomenal world we speak of the Self as *sat-cit-ānanda*."

Ramaṇa, not being overly interested in philosophy, was, more often than not, when asked, either silent or presented a *svarūpa-lakṣaṇa* definition of Reality. Unless pushed, he rarely

---

[1] TU *Bhāṣya* 2.1.1.

spoke of accidental definitions though, like the Upaniṣadic methodology, he always began with what is known to an individual, i.e. "I". On the other hand, he quite often spoke of the Reality as Existence *(Sat* in Sanskrit and *Ulladu* in Tamil). One should be aware that the term Existence in this context does not mean any particular existent, anything with name and form. It is not a predicate of an object. It should be noted here that this is a fundamental distinction propounded by Ramaṇa. If this is not correctly understood, inappropriate criticisms may rise, which they often did. Ramaṇa regarded Existence as the essential nature of the Reality. The Reality is Existence and Existence is the Reality. This Existence *(Sat)* is not the existence that is meaningful only in an object. Pure Being or *"Sat"* is not one being among beings. Existence, as it is usually used in both empirical and philosophical discourse, is a determinative description, a categorical expression, e.g., the man exists or the house exists. Ramaṇa was quick to point out that the Reality is neither "existent" nor "non-existent" in the ordinary sense of those terms. He said: "Reality must always be real. It is not with forms and names. Reality is that which is. It is as it is. It transcends speech and is beyond the expressions "existence, non-existence, and so on." The Reality merely *is,* and can never be designated exclusively as this or that. As it is pure Being, no causal relationship can be applied to it.

Ramaṇa would quote an analogy from the *Chāndogya Upaniṣad* to explain the relation between Reality as Existence and the various appearances that are existents, appearances with names and forms. Gold appears in a variety of forms, as rings, necklaces, bracelets, cups, plates, and so on. In the various objects, what is real is gold and the names and forms of each object are superimposed upon the gold. Gold persists while names and forms come and go. When the superimposition of names and forms is removed, all that remains is gold and gold alone. In his *Forty Verses on Existence*, Ramaṇa said: "The many ornaments are illusory. Say, do they exist apart from the gold which is real?"[1] The *Chāndogya Upaniṣad* says: "Just as . . . by one nugget of gold, all that is made of gold becomes

---

[1] *Forty Verses on Existence,* verse 13.

known."[1] In a similar way, the entire world with all its names and forms, all the existent particulars, are superimposed upon the Reality that is Existence.

Sometimes Ramaṇa would make use of another analogy from the *Chāndogya Upaniṣad.* Clay may take different forms in a potter's hands and thus become known as pots, cups, plates, and so forth. Really speaking, all these objects are but clay, through and through, though they are conventionally and individually called by various names. Each is a particular form in which the same clay appears. Even so, the Reality appears in different forms and is called by various names. To concentrate on the form makes one forget the basis. A potter is indifferent to the various manifestations and knows that each item is only clay in various shapes and sizes. The appearances are invested with a name and form but what abides is the Reality. The Sage Aruni said to his son, Śvetaketu:

> My dear, just as by one clod of clay all that is made of clay may be known, the difference being only a name, arising from speech, but the truth being that all is clay; and just as, my dear, by one nugget of gold all that is made of gold may be known, the difference being only a name arising from speech, but the truth being that all is gold.

This is the bold declaration of Ramaṇa, namely, whatever is, is nothing but the Reality, the Self, the Absolute. The entire manifold universe is nothing but *Brahman*. As *Brahman*, it always exists as pure Existence and never undergoes any change. To realize this is to realize that all names and forms really only refer to that Reality. Names and forms are like an illusion conjured up by a magician. When the real nature of the illusion is pointed out, what disappears is only the illusion that seemingly presented itself as something other than what it is. Being unsubstantial, the names and forms appearance have no ability to affect the nature of the Reality. Once one realizes this, never again will the existents as separate entities be taken for Reality and yet one can still perceive their appearances—but

---

[1] CU 6.1.5.

never again as anything other than gold, clay, the Reality. On this point Ramaṇa said:

> The ordinary man lives in the brain unaware of himself in the Heart. The Sage lives in the Heart. When a Sage moves about and deals with men and things, he knows that what he sees is not separate from the one supreme reality, Brahman, which he realized in the Heart, as his own Self, the Real. The Sage who has realized the supreme truth of his own Existence realizes that it is the one supreme reality that is there behind him, behind the world. In fact, he is aware of the One, as the Real, the Self in all selves, in all things, eternal and immutable, in all that is impermanent and mutable.[1]

Ramaṇa regarded the Absolute as that which is foundational to all experience though it is in no sense a substance. He replied when once asked the question, "what is reality?" "That which underlies all names and forms is the Reality. It underlies limitations being itself limitless. It is not bound. It underlies unrealities, itself being real." The Reality is that which is different from the phenomenal, the spatial, the temporal, and the sensible. It is not to be located in space, though seemingly it is everywhere—since all things imply, and depend upon it. It is seemingly nowhere since it is not a thing that has spatial relations to anything. Its nature is inexpressible since to say anything about it is to make it into a particular thing.

Living in a state of pure Consciousness was natural for Ramaṇa. It was constant, with no beginning or end; complete, full, ever Blissful, silent and peaceful. Memory did not keep it in place; when memories occurred they were the dependent ones. Even while perceiving things, mysteriously they were observed without dividing into separate objects. Consciousness was not broken or split into a knower, a known, and a process of knowing. Abiding as it is, the Self, appearances come and go, Though Ramaṇa moved about and dealt with people and things, never was he separated from the one supreme Reality.

---

[1] *Sat-Darshana Bhāṣya*, xx.

According to Ramaṇa, the Reality that is pure Existence is pure Consciousness or pure Awareness. He said: "The Self is pure Being, pure Awareness. You are Awareness. Awareness is another name for you. The body, which by itself is inert, does not say "I". From the perspective of an ordinary person there are three states of consciousness or awareness: waking, dreaming, and deep or dreamless sleep. (Ramaṇa and Advaita often speak of a fourth state *(turīya)* which is pure Consciousness that underlies and permeates these three). Listen to what Ramaṇa said:

> There is only one state, that of Consciousness or Awareness or Existence. The three states of waking, dream, and sleep cannot be real. They simply come and go. The Real will always exist. The "I" or existence that alone persists in all the three states is real. The other three are not real and so it is not possible to say they have such and such a degree of reality. We may roughly put it like this. Existence or Consciousness is the only reality. Consciousness plus waking, we call waking. Consciousness plus sleep, we call sleep. Consciousness plus dream, we call dream. Consciousness is the screen on which the pictures come and go. The screen is real, the pictures are mere shadows on it. Because by long habit we have been regarding these three states as real, we call the state of mere awareness or consciousness the fourth. There is, however, no fourth state, but only one state.[1]

In the waking state, you are there, aware, the sun is the light of the world, the world with all its multiplicity is perceived as real, and the world exists external to oneself. The gift of the waking state is that it creates an awareness in each individuality that there is a reality (even though what this reality actually is, is incorrectly understood). In the dreaming state, you are there, aware, the mind is the light of all you perceive, you create the experienced universe, and the world you perceive is internal to oneself. The gifts of the dreaming state reveal that the world

---

[1] Mudaliar, *Day by Day with Bhagavan,* I, 58.

may quite possibly and logically neither be real nor external to oneself and that it just may be the case that nothing ever really happens. The dream state also points to possibility that the waking state may be but a dream.

Last night you may have dreamed that you went to Los Angeles and had dinner with Brad Pitt. While the dream lasted, everything seemed real enough. But upon waking, did you really go to Los Angeles or have dinner there? Nothing of the sort really happened even though you experienced such. Dreams are taken to be real so long as the dream lasts. Yet, in the history of the world, there is not one philosopher who has been able to prove that the waking state is nothing more than an extended dream. Finally, in the deep sleep state, you are there; there are no desires, no dreams, no imperfections; you are aware as pure awareness (a fact which is revealed when you wake up and declare, "I slept so soundly I was aware of nothing"—(this experience of inertness is impossible without an element of awareness being present), and the world does not exist. The gift of deep sleep is that the world does not need to exist in order for you to. The Self is beyond desires and dreams. Though one's body is being ravaged by cancer or one has just won the lottery, there is neither pain nor pleasure, neither maleness nor femaleness, neither this nor that in this state—yet you are. Ramaṇa said: "A person says, "I had a dream; I was deep asleep; I am awake". You must admit that he is there in all the three states. That makes it clear that he is there all the time."

> Sri Bhagavān said: All mistake the mind-consciousness for Self-Consciousness. There is no mind in deep sleep; but no one denies his being in sleep. Even a child says on waking, "I slept well," and does not deny its existence. The "I" rises up, the mind turns outward through the five senses and perceives objects, this they call direct perception. Asked if "I" is not directly perceived, they get confused, because "I" does not announce itself as an object in front and only the perception with the senses can be recognized by them as knowledge: this habit is so strong with them. A stanza in the *Thevāram* says: "O Sages, eager to get over all misery, worry not about inferences and

examples! Our Light is ever shining forth from within! With mind clear, live in God!" This is direct perception. Will the common people admit it? They want God to appear in front of them as a bright Being mounted on a bull. Such a vision once originated must also end. It is therefore transient. *Thevāram* speaks of the Eternal and Ever-experienced Being. This *Thevāram* stanza takes one directly to the Reality.[1]

Ramaṇa likened Consciousness to a movie screen. He said:

The screen is always there but various pictures appear on the screen and then disappear. Nothing sticks to the screen, it remains a screen. Similarly, you remain your own Self in all the three states of existence. If you know that, the three states will not trouble you, just as the pictures which appear on the screen do not stick to it. On the screen, you sometimes see a huge ocean with endless waves; that disappears. Another time, you see fire spreading all around; that too disappears. The screen is there on both occasions. Did the screen get wet with water or did it get burned by the fire? Nothing affected the screen. In the same way, the things that happen during the waking, dreaming, and sleep states do not affect you at all; you remain forever your own Self.

Ramaṇa sometimes elucidated the nature of Consciousness by narrating a passage from the tenth chapter of Vidyāraṇya's *Pañcadaśī:*

Vidyāraṇya gives an example of the light that is kept on the stage of a theatre. When a drama is being played, the light is there, which illuminates, without any distinction, all the actors, whether they be kings or servants or dancers, and also all the audience. That light will be there before the drama begins, during the performance and also after the performance is over.

---

[1] Venkataramiah, *Talks with Sri Ramana Maharshi,* 288.

Similarly, the light within, that is, the Self, gives light to the ego, the intellect, the memory and the mind without itself being subject to the processes of growth and decay. Although during deep sleep and other states there is no feeling of the ego, that Self remains attributeless, and continues to shine of itself.

While the Self reveals everything, it itself is not revealed by anything. The Self is never an object to anything. As we observed earlier, the Self is called the knowing subject in ordinary, everyday external perceptions when it is associated with, and functions through, the mind. The indivisible non-dual pure Consciousness appears divided, dualistic in relational knowledge. This process necessarily and invariably involves the three distinct factors: the knower, the object known, and the resultant knowledge. Such knowledge is referred to as *vṛtti-jñāna* (knowledge derived from a modification of the mind). *Vṛtti-jñāna* or empirical knowledge is a blend of the modification of the mind and the reflection of Consciousness therein. It is an expression of pure Consciousness through a mental mode corresponding to an object. Fundamentally and primarily, knowledge is Pure Consciousness. When it is expressed through a mental mode it is called (secondarily) knowledge by courtesy.

The Self is called the witness *(sākṣin)* when it directly reveals the various internal mental modes. In the case of knowing the mind, there is nothing else to mediate between the Self and the mind. Thus, it is said that the mind is directly revealed by the Witness-Self. However, in whatever way Consciousness is said to function, it is never an object to anything. Nothing exists which can know Consciousness. Material objects are inert and can know nothing. The sense organs and the mind are also inert and cannot function without the light of Consciousness. Even Consciousness cannot know itself for It is one and non-dual and cannot split into a knowing subject and a known object. Thus, Consciousness is declared to be Self-luminous in the sense that, while Consciousness reveals everything, it itself is not revealed by anything.

Any type of knowledge requires and is dependent upon luminosity to reveal what was previously unknown. But the Self is not an object of knowledge. Nor can one say that Consciousness is unknown. Everyone knows that they exist. It would be totally absurd to declare, "I do not exist", for to deny oneself is to affirm oneself. Who is doing the denial? Thus, Consciousness must be Self-luminous. As long as one believes that one has the body, with such and such characteristics, the Self is spoken of as being Existence, Consciousness, Self-luminous and so on and such descriptions are not applicable to any other entity. Further, this does not mean they are characteristics of the Self. Such are the limitations of language.

If one were to speak about knowing the Self, there would have to be two selves—one a knowing self and the other the self which is known, as well as the process of knowing. As the Self, as Consciousness, is non-dual, who is to know what? A person can only be the Self. One does not attain Consciousness, attain something new or reach some far away goal. Consciousness has been there all along, persisting throughout the three states of experience. All that is required is to give up one's false notions of what the Reality is.

Finally, the Self is Bliss. Ramaṇa said:

> Perfect Bliss is *Brahman*. Perfect Peace is of the Self. That alone Exists and is Consciousness. That which is called happiness is only the nature of the Self; Self is not other than perfect happiness. That which is called happiness alone exists. Knowing that fact and abiding in the Self, enjoy Bliss eternally.

To live experientially as *Brahman* is Bliss. The Self is such incomparable Bliss that no words could ever approach it. Such Bliss cannot be talked about; it can only be experienced. It does not depend on any external factor but is completely independent and unconditioned.

Obviously, true happiness cannot be due to external causes such as objects, possessions, or emotions. If this were true, then a person's happiness would increase with the increase of possessions and decrease with the decrease of possessions. If one chocolate bar produces some happiness, then one hundred bars eaten consecutively should produce one hundred times the happiness. But this is not the case. Owning everything in the universe is not humanly possible and just because a person owns nothing does not necessarily imply that they have no happiness at all. In the state of deep sleep a person has no possessions, including his own body and thoughts, but instead of being unhappy, he is extremely happy. Bliss must be natural, the very nature of the Self.

In the ordinary scheme of life, an individual feels satisfaction when an object of their desire is obtained. Upon obtaining an object of one's desire, the mind temporarily turns within and rests in itself with a sense of satisfaction and contentment. However, it is the way of the world that soon, usually immediately, another desire arises and the process repeats itself. Doesn't this reveal that lasting happiness does not lie in objects of desire? Ramaṇa would point out that the Self is Bliss, and this Bliss is natural, unvarying and constant. Objects come and go and will eventually be abandoned. However, the Self can neither be taken up nor abandoned. One can take up that which one doesn't already have and one can abandon that which has once been taken up. But the Self is of the nature of unconceivable, unending Bliss. Ramaṇa remarked: "For one, who, having destroyed the ego, is awake to the nature of the Self which is Bliss, what is there to be accomplished?" And, "You can have, or rather you will yourself be, the highest imaginable kind of happiness. All other kinds of happiness which you have spoken of as "pleasure", "joy", and "bliss" are only reflections of the Bliss *(ānanda)* which is your true nature, you are."

The Self is Existence, Consciousness, Bliss. In one of his hymns to Aruṇācala, Ramaṇa interpreted the three syllables in the name A-ru-na to stand for Existence, Consciousness, Bliss. In another hymn to Aruṇācala, he describes Aruṇācala as "Being and Consciousness," and as the "Ocean of Bliss."

Ramana and Maya

Is the world real? Has it ever come to you and said, "I am real" or asked "Why do I exist, how was I created"? Or is it your mind that has determined that the world is real and seeks answers to its existence? Are you in the world or is the world in you? From the perspective of an ordinary person who is ignorant of the Self, the world is obviously real and external to oneself. To a Sage who embodies the supreme Reality and lives in the one, non-dual Consciousness, the world, as a composition of diverse objects, is not real.

When one sees a snake superimposed upon a rope, one does not see the rope. When one sees water superimposed upon the sand, one does not see the sand. When one sees silver superimposed upon a shell, one does not see the shell. Ramaṇa often employed these analogies. When a person forgets that they are the Self and deludes themselves into thinking they are a mind-body complex living in the universe, they must be reminded that the world that they think is real is but a delusion, an illusory appearance.

The mind of a deluded person habitually flows towards the world and not towards the Self. Further, even if one occasionally is able to turn their mind away from the world and concentrate it on the Self, it almost immediately loses its concentration and wanders back to the world. Why does this happen? Ramaṇa said it is because one believes that the world is real. "But for your belief that the world is real, it would be quite easy for you to obtain the revelation of the Self." The greatest wonder, Ramaṇa declared, is that, being always the Self, one is striving to become the Self.

Quoting the *Kaivalya Navanīta* about *māyā*, Ramaṇa said that the text asked and answered six questions, and that the questions and answers were instructive:

> The first question is: What is *māyā?* And the answer is: It is *anirvacanīya* or indescribable.
>
> The second question is: To whom does it come? And the answer is: To the mind or ego who feels that he is a separate entity, who thinks: "I do this" or "this is mine".
>
> The third question is: Where does it come from and how did it originate? And the answer is: Nobody can say.

The fourth question is: How did it arise? And the answer is: Through non-*vicāra*, through failure to ask: who am I?

The fifth question is: If the Self and *māyā* both exist does not this invalidate the theory of Advaita? The answer is: It need not, since *māyā* is dependent on the Self as the picture is on the screen. The picture is not real in the sense that the screen is real.

The sixth question is: If the Self and *māyā* are one, could it not be argued that the Self is of the nature of *māyā*, which is illusory? And the answer is: No; the Self can be capable of producing illusion without being illusory. A conjuror may create for our entertainment the illusion of people, animals and things, and we see all of them as clearly as we see him; but after the performance he alone remains and all the visions he had created have disappeared. He is not a part of the illusion but is real and solid.

Why is it that one's belief that the world of multiplicity is real, prevents one from realizing the Self that they are? Is it not the case that whatever one believes to be real possesses a certain capacity? It is an object separate from and other than the perceiver. It can come and it can go. The believed-to-be-real has an unquestionable right of entry to the mind. So long as the mind believes something is real, no thought can deny it. As long as the snake, water, silver are believed to be real, the rope, sand, and shell are denied. Further, once the mind regards the world as real in a sense that it is not, it becomes impossible to realize the Self until that delusion is destroyed. The very thing one takes as real is the very thing that obscures the Self.

We have observed that for both Ramaṇa and Advaita, the real is that which is eternal, which suffers no sublation, while the unreal is that which never is. They say that the unreal can *never* appear, not even in one's wildest dreams, e.g., the child of a barren woman. Because appearances are *perceived* they cannot be said to be unreal *(asat)*. Similarly, because the real *(Sat)* never changes, appearances, which change, cannot be called real *(Sat)*. Therefore, appearances must be indeterminable. How miraculous, mysterious, inscrutable! All that is perceived as "other than you" is neither real nor unreal! There never has been, nor is, nor ever will be water in a mirage and yet, somehow, it is perceived. There never has been a separate individual mind-body complex and yet, somehow, it is perceived. All appearances are "what is other than the real or the unreal" *(sadasat-vilakṣaṇa).* It is only in this sense that the seeming plurality of the universe, including individuals, is called "illusory" *(māyā).*

Now, let us dig deeper, for contained within Ramaṇa's teachings is an aspect of this illusoriness *(māyā)* that is often overlooked. The way the world is a superimposed appearance of Brahman differs from the way an individual is a superimposed appearance of *Brahman.* That is, the diversity displayed by the various objects of the universe differs from the diversity displayed by individuals (who are part of the universe) and further, the way that each diversity is negated differs. Take the following two examples. A person, walking in a forest at dusk, happens to see a snake but upon closer scrutiny realizes it is really a rope. This later correcting knowledge affirms the existence of a rope while negating the prior knowledge of a snake. Now, take a person looking at a white conch shell through a sheet of yellow glass. This person is not aware of the yellow glass and thus takes the white conch shell to be yellow. Subsequently this person learns that the yellowness belongs to the glass and not the shell. Here, as in the previous case, the later knowledge affirms the existence of some reality; unlike it however, it does not deny the object (the shell) of which it appeared. What it denies is only an aspect of it, that is, its yellowness. The shell is still seen. The illusion in the first example consisted of mistaking a given object (rope) for another (snake) that is not given. The illusion in the second example consists merely in attributing to an object (shell) that is perceived, a feature that does not really belong to it. In this second example, but for the superimposition of a sheet of glass to which the yellow actually belongs, there would be no illusion at all.[1]

---

[1] In Advaita the classic example used is of a jaundiced person observing a white conch as yellow and Ramana would sometimes quote this example. Hiriyanna changed the example to a sheet of yellow glass and I have paraphrased his analysis.

With the help of these two examples we are now in a position to see that the illusory nature of the world is not exactly like the illusory nature of the individual, notwithstanding the fact that both are illusory. While one and the same *Brahman* appears as both the world and as the individual, it is what the individual adds to the illusion that distinguishes them. In an individual, it is the ego, the inner organ *(antaḥkaraṇa),* the dualistic mind that needs to be negated. The shell is seen as shell though not as it is, i.e. a white shell. It is but the yellowness in the glass that is preventing one from seeing it as it is. An individual is already *Brahman* and this is partially known and revealed by the presence of "I" in each individual. No one says, "I do not exist." This "I"-notion is not fully understood. Under the sway of ignorance, an individual takes the "I" to be a "me", my body, my mind, and so on. Regarding the world, the illusion is total. The snake is seen all by itself and the rope is not seen while in regards to individuals, the shell is seen, though incorrectly, as something is being superimposed upon it to distort its reality from being seen as it truly is. *Brahman* is the sole Reality and the objective universe and the individual subject are said to be superimposed upon It. However, while the world is an illusory manifestation of *Brahman*, the individual is *Brahman* itself appearing under the limitations that form part of that illusory universe.

Why do I point out this distinction? I do so because Ramaṇa's focus was always on the Self. The world was not of primary importance; the individual was. He said, "Why worry yourself about the world and what happens to it after Self-realization? First realize the Self." He was not merely a philosopher espousing a theory. The world is known as what is seen. The individual is considered a seer as well as the seen. While all of the objects in the world are illusory, only part of the seer is. The individual is a complex of the Self and the not-Self. This is obvious from such statements as "I know myself where "myself" is referring to some aspect of the mind-body complex. Remember that while the world is a superimposition upon *Brahman*, *Brahman* is not a superimposition upon the world. On the other hand, there is a mutual superimposition between the Self (Atman) and not-Self *(anātman)*, i.e. features of the *Atman* are superimposed upon the inner organ and features of the inner organ are superimposed upon the *Atman*. Because of this, the inner organ, which is inert, appears conscious and the Self, which is infinite, appears finite. Realization consists in destroying, not the individual as a spiritual being, but only aspects of it, like its finitude and separateness from other selves.

By the criterion of nonsublatability, the Self alone is absolutely real. All else is called "real" only by courtesy. The distinction between one individual and another, the existence of a plurality of things, the superimposition of attributes on the Absolute are all concessions to the Truth made from the relative point of view. By this criterion, *māyā* is not a second entity. Only a person under the spell of ignorance perceives its effects. The sun does not ask, "Where is this darkness you speak about?" Because one denies what one is, the Self, and superimposes upon the Self what is not, the not-Self, does not therefore make the world, the not-Self, real.

Maya is the means, not the end. Within Advaita, any "means" exists only at the relative level. From the absolute perspective, one is the Self, one does not become the Self. Thus, *māyā* is a provisional explanation as to how the eternally all-pervasive Self appears otherwise. Though *maya* is not ultimately real, its importance cannot be exaggerated for the role that it plays. No one can deny that individuals seemingly *perceive* multiplicity and distinctions. How does this happen?

> *Atman,* the self-luminous, through the power of one's own *māyā,* imagines in oneself, by oneself (all the objects that the subject experiences within or without). This unborn changeless, non-dual *Brahman appears* to undergo modification only on account of *māyā* and not otherwise.[1]

The entire phenomenal world is said to be neither real nor unreal. A two-valued logic is not applicable here. To say that the world is not real is not to say, by logical implication, that the world is thus real or *vice versa*. The Advaitin's conception of unreality is both a logical impossibility and an empirical impossibility, i.e. a son of a barren woman. But the world of

---

[1] MaU with Gauḍapāda's *Kārikā* and Śaṅkara's Commentary, 2.12; 3.19.

māyā is neither logically impossible nor empirically impossible—though it may be conceptually indeterminable.

The world of *māyā* is comprised of illusions, dream-like objects and experiences, the entire realm of multiplicity. Anything that is perceived or experienced is attributed some sort of existence. The question is "what sort of reality?" What is to be clearly understood is that the reality that is given to such objects of perception is not the reality that is given to *Brahman*. Advaita admits of three levels of reality for discussion purposes: that which is apparently real *(prātibhāsika),* that which is empirically real *(vyāvahārika),* and that which is absolutely real *(pāramārthika).* That which is apparently real has a reality that is very much restricted. Such existents are real to an individual at the time they are experienced. But once the earlier cognition suffers sublation, they cease to be real. Their reality is subject to given individuals at a given time. A good example to show that perceptions are possible of objects that do not necessarily exist in empirical reality is the case of dreams or hallucinations.

Dreams are inscrutable phenomena and Ramaṇa made frequent use of dreams to illustrate the nature of reality:

> All that we see is dream, whether we see it in the dream state or waking state. On account of some arbitrary standards about the duration of the experience and so on, we call one experience a dream and another waking experience. With reference to reality both the experiences are unreal. A man might have such an experience as getting grace in his dream and the effects and influence of it on his entire subsequent life may be so profound and so abiding that one cannot call it unreal, while calling real some trifling incident in the waking life that just flits by, is casual and of no moment and is soon forgotten.[1]

In a dream, note that every dream-object, inert or living, human or demonic, pleasurable or painful, including oneself and anything else in any shape or form, all enjoy the exact same ontological status. The reality of the most expensive diamond is

---

[1] Mudaliar, *Gems from Bhagavan*, 24.

exactly the same as a speck of dirt. This aspect of dreams helps to convey some understanding of the state of a Sage. Ramaṇa remarked: "Does a man who sees many individuals in his dream persist in believing them to be real and enquire after them when he wakes up?"[1] "When a man dreams, he creates himself (i.e. the ego, the seer) and the surroundings, all of them are later withdrawn into himself. The one becomes many, along with the seer."[2]

In addition to this, dreams are a helpful aid in a spiritual seeker's spiritual practices. A seeker is advised to look upon everything in the world as possessing the same value, since nothing in the world actually possesses any real value. If the world is viewed as a dream containing dream objects, an individual is less likely to foster desires and strive to accumulate possessions.

> A dreamer dreams a dream. He sees the dream world with pleasures, pains, etc. But he wakes up and then loses all interest in the dream world. So it is with the waking world also. Just as the dream-world, being only a part of yourself and not different from you, ceases to interest you, so also the present world would cease to interest you if you awake from this waking dream *(samsāra)* and realize that it is a part of yourself and not an objective reality. Because you think that you are apart from the objects around you, you desire a thing. But, if you understand that the thing was only a thought-form you would no longer desire it.[3]

The dream world is thus very useful but all the dream world can inform us of is that the Reality is "not-this", "not-this." If the world is but an extended dream, this tells us that it is not real, but it can't tell us what is Real. We live in this seemingly real world and never doubt its veracity. Even if we learn that this world is a dream, all that informs us of is that all this is not real. It doesn't tell us what is real. A Sage is like an awakened

---

[1] Venkataramiah, *Talks with Sri Ramana Maharsi*, 530.

[2] Ibid, 451.

[3] Ibid, 588.

one who speaks to us in our dreams. Picture yourself at home in your bed asleep. Your father, who is awake, comes in and speaks to you. You may hear his words, but you will distort them. The closer you are to waking, the more precisely will you understand him. If you are fast asleep, you will hear nothing. A devotee of Ramaṇa put it wonderfully:

> Do you understand that you cannot ask a valid question about yourself because you do not know whom you are asking about. In the question, "Who am I?" the "I" is not known and the question can be worded as, "I do not know what I mean by "I"." What you are, you must find out. I can only tell you what you are not. You are not of the world, you are not even in the world. The world is not, you alone are. You create the world in your imagination like a dream. As you cannot separate the dream from yourself, so you cannot have an outer world independent of yourself. You are independent, not the world. Don't be afraid of a world you yourself have created. Cease from looking for happiness and reality in a dream and you will wake up. You need not know all the "why" and "how," there is no end to questions. Abandon all desires, keep your mind silent, and you shall discover.[1]

The dream analogy has so many facets to it and explicates what else may remain puzzling *vis-a-vis* non-dualistic teachings. Another aspect that the dream analogy clarifies is the rather incredible claim that one is not, as is generally believed, in the universe, but rather the universe is in oneself. Dreams and everything contained within them are within the dreamer. Ramaṇa said: "You dream of finding yourself in another town. Can another town enter your room? Could you have left and gone there?"[2] In dreams, the dreamer is the light of that world, the dreamer creates the entire dream universe, experiences various things, and then withdraws them.

A most intriguing question arises when an experience

---

[1] Sudhaker Dikshit, *I am That: Conversations with Sri Nisargadatta Maharaj*, 452-53.

[2] *Conscious Immortality*, 98.

makes one question one's certainty about what is real and what is not. Dreams, according to Ramaṇa, suggest that the dream state and the waking state partake of the same reality. Dreams have the ability to put into doubt the reality of waking experiences which one takes for granted as real. What are the reasons why one would make such a bold claim? Even if it is true that objects come and go in both states, there seem to exist many differences between them.

Ramaṇa said: "In the waking state, the ego identifies itself with the physical body; in the dream state it identifies with the subtle mind. The ego and the mind are one and the same."[1] Just because Ramaṇa declares that whatever is seen by the mind is unreal, does not seem to prove the point. Even if one were to grant this, how does this show that objects are not real in either case? This seems to fly in the face of everyone's everyday experience.

Dream objects differ from waking objects in a number of aspects. Objects found in the waking state are practically efficient. One can actually drink water in the way one can't drink dream water. Dream objects are often bizarre, abnormal, and incredible. In the waking state one is aware that one is awake but in the dream state one is not usually aware that one is dreaming. Dreams take place within the mind/body while the waking state involves the external world. Dream objects are often imprecise and ethereal while waking objects are definite and solid. Dream objects last only so long as the dream lasts while waking objects are perceived before and after a dream. Ramaṇa remarked:

> There is no difference between dream and the waking state except that the dream is short and the waking long. Both are the result of the mind. Because the waking state is long, we imagine that it is our real state. But, as a matter of fact, our real state is *turīya* or the fourth state which is always as it is and knows nothing of the three states of waking, dream, or sleep.[2]

---

[1] Venkataramiah, *Talks with Sri Ramana Maharshi*, 396.

[2] Mudaliar, *Day by Day with Bhagavan*, 90.

Further, consider the fact that waking objects outlast the duration of dream objects *only* from the vantage point of the waking state. What status waking state objects have from within the dream state is unknown. Why privilege one vantage point over another? In an attempt to determine what is real, one cannot presuppose that the criteria of the waking state is valid when that is the very thing one is attempting to prove. Isn't it obvious that dream objects last as long as the dream lasts and waking objects last as long as the waking state lasts. No advantage to either side. Ramaṇa remarked: "Because you find the dream creations transitory in relation to the waking state there is said to be a difference. The difference is only apparent and not real."[1] Again, on this aspect he said, confronted with a person who was objecting that a dream is fleeting and unreal, besides being contradicted by the waking state:

> The waking experiences are similar. You go to sleep and dream a dream in which the experiences of fifty years are condensed within the short duration of the dream, say five minutes. There is a continuity in the dream. Which is real now? Is the period covering fifty years of your waking state real or the short duration of five minutes of your dream? The standards of time differ in the two states. That is all. There is no other difference between the experiences.[2]

The objection that dream objects are not similar to waking objects cannot be supported on the contention that, while objects experienced in the waking state are practically efficient, those seen in a dream are not. When confronted with this objection, Ramaṇa replied: "You are not right. There are thirst and hunger in dream also. You might have had your fill and kept over the remaining food for the next day. Nevertheless you feel hungry in dream. This food does not help you. One's dream-hunger can be satisfied only by eating dream-food. Dream-wants are satisfied by dream-creations only."[3] Objects of

---

[1] Venkataramiah, *Talks with Sri Ramana Maharshi,* 218.

[2] Ibid, 273.

[3] Ibid, 274.

the waking state *only* have efficiency in the waking state. Dream objects are useful in their own way in the dream state. Dream water cannot quench a waking thirst, but it does quench a dream thirst; and it is equally true that waking water cannot quench a dream thirst even though it does quench a waking thirst. Again, listen to Ramaṇa:

> A phenomenon cannot be a reality simply because it serves a purpose or purposes. Take a dream for example. The dream creations are purposeful; they serve the dream-purpose. The dream water quenches dream thirst. The dream creation is however contradicted in the waking state. The waking creation is contradicted in the other two states. What is not continuous cannot be real. If real, the thing must ever be real—and not real for a short time and unreal at other times. So it is with magical creations. They appear real and are yet illusory. Similarly the universe cannot be real of itself—that is to say, apart from the underlying Reality.[1]
>
> It is like a man satisfying his dream wants by dream creations. There are objects, there are wants and there is satisfaction. The dream creation is as purposeful as the waking world and yet it is not considered real. Thus we see that each of these illustrations serves a distinct purpose in establishing the stages of unreality. The realized Sage finally declares that in the regenerate state the waking world also is found to be as unreal as the dream world is found to be in the waking state. Each illustration should be understood in its proper context; it should not be studied as an isolated statement. It is a link in a chain. The purpose of all these is to direct the seeker's mind towards the one Reality underlying them all.[2]

---

[1] Ibid, 165.

[2] Ibid, 219.

Thus it cannot be said that waking objects alone are useful, fruitful, or practically efficient. Dream objects work in dreams just as waking objects work in the waking state. Take another example. I am sleeping peacefully in my bed. I begin dreaming that I am walking down a path in the forest when suddenly I see a tiger behind me. I realize that I am about to be eaten by the tiger. I begin to run. I run faster and faster but the tiger remains right behind me. I turn and look and see the tiger crouching, ready to spring. The tiger lunges at me and just before he strikes, I observe his claws are open and about to rip into me. At that moment, I cry out and wake, in a sweat with my heart pounding. Now, was there ever a tiger there? No, you reply, it was only a dream. Then why am I sweating and my heart pounding? An unreal tiger produced real effects (from the waking perspective). Thus, it isn't the case that an illusory something cannot produce real effects. Not only that, this dream, which some call a nightmare, had the effect of waking me up. Thus, the issue is still out on whether the waking state can be proven to be different from the dream state.

Another argument was advanced stating that dreams are strange and contain bizarre objects, while the waking state is normal. Śaṅkara addressed this issue in his commentaries on the *Brahmansūtras* and the *Gauḍapāda-kārikās:*

> It may be argued that, since the contents of dream are quite different from the objects of waking, they cannot constitute the illustration for proving the illusoriness of the waking world. The *dream-contents* are strange and abnormal, and are not the replica of what are experienced in waking. It has been said that the things seen in dreams are strange and abnormal. But when and to whom do they appear abnormal? To him who has returned to waking after a dream. In the dream-state itself the contents are not realized to be strange. It is from the side of waking that the dream-contents seem abnormal, but in themselves they are quite normal.[1]

[1] See William Indich, *Consciousness in Advaita Vedanta*, 63.

> Just as a traveller who is well-instructed goes to a place and sees there strange things which are but natural to that place, so the dreamer transported as he is to the dream-world, experiences strange things. Each state or circumstance has its own peculiarity. But that cannot prevent comparison of the waking-world with the *contents* of dream.[1]

There do exist strange and unusual events and objects in the waking state, even if they may be rarer than the ordinary and commonplace. Sometimes, quite often in fact, dream contents are ordinary, too. The *Brahmasūtras* say: "The dream is only an illusion, for its nature is not completely manifest (compared to waking)."[2] However, dreams are sometimes quite vivid and lucid while perceptions in the waking state are sometimes fuzzy and unclear. But this is not the crucial issue here. In dreams, the senses function unaided by the external sense organs while the sense organs function in the waking state. Yet, is it the case that what the external sense organs perceive is Reality? What is important to note is that the logic of one state need not conform to another in order for both to be dream-states. Dreams can take many forms and merely because of variations one need not conclude that something is not a dream. As Ramaṇa remarked:

> Again, consider it from another point of view: You create a dream-body for yourself in the dream and act with that dream-body. The same is falsified in the waking state. At present you think that you are this body and not the dream-body. In your dream this body is falsified by the dream-body. So that, you see, neither of these bodies is real because each of them is true for a time and false at other times. That which is real must be real for ever. But you say "I". This "I"-consciousness is present all through the three states. There is no change in it. That is alone real. The three states are false. They are only for the mind. It is the mind which obstructs your vision of your true nature. Your true nature is that

[1] See T.M.P. Mahadevan, *Gauḍapāda: A Study in Early Advaita*, 123-24.

[2] BS III.2.3.

> of infinite spirit. That was the case in your sleep. You note the limitations in the other two states. What is the difference due to? There was no mind in sleep, but it exists in the dream and the waking states. The feeling of limitation is the work of the mind. What is mind? Find it. If you search for it, it will vanish by itself. For it has no real existence. It is comprised of thoughts. It disappears with the cessation of thoughts.[1]

Another aspect of dreams Ramaṇa remarked about was the charge that a person makes no conscious effort to get rid of a dream and awaken. Dreams come to an end spontaneously without any effort on one's part. If the waking state is a dream, then why doesn't it come to an end without any effort on our part? Why should an individual attempt to realize the Self?

> Your thinking that you have to make an effort to get rid of this dream of the waking state and your making efforts to attain or real awakening are all parts of the dream. When you attain *jñāna* you will see there was neither the dream during sleep, nor the waking state, but only yourself and your real state.[2]

> In a dream, you have no inkling that it is a dream and so you don't have the duty of trying to get out of it by your effort. But in this life you have some intuition, by your sleep experience, by reading and hearing that this life is something like a dream, and hence the duty is cast on you to make an effort and get out of it. However, who wants you to realize the Self, if you don't want it? If you prefer to be in the dream, stay as you are."[3]

It has been said that the waking world can be distinguished from the dream world because in the waking state one is aware that one is awake, but one is not aware that one is dreaming in

---

[1] Venkataramiah, *Talks with Sri Ramana Maharshi,* 175.

[2] Mudaliar, *Day by Day with Bhagavan,* 85.

[3] Ibid, 49.

the dream state (except perhaps in what are called lucid dreams). The reason given for this claim is that objects are external to oneself when one wakes while, upon waking, one believes the dream objects were internal. Ramaṇa pointed out that it is only upon awakening that one realizes that the dream objects which had appeared as external to the dreamer in the dream, were actually internal. In a similar manner, upon Self-realization, true awakening, one realizes that the objects of the world that were perceived as external, are really internal. Even as the waking state reverses the experience of the dream state, so does Self-realization reverse the experience of the waking state. In this way, the waking and dreaming states are not less, but more compatible.

How does one know that there are external physical objects in the waking state and merely internal mental objects in a dream? When dreaming, objects are perceived as real and as external to the perceiver. It is only upon waking that one renounces these perceptions as being mere mental creations, internal, and illusory. Judged from the perspective of within a dream, there is no way to tell that such perceptions are internal. Then the question may arise if a truly awakened person, a *jīvan-mukta,* has dreams, because it is said that *jīvan-muktas* do not sleep like ordinary individuals. Ramaṇa said:

> If the *jñāni* can have a waking state, what is the difficulty about his having a dream state? But of course, as his waking state is different from the ordinary man's waking state, so his dream state also will be different from the ordinary man's dream state. Whether in waking or in dream, he will not slip from his real state, which is sometimes called the fourth or *turīya* state.[1]

> Of course, the *jīvan-muktas* are having *brahmākāra vṛtti* always, even during sleep. The real answer to the question, and the whole set of questions, is that the *jñāni* has neither the waking, dreaming, or sleeping states, but only the *turīya* state. It is the *jñāni* that

[1] Mudaliar, *Day by Day with Bhagavan,* 5.

sleeps. But he sleeps without sleeping or is awake while sleeping.[1]

Thus, we see that Ramaṇa often used the dream analogy to elucidate how *māyā* operates as well as to reveal the unreality of the world. In fact, it seemed to be his favorite analogy. Why he did this was not to formulate an intellectual theory, though we see him discussing various aspects of the dream world—he did it so as to direct the seeker's mind towards the one Reality underlying both the waking and dreaming states. The key, or heart, of the issue rests in his contention that the entire universe, with all its infinite multiplicity, is built upon a single mental thought, the "I"-thought. A person mistakes the "I" for a "me".

There remains the problem that if the waking state is similar to the dream state, then why doesn't the waking world disappear when one wakes up, that is, becomes enlightened? Yet, as we just saw in Ramaṇa's own words, the *jñāni* continues to perceive the world even after Self-realization has occurred—though the *jñāni* perceives the world as Brahman rather than apart as separate and distinct objects. To this objection Ramaṇa replied:

> There are different methods of approach to prove the unreality of the universe. The example of the dream is one among many. Waking, dreaming, and deep sleep are all treated elaborately in the scriptures in order that the Reality underlying them might be revealed. It is not meant to accentuate differences among the three states. The purpose must be kept clearly in view.
>
> Now they say that the world is unreal. Of what degree of unreality is it? Is it like that of a song of a barren mother or a flower in the sky, mere words without any reference to fact? Whereas the world is a fact and not a mere word. The answer is that it is a superimposition on the one Reality, like the appearance of a snake on a coiled rope seen in dim light. But here too the wrong identity ceases as soon as the friend points out that it is a rope. Whereas in the matter of the

---

[1] Ibid, 183.

world it persists even after it is known to be unreal. How is that? Again the appearance of water in a mirage persists even after the knowledge of mirage is recognized. So it is with the world. Though knowing it to be unreal, it continues to manifest.

But the water of the mirage is not sought to satisfy one's thirst. As soon as one knows that it is a mirage, one gives it up as useless and does not run after it for procuring water.

(How can the world be false when, after being repeatedly declared to be false, one cannot resist satisfying one's desires from the world?) It is like a man satisfying his dream wants by dream creations. There are objects, there are wants, and there is satisfaction. The dream creation is as purposeful as the waking world and yet it is not considered real.

Thus, we see that each of these illustrations serves a distinct purpose in establishing the stages of unreality. The realized Sage finally declares that in the regenerate state the waking world also is found to be as unreal as the dream world is found to be in the waking state.

Each illustration should be understood in its proper context; it should not be studied as an isolated statement. It is a link in a chain. The purpose of all these is to direct the seeker's mind towards the one Reality underlying them all.[1]

We see Ramaṇa acknowledging that, from a certain perspective, a mirage, unlike a dream, more accurately conveys how an illusion can continue to exist even after it is known to be an illusion. If one persists by questioning the mirage analogy: although it is true that water drunk by a *jñāni* quenches his thirst, while mirage-water does not, one should remember that any given analogy is advanced to give a particular insight and that one should never push an analogy beyond its intended purpose—otherwise, one's questions will be unending.

---

[1] Venkataramiah, *Talks with Sri Ramana Maharshi*, 372.

Ramana and Causality

We have noted that Ramaṇa was not particularly interested in theory. He discouraged theoretical questions and generally either remained silent when such questions were asked or else asked the questioner to find the source of the "I" that was asking the question. When he spoke, he spoke freely and often with laughter and humor. If a questioner was particularly insistent, Ramaṇa would sometimes relent and give an explanation. If the questioner was not satisfied, he was free to object and ask further questions. Such explanations were usually rather short and if the questioner persisted too long with the topic, or if they moved in the direction of mere intellectualism, Ramaṇa would change the topic and direct the attention of his questioners towards more practical matters.

Among such topics, those that centered around the nature and origin of the world often arose. Ramaṇa expressed, when pushed, that there are three traditional modes of approach or standpoints to the metaphysical problem of creation:

> The *ajāta* school of Advaita says, "Nothing exists except the one reality. There is no birth or death, no projection or drawing in, no *sādhaka* (practicer), no *mumukṣu* (one who desires to be liberated), no *mukta* (one who is liberated), no bondage, no liberation. The one unity alone exists for ever." To such that find it difficult to grasp this truth, and ask, "How can we ignore this solid world we see all around us?" the dream experience is pointed out and they are told, "All that you see depends on the seer." This is called *dṛṣṭi-sṛṣṭi-vāda* or the argument that one first creates out of his mind and then sees what his mind itself has created. To such that cannot grasp even this and who further argue, "The dream experience is so short, while the world always exists. The dream experience was limited to me. But the world is felt and seen not only by me but by so many and we cannot call such a world non-existent," the argument called *sṛṣṭi-dṛṣṭi-vāda* is addressed and they are told, "God first created such and

such a thing out of such and such an element and then something else and so forth." That alone will satisfy them. Their mind is not otherwise satisfied and they ask themselves, "How can all geography, all maps, all sciences, stars, planets and the rules governing or relating to them, and all knowledge be totally untrue?" To such it is best to say, "Yes, God created all this and so you see it." All these are only to suit the capacity of the hearers. The Absolute can only be one.[1]

Ramaṇa said that *ajāta-vāda,* or the theory of non-origination, is the closest or most compatible with the Truth (the Truth is beyond conceptualization—*ajāta* is meaningful only if one presumes birth or *jāti).* Remember, this is also a theory and unless one assumes that there is creation there would be no reason to deny it. People often say that Ramaṇa, himself, held the *ajāta-vāda* theory. He remarked: "I do not teach only the *ajāta* doctrine." If this theory was too difficult to grasp, Ramaṇa was insistent that a serious seeker should be satisfied with the doctrine of simultaneous creation, since it is the most beneficial attitude to adopt if a seeker is seriously seeking the Self.

Let me give a rather lengthy quote by David Godman on the three theories, as it is so very well put:

> 1 – *Ajāta-vāda* (the theory of non-causality). This is an ancient Hindu doctrine which states that the creation of the world never happened at all. It is a complete denial of all causality in the physical world. Sri Ramaṇa endorsed this view by saying that it is the *jñāni's* experience that nothing ever comes into existence or ceases to be, because the Self alone exists as the sole unchanging reality. It is a corollary of this theory that time, space, cause and effect, essential components of all creation theories, exist only in the minds of *ajñānis* and that the experience of the Self reveals their non-existence.
>
> This theory is not a denial of the reality of the world, only of the creative process which brought it into

[1] Mudaliar, *Gems From Bhagavan,* 3-4.

existence. Speaking from his own experience, Sri Ramaṇa said that the *jñāni* is aware that the world is real, not as an assemblage of interacting matter and energy, but as an uncaused appearance in the Self. He enlarged on this by saying that because the real nature or substratum of this appearance is identical with the beingness of the Self, it necessarily partakes of its reality. That is to say, the world is not real to the *jñāni* simply because it appears, but only because the real nature of the appearance is inseparable from the Self.

The *ajñāni,* on the other hand, is totally unaware of the unitary nature and source of the world and, as a consequence, his mind constructs an illusory world of separate interacting objects by persistently misinterpreting the sense-impressions it receives. Sri Ramaṇa pointed out that this view of the world has no more reality than a dream since it superimposes a creation of the mind on the reality of the Self. He summarized the difference between the *jñāni's* and the *ajñāni's* standpoint by saying that the world is unreal if it is perceived by the mind as a collection of discrete objects and real when it is directly experienced as an appearance in the Self.

2 – *Dṛṣṭi-sṛṣṭi-vāda.* If his questioners found the idea of *ajāta* or non-causality impossible to assimilate, he would teach them that the world comes into existence simultaneously with the appearance of the "I"-thought and that it ceases to exist when the "I"-thought is absent. This theory is known as *dṛṣṭi-sṛṣṭi,* or simultaneous creation, and it says, in effect, that the world which appears to an *ajñāni* is a product of the mind that perceives it, and that in the absence of that mind it ceases to exist. The theory is true in so far as the mind does create an imaginary world for itself, but from the standpoint of the Self, an imaginary "I" creating an imaginary world is no creation at all, and so the doctrine of *ajāta* is not subverted. Although Sri Ramaṇa sometimes said that *dṛṣṭi-sṛṣṭi* was not the ultimate truth about creation, he encouraged his followers to accept it as a working hypothesis. He

justified this approach by saying that if one can consistently regard the world as an unreal creation of the mind, then it loses its attraction and it becomes easier to maintain an undistracted awareness of the "I"-thought.

3 – *Sṛṣṭi-dṛṣṭi-vāda* (gradual creation). This is the common-sense view that holds that the world is an objective reality governed by laws of cause and effect which can be traced back to a single act of creation. It includes virtually all western ideas on the subject from the "big bang" theory to the biblical account in Genesis. Sri Ramaṇa only invoked theories of this nature when he was talking to questioners who were unwilling to accept the implications of the *ajāta* and *dṛṣ ṭi-sṛṣṭi* theories. Even then, he would usually point out that such theories should not be taken too seriously as they were only promulgated to satisfy intellectual curiosity.[1]

A number of important points in the above quote are worth mentioning. The non-creation theory is an attempt to describe the *jñāni's* personal experience. Truly speaking, for a *jñāni*, there is nothing to say and no one to say it to. It is only because a person assumes that there is birth *(jāti)* that the *jñāni*, out of compassion, opens his mouth and denies it—his words being but an intellectual statement or theory for the listener—the truth lies in the experience, not in the theory. One should not mistake map for territory, a finger pointing at the moon for the moon itself.

Secondly, the theory of non-origination is *not* a denial of the reality of the world, but only of the creative, causal process that brought it into existence. Ramaṇa often said, and his speech and actions only confirmed such, that the *jñāni* is aware that the world is real – *not* as separate objects, but as an *uncaused* appearance of the Self. The world's appearance is perceived by the *jñāni*, but it is not its appearance that makes it real, it is real because its appearance is inseparable from the Self. On the other hand, an *ajñāni* creates with his mind an illusory world of

---

[1] David Godman, *Be As You Are: The Teachings of Sri Ramana Maharshi*, 174-76.

separate objects by continually misinterpreting the sense-impressions it receives. In both cases, sense-impressions are perceived. Where they differ, and it makes all the difference, is that the ego, the me/my thought is absent in the *jñāni* and present in the *ajñāni.* Thus, the *jñāni* perceives the Self, or better, reposes in the Self, while in the *ajñāni's* mind, thoughts create a false separation between the Self and the not-Self.

The simultaneous creation theory, though not as close to the truth as the non-origination theory, has an extremely useful aspect to it. While non-origination is a breathtakingly wonderful theory, it is more or less an intellectual theory. On the other hand, according to Ramaṇa, the simultaneous creation theory is a theory that can be practiced and he encouraged his followers to accept it as a working hypothesis. If one accepts the idea that the world is an unreal creation of the mind, then it will begin to lose its attractiveness, thus making it easier to focus on the source of the "I"-thought.

Ramaṇa remarked on many occasions when individuals would ask about which of the gradual creation theories are correct:

> There are many (gradual creation theories) and they are meant to indicate that the creation has a cause, and a creator should be posited so that one might seek the cause. The emphasis is on the purpose of the theory and not on the process of creation. Moreover, the creation is perceived by some one. There are no objects without the subject, i.e., the objects do not come and tell you that they are, but it is you who say that there are the objects. The objects are therefore what the seer makes of them. They have no existence independent of the subject. Find out what you are and then you understand what the world is. That is the object of the theory.[1]

The important point to be noted in the gradual creation theory, with its myriad variations, is that it generally only serves to satisfy intellectual curiosity. Ramaṇa said:

---

[1] Venkataramiah, *Talks with Sri Ramana Maharshi,* 353-54.

> There are only two ways in which to conquer destiny or be independent of it. One is to enquire who undergoes this destiny and discover that only the ego is bound by it and not the Self, and that the ego is non-existent. The other way is to kill the ego by completely surrendering to the Lord, by realizing one's helplessness and saying all the time, "Not I, but Thou, O my Lord", and giving up all sense of "I" and "mine" and leaving it to the Lord to do what he likes with you. Surrender can never be regarded as complete so long as the devotee wants this or that from the Lord.[1]

Gradual creation theories do not meet either of these criteria. As well, gradual creation theories are full of logical contradictions and inconsistencies.

There are two traditional positions with regard to the cause-effect relation that lies at the heart of gradual creation theories: Either the effect is pre-existent in the cause or else the effect is non-existent in the cause prior to its production. However, both positions are riddled with inconsistencies. The basic position of those who hold that the effect is a *de novo* creation from the cause is that if such were not the case, causation itself would be meaningless. If the effect is pre-existent, then why does it need to be produced? Thus the cause and effect must differ and the effect must be non-existent before its production by the cause. But this position raises two fundamental problems. First, the cause and effect relation regarding the material cause is unsatisfactory. Nothing can come out of something unless it is already existent in that something. If such were not to be the case, then it would amount to disclaiming the need for a material cause for the production of an effect. And secondly, if the efficient cause is separate from the material cause, then this implies a limitation to God. God, being the efficient cause, would be bound to work upon material independent of him. Furthermore, he would be limited to creating only those forms of which this given material would admit.

Those who hold that the effect is pre-existent in the cause counter the objection that if such were the case, then causation

---

[1] Mudaliar, *Day by Day with Bhagavan,* 57.

itself would be meaningless, by saying that if the effect is not pre-existent in the cause, then anything could come out of anything. There would be no determinative cause for a specific effect. Milk could come out of sand and then, only sometimes. In rebuttal, the opponents object that if the effect pre-exists in the cause, why does it need to be produced? The reply is that the effect is not in the cause as such—it is latent in the cause and has to be brought out. Thus, what is latent must become patent. Yet, still difficulties persist. Is the cause wholly transformed or only partially transformed in this process? If the whole cause is transformed, then the cause ceases to be, and what happens to the cause in which the effect is said to pre-exist? And if only a part of the cause changes into the effect, with the other part maintaining its substance, it will be like killing one-half of a hen to eat and trying to keep the other half to lay eggs with.

The reply to this is that what is meant in saying that the cause is transformed into the effect is that what was not previously manifested is now made manifest. The clay as cause does not disappear when the pot, as effect, is produced. What was the cause is now the effect, persisting in it. Yet still the dialectic continues by asking exactly what does this "manifestation" mean? Again one is caught between the horns of a dilemma involving either the case that causation is redundant or else impossible.

Thus it is that these two theories of causation destroy each other's position. If the effect is already existent, it is redundant to say that the already existent is created. And if the effect is non-existent, it can never be produced. Either alternative fails to satisfy the demands of logic. Thus it is that the Advaitin propounds the doctrine of non-origination.

According to the ontological position of Advaita, the causal relationship cannot apply to the Absolute due to the fact of its being merest Being. Being is said to be the constitutive stuff of everything that is. It must not be thought of as the greatest common factor. As the constitutive reality of things it is the essence of all conscious and unconscious referents. As well, it is the source and ground of everything. Thus, it is the irreducible substratum, the most elementary, the simplest, the only non-composite. Merest Being cannot be one member in a causal series, even if that one be held to be the highest or the greatest. If it were a member of a series, then it would not be merest Being itself. Nor can merest Being be a product of evolution. For this would imply that the world came into being from non-being that is logically absurd. Non-being is not the cause of anything whatsoever precisely because it is nothing. Even to deny it, and have the negation be real, must mean that Being is embedded therein.

The provisional Advaita Vedānta theory of causation implies six requisites: (1) There is a relation in terms of succession in the cause-effect relationship. The cause is earlier and the effect is later. (2) The relationship between the cause and the effect is an irreversible relationship. The cause always precedes the effect and never *vice-versa*. (3) The relationship between the cause and the effect is a necessary relationship and not a contingent one. (4) Cause and effect are not completely identical nor are they totally different. (If any two entities are absolutely different, they are not related by cause and effect, and if they are absolutely identical, then they are the same entity.) (5) The relationship between cause and effect is a one-sided relationship. The effect is always dependent upon the cause and not vice-versa. (6) Between the cause and the effect, the cause alone is real.

This analysis will logically lead an individual to discover the impossibility of a causal scheme. From the seeming reality of the causal scheme at the empirical level, one is led to discover that philosophically speaking, there is no causation. By applying this criterion to the famous rope-snake example, the Advaita theory of causality will become clear.

The rope is the cause of the snake in the sense that the snake pre-existed (so to speak) in the rope. It was sustained by the rope and finally disappeared back into the rope. All the time there was nothing other than the rope. The rope never ceased being a rope, even while it appeared as the snake. This is the very essence of the idea; a thing appearing differently without ceasing to be itself even during the different appearance.

Because every effect has a cause, the Absolute is cosmologically said to be the cause of the Universe. This needs some elucidation. Whenever the Advaitin speaks of causation, it is with regard to God *(Īśvara)*. Whenever the Advaitin speaks of appearance, it is with regard to the Absolute *(Brahman)*. Since the Absolute *(Brahman)* is the only Reality, and if we seek a cause for the world as we see it given in experience, we employ the language of cosmology and say, the Absolute alone, if anything, could be the cause of the world and not anything else.

Theologically, Advaita is aware of the theoretical difficulties of a mere theism. Thus, this is only a provisional acceptance purely as a methodological device later to be abandoned for a purer concept of non-duality. Accordingly, the Absolute *(Brahman)* is considered as the substrate *(adhiṣṭhāna)* of an illusory appearance of the world.

If God is the creator of the world, the theists run into difficulty relating to the material out of which the world is fashioned and its subsequent implications with regard to the efficient cause or Creator. Was this material pre-existent and independent of God? What is the material itself made of? Is it a part of God? Does all of God change or only a part of him if this material is somehow God? What is the relationship therein? Is the universe a *de novo* creation or a transformation of something pre-existent?

Supposing there is a world and God is the cause of it, the following questions must be answered. Why does a non-creative God suddenly become creative? What is the purpose of God's creation? If there is something left for God to achieve, then his perfection has been compromised and if there is not, then creation must be redundant. God is infinite and creation is finite. What could an infinite God desire from a finite creation? Yet, as the *Brahmasūtrabhāṣya* asks: "If *Īśvara* has no purpose, then how do we explain creation?"[1]

One attempt to overcome this dilemma is to propound the theory that creation provides a place in which individuals may work out their past merits and demerits. Ramaṇa said:

> The purpose of creation is only to give rise to asking the question, "what is the purpose of creation. Investigate the answer to this question, and finally

[1] Ibid.

> abide in the Supreme or rather the primal source of all, the Self. The investigation will resolve itself into a quest for the Self and it will cease only after the non-self is sifted away, and the Self realized in its purity and glory.[1]

However, the flaw in saying that the universe exists to work out past-*karma* is that past deeds themselves also require a place and time in which they were performed, *ad infinitum*. The solution is merely postponed, but not solved. And to postulate a beginningless creation is to silence one's critics, but not to explain the phenomena of creation.

The theory of origination postulates an efficient cause (God) and a material cause (atoms) and the effect is said to be a new production from the cause. Yet the defects of this theory include limiting the creative powers of God. If God is forced to work with the atoms given, which are co-eternal with and independent from God, then only those forms that the nature of the material admits of can be created. And what is the relationship between God and this material? If there is no relationship between them, then the two merely exist side by side, not affecting each other. Yet, as this does not explain creation, there must be some sort of relation. If there is a relation, then what affects one must affect the other. It is all very well for creation to undergo change, but it plays havoc to have to accept the fact that God as well must undergo change. To propound the relation as one of "identity in difference" will not alleviate the problem. How is it possible for a thing to undergo change and yet at the same time to remain the same? Such is a logical impossibility. If there is a connection between the two causal correlates, then either both sides are affected, or else they are not related at all. One cannot have it both ways. To maintain both change and identity in the same entity is to divide that entity itself.

The Sāṅkhya theory of *pariṇāma-vāda* or *satkārya-vāda* says that the effect pre-exists in the cause. Yet as we saw earlier, this has unwelcome consequences in regards to the transformation of the cause. Since Sāṅkhya denies the need for an efficient cause (God), the problems with God undergoing change do not

---

[1] Venkataramiah, *Talks with Sri Ramana Maharshi*, 341.

affect their theory. But, at the same time, it is unthinkable for an insentient matter *(prakṛti)* to produce the world by itself. An intelligent agent seems a necessary presupposition for the creation of things having a design.

Advaita provisionally accepts the Sāṅkhya theory of *pariṇāma-vāda*, but modifies it in that *māyā* is the material cause in association with God as its power. However, since difficulties eventually do present themselves, the entire conception of creation is held to be (in the final analysis) without any ultimate significance to the Advaitin. It does have practical implications, but is not logically defensible. Thus, for all practical theological purposes, the world may be said to be an actual change of *māyā* as the power of God. However, in the ultimate analysis, it is but an appearance of *Brahman*. In other words, the world is non-existent in *Brahman*.

Thus, the theory of transformation is held to be only provisionally correct. It is a preliminary teaching device to the theory of the appearance of *Brahman* as the world. It is a concession and, as a theory of creation, it may be more plausible than others. But any creation theory is beset by certain fundamental difficulties that are inherent in the very idea of change. It is said within Advaita Vedānta that the creation-stories have not a metaphysical import but a metaphorical one. There is nothing absolutely to be gained by the knowledge of creation. It is the identity of the Self with *Brahman* that is the purport of the creation texts.

The real is the Absolute. Theologically speaking, this *Brahman* in association with *māyā,* is called *Īśvara* or *saguṇa Brahman*. And it is this *saguṇa Brahman* that creates the world. But philosophically speaking, there is no causation at all.

It is only by assuming the existence of the world that its cause is sought for. Cause and effect are relative terms. Any event that is the cause of another event requires to be explained in terms of its own antecedent. Such a process leads to an *infinite regress*. To arbitrarily draw a line somewhere is to compromise with logical consistency. There is no reason to presuppose an uncaused cause after asserting that every event has a cause. If such were the case, what is to prevent one from postulating that each event was itself uncaused? And then where is the question of causality at all?

Utmost care should be taken not to interpret *ajāta-vāda* statements as advocating an invisible being or entity behind the phenomena. The non-origination theory of non-duality expresses the absence of difference of every kind. The purport of its message is just to convey this knowledge. That which is, is all there is. To posit a being behind the scenes is to posit something over and above what is given. Ramaṇa was keen to point to what should be the most obvious fact of any experience. He affirmed the pure experience that always is. In every reference to an individual's "I", the Reality is manifesting itself. Though the total significance of the "I" may not be exactly cognized or appreciated, no experience takes place without it. It is the nature of this "I" which Ramaṇa is always referring to.

The problem of causality is a problem about mere illusional and intellectual matters and what they imply regarding the nature of Reality. Always Ramaṇa's preference was to single out the "I"-"I", the Self for this analysis since all other understanding not only presupposes this Self, but is dependent upon it. The second and third level creation theories presuppose that the things it identifies are different. Ramaṇa and *ajāta-vāda* state that the "two things" are really identical. They express the absence of another. They are not mere emotional or conceptual possibilities. They state a fact and this fact is self-existent. And that which is self-existent, which has being in itself and for itself, is complete and immutable.

Ramaṇa said about all these theories:

> Various accounts (of creation) are given in books. But is there creation? Only if there is creation do we have to explain how it came about. We may not know about all these theories but we certainly know that we exist. Why not know the "I" and then see if there is a creation?[1]

Ramaṇa remarked:

---

[1] Mudaliar, *Day by Day with Bhagavan*, 132.

> Of what use are disputes about the world, saying that it is real, that it is an illusory appearance, that it is conscious, that it is insentient, that it is happy, that it is miserable? We have observed that the Self alone exists. From the perspective of the Sage, the world presents no problems.

Again, he explained:

> Brahman is real. The world is illusion. Others say that the world is real. Both statements are true. They refer to different stages of development and are spoken from different points of view. The aspirant starts with the definition "that which is real exists always". Then he eliminates the world as unreal because it is changing. The seeker ultimately reaches the Self and there finds unity as the prevailing note. Then, that which was originally rejected as being unreal is found to be a part of the unity. Being absorbed in the reality, the world also is real. There is only Being in Self-realization, and nothing but Being.

Ramana and the Individual

Ramaṇa's descriptions of the individual self *(jīva)* are very much in keeping with Advaita's definitions and descriptions. However, other than the parts of Ramaṇa's definitions that are virtually identical with Advaita's, Ramaṇa also had his own unique description. We will look at some examples of both.

The individual self (human being) is called *"jīva"* because it is characterized by life (from "*jīv*" = "to live, breathe"). Ramaṇa said, *"Jīva* is so called because the individual self *sees* the world." This tells us something about the *jīva* and how it differs from the Self because the Self is not the one who sees. The *jīva* is the Self appearing through the limiting adjuncts of the psycho-physical complex. It is comprised of a physical body with its five cognitive sense organs, as well as an inner organ *(antaḥkaraṇa)* comprised of the mind, intellect, ego, and consciousness. In the *jīva*, the inner organ *(antaḥkaraṇa),* which is not conscious in nature, appears conscious and the Self, although infinite in nature, appears limited to the inner organ. When the identity of the Self with Brahman is realized in one's own experience, what is destroyed is not the essential nature of the *jīva* but only certain aspects of it, such as its finitude, mortality, its separateness from other individuals, and so on.

Every conscious activity of the mind or body of an individual revolves around their assumption that there is an "I", which they take to be a "me" who is doing something. This "I" is the common factor involved in every thought, word, or deed and this "I" assumes it is responsible for all these activities. Everyone believes they are the doer. Ramaṇa described this common factor the "I"- thought. The technical term for this "I"-thought is *"aham-vṛtti,"* i.e. a mental modification of the "I". When a one's mind flickers, one's personality or what is called the ego, takes responsibility for whatever happens. This is an illusion. The Self or real "I" never moves, never imagines that it is doing or thinking anything. The "I" that is imagining all this is but a mental fiction, a delusion. Ramaṇa upheld the traditional Advaita view that the notion of individuality is only this "I"-thought manifesting itself, flickering, in different ways. No matter in which way the "I"-thought moves, be it as the ego, memory, emotions, intellect and so on, they are all but thoughts, all but different forms of the phantom "I"-thought. Ramaṇa said:

> The mind is nothing other than the "I"-thought. The mind and the ego are one and the same. The other mental faculties such as the intellect and the memory are only this. Mind, intellect, the storehouse of mental tendencies, and the ego; all these are only the one mind itself. This is like different names being given to a man according to his different functions. The individual soul *(jīva)* is nothing but this ego.[1]

Giving a wonderful description of the *jīva*, Ramaṇa said:

---

[1] M. Spenser, 'Sri Bhagavan's letter to Ganapati Muni', *The Mountain Path*, 1982, Vol. 19, 96.

> Arranging thoughts in the order of value, the "I"-thought is the all-important thought. The second and the third persons (he, you, that, etc.) do not appear except to the first person (I). Therefore they arise only after the first person appears, so all the three persons seem to rise and sink together. Trace, then, the ultimate cause of "I" or personality.[1]

In Advaita, an individual is said to be enveloped by five sheaths *(kośa).*[2] A picture is drawn, as it were, of five men one within the other, and all veiling the true Self. The five men are the five sheaths, each with a head, limbs, trunk, and support. As we go from the outermost to the inner sheaths, we get nearer the truth. Each outer sheath stands to the inner in the relation of the filled to the filler. By the inner is the outer filled. As the Sage Varuṇa instructs his son, Bhṛgu: *Brahman* is that from whence all beings are born, wherein having been born they reside, and whereunto they return at the end. Bhṛgu makes a journey into the realm of truth. He comes across the five sheaths, one by one, each time thinking that the sheath he is faced with is the reality, and each time going beyond, not being satisfied with his own discovery, till he arrives at the final truth that Bliss is *Brahman.*

The sheaths *(kośa)* are so called because they veil the Self, hiding it from one's view. The five sheaths are: the food sheath *(annamaya),* the vital air sheath *(prānamaya),* the mental sheath *(manomaya),* the intellect sheath *(vijñānamaya)* and the bliss sheath *(ānandamaya). Annamaya* is the sheath made of food, the physical body. Its constituents are the quintuplicated elements, *i.e.* earth, air, fire, water, and space—elements, not in their pure form, but in their varying grades of mixture. Of the same stuff as the physical body are the things of the experienced world made. *Prāṇamaya* is the vital sheath; it is that which makes for life, and its expression is the breath. The *prāṇas* are said to be the products of the *rajas* aspect of the pure (non-quintuplicated) elements. To the sheath of *prāṇa* belong also the five organs of action *(karmendriya)*—those of speech, grasping, locomotion, excretion, and generation. *Manomaya* is the sheath of

---

[1] Venkataramiah, *Talks with Sri Ramana Maharshi*, 25.

[2] See TU, *Brahmānanda* chapter and Varuṇa's instruction to his son, Bhṛgu.

consciousness. Desiring and doubting are the functions of the mind. It arises out of the *sattva* phase of the pure elements. Its channels are the five organs of knowledge *(jñānendriya)*—those of hearing, touch, sight, taste and smell. *Vijñānamaya* is the sheath of self-consciousness; it is what is called intellect *(buddhi),* the agent of actions and the enjoyer of the fruit of actions. It is the empirical individual migrating from one physical body into another. *Ānandamaya* is the sheath of bliss. It is not the original bliss that is *Brahman* but a pseudo-bliss, and is the root-cause of transmigration. *Ānandamaya* is another name for ignorance *(ajñāna)* or nescience *(avidyā).*

The five sheaths may also be rearranged into three bodies. *Annamaya* is the gross body *(sthūla-sarīra).* The next three, *prānamaya, manomaya* and *vijnānamaya,* constitute the subtle body *(sukṣma-sarīra).* And, *ānandamaya* is the causal body *(kāraṇa-sarīra).* It is as endowed with these five sheaths, or three bodies, that an individual experiences the external world in the waking state. In dream-experiences, the gross body does not function but the other two bodies are active. While the wakeful enjoyments are gross, those pertaining to dreams are subtle. In deep sleep, the individual experiences neither the gross objects of the world without, nor the subtle objects of the world within. But the causal body, *viz.*, nescience, persists. And, it is on account of this that we dream and become awake again.

Ramaṇa, in his own inimitable style, made clear what is not so obvious in this traditional Advaita analysis of the three bodies: the gross, the subtle, and the causal. In his characteristic way he goes right to the heart of the matter and elucidates why the "I"-thought is where one's focus must be turned. In effect, he turns what is an intellectual analysis into a personal practice. He said:

> The ego is described as having three bodies, the gross, the subtle, and the causal, but that is only for the purpose of analytical exposition. If the method of enquiry were to depend on the ego's form, you may have to take it that any enquiry would become altogether impossible, because the forms the ego may assume are legion. Therefore, for the purpose of Self-enquiry you have to proceed on the basis that the ego

> has but one form, namely that of the *aham-vṛtti.* Although the concept of "I"-ness or "I am"-ness is by usage known as *aham-vṛtti,* it is not really a modification *(vṛtti)* like other *vṛttis* of the mind. Because, unlike the other *vṛttis* which have no essential interrelation, the *aham-vṛtti* is equally and essentially related to each and every *vṛtti* of the mind. Without *the aham-vṛtti* there can be no other *vṛttis*, but the *aham-vṛtti* can subsist by itself without depending on any other *vṛtti* of the mind. The *aham-vṛtti* is therefore fundamentally different from other *vṛttis*. So then, the search for the source of the *aham-vṛtti* is not merely the search for the basis of one of the forms of the ego, but for the very source itself, from which arises the "I am"-ness. In other words, the quest for, and the realization of the source of the ego in the form of *aham-vṛtti,* necessarily implies the transcendence of the ego in every one of its possible forms. . . . From the functional point of view, the ego has one and only one characteristic. The ego functions as the knot between the Self which is pure Consciousness and the physical body which is inert and insentient. The ego is therefore called the knot between Consciousness and the inert body *(cit-jaḍa-granthi).* In your investigation into the source of *aham- vṛtti*, you take the essential Consciousness *(cit)* aspect of the ego. For this reason the enquiry must lead to the realization of pure Consciousness of the Self.[1]

Advaita Vedānta adopts an enquiry into the three states of experience *(avasthā-traya-vicāra)* to reveal the real nature of the Self. By analyzing life as a whole, and not merely the waking state as most philosophical systems are prone to, Advaita reveals a comprehensive approach. An analysis of the waking state shows that the individual self resides in a physical body and employs its instruments to enjoy the objects of the external world. But the Self is not the not-Self. The former is conscious while the latter is inert. The analysis of the dream state reveals

---

[1] Venkataraman, *Maharshi's Gospel,* 83-85.

that the Self does not really act and is unattached. In dreams, the Self appears to interact with a myriad of things. But upon waking, it is realized that there were no dream objects and no interaction. And an analysis of the deep-sleep state shows that the Self is relationless. Here there are no distinctions whatsoever. There is no knowing subject, nor known objects. There is no within and no without as all empirical distinctions have vanished. Objective consciousness has disappeared though pure Consciousness remains. Thus, though the three states exist, they and their contents are not persistent. But underlying them and persisting throughout is the Self. The "I" that was there in the waking state, was also there in the dream and deep-sleep states. The states pass and vary, but the underlying consciousness remains the same. The *Kena Upaniṣad* says: "The world which shines in the states of waking, dream, and dreamless sleep, knowing as the Absolute—who I am, one is freed from all bonds."[1]

Philosophers say metaphysics deals with three basic entities: God/Absolute; the world; and the individual.[2] If the individual is a part of the world, why is it given a special place? Unlike the myriad things comprising the world that are always known as objects, the individual human being is both a subject and an object. It is both a subject who knows and it is also an object to itself which is known. The individual is thus distinguished from the world of matter in that it is a living and conscious being. The word *jīva* is really a contraction of the word *jīvātman*. In its capacity as *jīva*, the subjective individual is involved in duality, and in its capacity as *Atman*, it is identical with *Brahman*.

Ramaṇa, and the Advaitins before him, had to somehow explain or at least address the issue of how the one undifferentiated Consciousness could be understood as functioning in various different individuals or, more concise, how does the One appear as the many? If the ultimate Reality is one and non-dual, how to explain the apparent plurality of the world? Also, how to vindicate the apparent plurality of

---

[1] KeU 1.6. Also see BU 3.4.2 and *Kaivalya Upaniṣad* 1.17.

[2] See verse 2 of *Forty Verses on Existence* where Ramana says, "All systems of thought postulate the three principles (i.e., the world, soul, and God)".

individual beings *(jīva),* for the *jīva*, unlike the objects of the world, are said to partake of, and essentially be, the one non-dual Reality. It is, however, easy to explain and understand how plates, cups, and so on may emerge from the same clay, rather than explaining how the one undifferentiated, unmoving Consciousness appears as a multitude of conscious individuals. After all, plates and cups are not aware of anything, while individuals possess awareness with a desire for change.

Regarding this seeming enigma, and keeping in mind that Ramaṇa had no desire to formulate logical theories, he gave analogies or metaphors such as: the reflection of the sun in various pots of water; the reflection of color in a crystal; the sun and shadows; the cinema screen; ocean and waves, and sweets of various shapes. Unlike Ramaṇa, Śaṅkara, and the ancient Sages who merely resorted to metaphors in an attempt to address the issue, post-Śaṅkara Advaita philosophers both can and did develop these metaphors into metaphysical philosophical theories. Thus, there came about three basic theories in their attempts to establish the essential non-difference of the individual *(jīva)* from *Brahman*: the theory of reflection *(pratibimba-vāda),* the theory of limitation *(avaccheda-vāda),* and the theory of manifestation or appearance *(ābhāsa-vāda).*[1]

Śaṅkara explains that *jīvas* are mere appearances or reflections of the Self, as when the sun is reflected in rippling water.[2] He was addressing the question, "if there is only one Self, operating in all the various individuals, why don't the actions of the various individuals get mixed up?" It was also a reply to the question, "How does the one undifferentiated, unmoving Consciousness appear as a multitude of conscious individuals?"

The reflection of the sun in a body of water varies according to the state of the water, be it calm or turbulent, clean or dirty. Likewise, the reflection of the one undifferentiated Self

---

[1] It is often remarked that there are two basic theories and *abhāsa-vāda* is but a variation of the *pratibimba-vāda.* See Mahadevan, *Gauḍapāda: A Study in Early Advaita,* 163ff. The Vivaraṇa school of Advaita holds the *pratibimba-vāda*; the Bhāmati school holds the *avaccheda-vāda*; and Sureśvara posited the *abhāsa-vāda.*

[2] See BSB II.2.20.

varies according to the state of ignorance in which it is reflected. The minds of all the myriad individuals vary. Some are more, some are less, under the influence of passion and desire, capable of intellectual discrimination or not, and so on. The one undifferentiated Consciousness appears differently as it is reflected according to the differences in the reflected medium, i.e. individuals. Individuals have perceptions of sense-data, and their mind interprets that data as being an object, as being other than oneself. Even a little reflection will reveal that one is not their body, but that their body is theirs. Everyone says, "this is my body", "this is my hair"; "this is my thought", "this is my emotion" and so on. "My" is a personal pronoun signifying possession. These things belong to you, the perceiver, the owner and the user. Who are you?

The role of an illustration is to refer to some common feature(s). When two things are compared, they are compared only with reference to some particular point(s) they have in common. It is well-known that no comparison is ever totally equal, for, if that were the case, there would not be a comparison but identity. The special feature of the sun that warrants comparison in this case is known as "participation in increase and decrease". The reflected image of the sun increases when the water expands, and contracts when the water shrinks. Further, the reflected image trembles when the water is agitated and divides itself when the water is divided. Thus, the reflected image participates in all the conditions and attributes of the water, even as the real sun remains unaffected all the while. Similarly, the Self, although changeless, participates, as it were, in the attributes and states of the body. One's image of who they are seemingly grows, shrinks, and so on, as the body grows, shrinks, and so on.

One may note that while Ramaṇa was living in the Virupākṣ a cave, he was given a copy of the *Vivekacudāmani* and he felt that a prose paraphrase of the book in Tamil would be useful for spiritual aspirants and so he wrote one. Thus, Ramaṇa was very aware of the analogies given therein and often employed them himself.

In the *Vivekacūḍāmaṇi*, the following verses are pertinent:

> Even if *sattva* is pure like water, yet, in combination with *rajas* and *tamas*, it generates worldly existence. But, when the original, the light of the Self, gets reflected in *sattva* alone, then, like the sun, it illumines the entire inanimate world.[1]

> Just as you do not identify yourself with your body's shadow, or your reflection, or your dream body, or when you imagine it in your heart, so too, do not identify yourself with your living body.[2]

> Looking at a reflection of the sun, mirrored in the water of a jar, a fool thinks it is the sun itself. Similarly, a stupid person, through delusion, imagines that the reflection of Consciousness appearing in the limiting adjunct is the Self.[3]

> A wise person rejects the pot, the water, and the sun's reflection in it and, indifferent and independent of them all, so sees the self-luminous sun in the sky which illuminates these three.[4]

> Being yourself the ever-existent Reality, which is the self-luminous foundation of everything, abandon the universe and your individual body like vessels filled with impurities.[5]

When a person's attention is on the reflection he ignores the real sun in the sky. In order to perceive the original, one must turn one's attention from the reflection to the prototype. The sun does not include the pot, the water, and the reflection. If anything, they are there only to turn one's attention to the original. One should not mistake the reflection for the original.

---

[1] V 119.

[2] Ibid, 165.

[3] Ibid, 220.

[4] Ibid, 221.

[5] Ibid, 290.

Interestingly, Śaṅkara's analogy of the sun being reflected in various pots of water helps to explain how it is that the Self "enters" the universe and *jīvas*. Though the Self goes nowhere, does nothing, and thus cannot "enter" literally, it "enters" the universe and *jīvas* just as the sun "enters" the water by being perceived there in its reflection. Of course the sun does not "enter" the water literally but merely as a reflection.

The above-mentioned analogy helps to explain how it is that the individual is not the "doer" of actions. "When the limiting adjunct moves, the movement of its reflection is ascribed by fools to the original, like the sun which is unmoving. Likewise, one thinks "I am the doer", "I am the enjoyer", "I am lost", alas!"[1] From the perspective of the sun, it does not move, but from the perspective of an ignorant person on the earth, it appears to rise and set; it is perceived to move though in actuality it does not!

Again, the *jīva* is said to be a reflection of the Self on the mirror of ignorance.[2] From a particular perspective, the reflection is the prototype. A person's face reflected in a mirror is not really different from the face in front of it and does not have an independent life of its own. Further, the reflection lasts only so long as the mirror remains. But how the reflection appears, what it looks like (being so independent, so object-like, so other than me) is due to the shape, size, clarity and so on, of the mirror. Obviously, the clearer the mirror, the more perfect will be the reflection and relation between the *jīva* and *Atman*.

Finally, the reflection theory powerfully demonstrates the main thrust of why such analogies are used in the first place. Liberation is the goal, the reason to be, of all such teachings. Breaking the pot means the destruction of ignorance of the ego.

> As when the pot is broken, the space (within) becomes one with the space (without), so too, the supreme

---

[1] Ibid, 509.

[2] Ibid, 292. "That, wherein this reflection of the world is like a city in a mirror, that Absolute am I." Actually this analogy pertains to the *jīva's* relationship to the world, but a variation of it is used in the reflection theory to illustrate our point.

> knower of the Absolute becomes the Absolute itself when the limiting adjuncts vanish.[1]

The *ābhāsa-vāda* or appearance theory posits that the individual *(jīva)* is a seeming or illusory appearance of the Absolute *(Brahman).* All manifestations of name and form, of being independent separate objects, are an appearing-to-be what it is not. The unity of Being, the Self, instead of being realized, appears to an individual as a world of multiplicity. Those ignorant of the undifferentiated Self assume the diversity to be real, whereas it has no real independent status, it is the figment of a fractured mind.

Sureśvara, who formulated the appearance theory, said "*jīvas* are reflections of *Brahman (cidābhāsa)* on individual ignorant minds with their latent tendencies". Reflection of the Self on the ignorant mind is the *jīva.*" He said:

> The one seer (Self) in all being, shines as if different because of the objects, even as the sun with his wealth of rays shines as many (as reflected on account of the different water-containers).[2]

> Just as for one and the same person the state of being friend, neutral, or foe is imagined by other people, so also, of the non-different pure Consciousness, difference is dependent on the internal organ.[3]

Padmapāda presented two other analogies for the reflection theory. He proposed the red crystal and the mirror examples to demonstrate how the undifferentiated Self is reflected in *jīvas.* In the case of the red crystal, the crystal's nature (its color) is different from that of the (red) flower. The error comes in identifying the red color with the crystal which of itself, has no color. The mirror analogy shows how the prototype is identical with the reflected face in the mirror. Thus, the ego of a person is (essentially) identical with *Brahman* (and not just similar to it).

---

[1] V 566.

[2] NS 2.47.

[3] Ibid, 2.48.

With the reflection theory, one can understand how it is that just because one realizes the identity of the *jīva* and *Brahman*, it does not follow that the reflecting medium (the internal organ) is destroyed. When one realizes that one's face is identical with the reflected face in the mirror, the mirror is not thereby destroyed. This explains the fact that even after a person realizes the Self, the body of the *jīvan-mukta* does not disappear.

The limitation theory, looking at the dilemma from another angle, states that the one, undifferentiated pure Consciousness, being without attributes or qualities, cannot be reflected (as in a mirror or a pot of water) and thus, it would be more accurate to say that the individual is not so much a reflection of Consciousness, as to say that *jīvas* are limitations of it. Remember, this objection arises only when one stretches the analogy beyond its legitimate point. In Śaṅkara's writing both types of analogies are found and thus, two philosophical theories emerge. The point of the reflection theory is that the *jīva* is adventitious. The theory has its own insights and it behooves the reader to take what it is attempting to reveal, and not reject it as inaccurate merely because no analogy can explain everything. Ramaṇa remarked:

> But, why all this objection and counter-objection, analysis and counter-analysis? Can the world exist apart from the Self? The "I" is always Brahman. Its identity need not be established by logic and practice. It is enough that one realize the Self. The Self is always *Brahman*.[1]

That being noted, the limitation theory arose because of the beauty and appropriateness, the illustrative power of examples like, "the space within a pot". This theory elucidates that the individual *(jīva)* is but a limitation of consciousness. This limitation is constituted of the limiting condition or adjunct *(upādhi)* of ignorance. Advaita philosophers frequently employ the term *"upādhi"* and use it in the sense that the *upādhi* is a qualification or limitation of one thing by another. Thus, in this context, it refers to the mind superimposing upon the infinite

---

[1] Venkataramiah, *Talks with Sri Ramana Maharshi*, 597.

Self limitations and conditions that do not properly belong to it. So long as this ignorance lasts, individuals engage in this false superimposition and do not know the Self as it is. Individuals thus view themselves as individual, separate, distinct, conditioned, and finite. In a similar way, space is really one and indivisible but is perceived through limitations as if it were divided into particular spaces like the space in a pot, a house, and so on.

> As the space in a pot merges into the universal space, merge the individual in the great Self and be ever silent, O Sage[1]
>
> Space is universal, located everywhere. Space enclosed in a pot is known as *ghaṭākāsa.* This enclosed space is merely conventional. In actuality, space is space. Likewise, the Self appears enclosed by the body and its adjuncts but in actual fact, this is only seemingly so.[2]
>
> Space, divested of hundreds of limiting adjuncts such as a pot, a jar, a receptacle for grain, the eye of a needle, and so on, is one and not diverse. So too, the supremely pure Self is one only, when divested of limiting adjuncts such as egoism, and so on.[3]
>
> Though connected with a jar, space is not tainted by the odour of the liquor in it. Similarly, the Self is not tainted by the qualities of the limited adjuncts with which it is connected[4].
>
> It is not born; it does not die; it does not grow; it does not decline; it does not change. It is eternal. Even if this body is destroyed it does not cease to exist, just as the

---

[1] V 289.

[2] Ibid. See *V* 136, 383, 386, 451, 566 per space in a pot.

[3] Ibid, 386.

[4] Ibid, 451.

> space in a pot does not become extinct when the pot is broken.[1]

> As when the pot is broken, the space (within) becomes one with the space (without), so too, the supreme knower of the Absolute becomes the Absolute itself when the limiting adjuncts vanish.[2]

An advantage of the limitation theory over the reflection theory is that the former gives a greater empirical reality to the *jīva* than the latter. In the reflection theory the *jīva* is a mere fleeting reflection, while in the limitation theory it is a necessary practical reality in that individuals in the world, subject to ignorance, do perceive other individuals and objects in the world as separate, distinct realities.

Ramaṇa covers, in detail, all aspects of this discussion as follows:

> Multiplicity of individuals is a moot point with most persons. A *jīva* is only the light reflected on the ego. The person identifies himself with the ego and argues that there must be more like him. He is not easily convinced of the absurdity of his position. Does a man who sees many individuals in his dream persist in believing them to be real and enquire after them when he wakes up?

> This argument does not convince the disputant.

> Again, there is the moon. Let anyone look at her from any place at any time; she is the same moon. Everyone knows it. Now suppose that there are several receptacles of water reflecting the moon. The images are all different from one another and from the moon herself. If one of the receptacles falls to pieces, that reflection disappears. Its disappearance does not affect

[1] Ibid, 136.

[2] Ibid, 566.

the real moon or the other reflections. It is similar with an individual attaining Liberation. He alone is liberated.

The sectarian of multiplicity makes this his argument against non-duality. "If the Self is single, if one man is liberated, that means that all souls are liberated. In practice it is not so. Therefore Advaita is not correct."

The weakness in the argument is that the reflected light of the Self is mistaken for the original Light of the Self. The ego, the world and the individuals are all due to the person's latent tendencies. When they perish, that person's hallucinations disappear, that is to say one pitcher is broken and the relative reflection is at an end.

The fact is that the Self is never bound. There can therefore be no Release for It. All the troubles are for the ego only.

Jīva is called so because he sees the world. A dreamer sees many *jīvas* in a dream but all of them are not real. The dreamer alone exists and he sees all. So it is with the individual and the world. There is the creed of only one Self which is also called the creed of only one *jīva*. It says that the *jīva* is only one who sees the whole world and the *jīvas* therein. Then *jīva* means the Self here.

So it is. But the Self is not a seer. But here he is said to see the world. So he is differentiated as the *Jīva*.[1]

Ramaṇa invoked all these theories without saying that one was more appropriate or superior than another, but he does say that, in all cases, his own direct method of Self-enquiry is superior to any indirect method or theory. Citing the reflection theory, he explains:

---

[1] Venkataramiah, *Talks with Sri Ramana Maharshi*, 530.

> Some *Upaniṣads* also speak of 101 *nādīs* which spread from the heart, one of them being the vital *nādī.* If the *jīva* comes down from above and gets reflected in the brain, as the yogis say, there must be a reflecting surface in action. That must also be capable of limiting the Infinite Consciousness to the limits of the body. In short the Universal Being becomes limited as a *jīva.* Such reflecting medium is furnished by the aggregate of the latent tendencies of the individual. It acts like the water in a pot which reflects the image of an object. If the pot be drained of its water there will be no reflection. The object will remain without being reflected. The object here is the Universal Being-Consciousness which is all-pervading and therefore immanent in all. It need not be cognized by reflection alone; it is self-resplendent. Therefore, the seeker's aim must be to drain away the latent tendencies from the heart and let no reflection obstruct the Light of Eternal Consciousness. This is achieved by the search for the origin of the ego and by diving into the heart. This is the direct method for Self-Realization. One who adopts it need not worry about *nādīs*, the brain, the *suṣūmnā*, the *paranāḍī*, the *kuṇḍalinī, prāṇāyāma* or the six centers.[1]

The above passage is immediately followed by a passage from Ramaṇa that utilizes the *abhasa-vada* model:

> The Self does not come from anywhere else and enter the body through the crown of the head. It is as it is, ever sparkling, ever steady, unmoving and unchanging. The changes which are noticed are not inherent in the Self which abides in the Heart and is self-luminous like the Sun. The changes are seen in Its Light. The relation between the Self and the body or the mind may be compared to that of a clear crystal and its background. If the crystal is placed against a red flower, it shines red; if placed against a green leaf it shines green, and so

[1] Ibid, 333.

> on. The individual confines himself to the limits of the changeful body or of the mind which derives its existence from the unchanging Self. All that is necessary is to give up this mistaken identity, and that done, the ever-shining Self will be seen to be the single non-dual Reality. The reflection of Consciousness is said to be in the subtle body *(sukṣma sarīra),* which appears to be composed of the brain and the nerves radiating from it to all parts of the trunk, chiefly through the spinal column and the solar plexus.[1]

In the following passage, Ramaṇa elucidates the nature of the mind. The *jīva* believes that it is an individual and bound because of the mind and its "I"-thought. With the disappearance of the mind and its "I"-thought, the disappearance of a sense of individuality, there is Self-realization.

> What is called "mind" is a wondrous power residing in the Self. It causes all thoughts to arise. Apart from thoughts, there is no such thing as mind. Therefore, thought is the nature of mind. Apart from thoughts, there is no independent entity called the world. In deep sleep there are no thoughts, and there is no world. In the states of waking and dream, there are thoughts, and there is a world also. Just as the spider emits the thread (of the web) out of itself and again withdraws it into itself, likewise the mind projects the world out of itself and again resolves it into itself. When the mind comes out of the Self, the world appears. Therefore, when the world appears (to be real), the Self does not appear; and when the Self appears (shines) the world does not appear. When one persistently inquires into the nature of the mind, the mind will end leaving the Self (as the residue). What is referred to as the Self is the *Atman.* The mind always exists only in dependence on something gross; it cannot stay alone. It is the mind that is called the subtle body or the soul *(jīva).*[2]

---

[1] Ibid, 333-34.

[2] *Who Am I? (Nān Yār)*, verse 8.

Isn't it obvious that it is not the body that proclaims itself as "I"? Every baby knows that it is not "I" when it first becomes aware and talks of "baby wants this, baby wants that". Then its elders, who are far less wise than the baby and sadly have been conditioned by others, comes and with constant persistence tells the baby again and again that baby's body is baby's self. The poor child, upon hearing nothing but this from all sides, becomes more and more convinced of this falsehood until, having attained what is called maturity, the baby grows into an adult and is himself or herself now ready to denounce anyone who is so bold as to affirm that the body is not the Self.

V
Ramana and Ethics

On being asked whether it was not the duty of a Sage to act and preach the Truth to all people, Ramaṇa replied, ṢIf a man awakes from a dream, does he ask: 'Have those men that I saw in the dream awakened? This is like a dreamer saying, 'I shall not awake until all these dream-men awake.'

Introduction

Advaita's absolute non-dualistic thought has often been criticized for its lack of ethical doctrines. Ramaṇa was occasionally criticized for 'just sitting on the hill all those years and not actively engaged in helping the world'. These criticisms flow from a common misconception that the non-dual Self, when it manifests as an enlightened one, is beyond ethics, beyond right and wrong and therefore uninvolved with morality. There is a grain of truth here, but there is also a misunderstanding. If one correctly understands what the Self necessarily implies, such criticisms would not arise. It is correct that since the Self transcends all moral distinctions, it must be beyond good and evil. The *Upaniṣads* have numerous such statements: "When the seer sees . . . then the illumined one completely shakes off both virtue and vice."[1] "Tell me that which you see as different from righteousness *(dharma)* and different from unrighteousness *(adharma)*."[2] "Even if one

[1] MuU 3.1.3.

[2] KUp 1.2.14.

performs a great and holy work, without knowing this (the Self), that work is exhausted in the end."[1]

Ethics, both subjective and objective, belongs to the empirical world where the dualities of auspicious and inauspicious, good and evil, virtue and vice are found. However, since every aspect of the embodied Self is permeated with, its very nature is an embodiment of virtue, such a one is neither compelled nor troubled by good and evil. The sun's nature is to shine, water is wet; that is their nature. The Sage's nature embodies and displays virtues like love, humility, compassion, self-control—they are not other than the Sage but his very nature and they flow spontaneously from him. Ramaṇa remarked: "Good, God, Love, are all the same thing."[2] The *Upaniṣad* says: "Evil does not overtake him, but he transcends all evil. Evil does not trouble him, but he consumes all evil. He has become sinless, stainless, and free from doubts."[3] Thus, in one sense, an independent separate treatment of ethics becomes redundant in Advaita. Why? Because value questions are implied in every epistemological and metaphysical statement Advaita makes. For instance, in the treatment of the fundamental distinction between orders of being, the criterion used to establish these orders is at once value laden. The same goes for the self and consciousness and its modes of knowing. In Advaita, as with Ramaṇa, few separate ethical questions are raised for they are implicit in the treatment of every epistemological and metaphysical question.

We have seen that Advaita and Ramaṇa speak from different standpoints, corresponding to various levels of human experience and, for the unenlightened person, there are moral consequences for one's actions. Both Advaita and Ramaṇa hold that one who has not yet "attained" Self-realization is very much bound up with ethical judgments and must accept the scale of values by which his or her own judgment may be informed. Ramaṇa said: "So long as the feeling 'I am doing' is there, one must experience the result of one's acts, whether they

---

[1] BU 1.4.15.

[2] Mudaliar, *Day by Day with Bhagavan,* 94.

[3] BU.

are good or bad. So long as the ego lasts, effort is necessary. When the ego ceases to exist, actions become spontaneous."[1] "Until Self-realization there will be *karma*, that is, action and reaction. After realization there will be no *karma* and no world."[2]

Thus, we see that Ramaṇa views the issue of ethics from two standpoints. At the absolute level, the level of the enlightened Sage, there is no doer, nothing to be done, no world to improve or relieve of its sufferings, neither good or bad, yet at the relative level of duality, ethics does exist and play its appointed role.

The Advaita Vedānta system lays down an oft-quoted, well-known, four-fold requirement[3] qualifying an aspirant to pursue the path of knowledge. The third qualification is: possession in abundance of the six virtues, *viz*., calmness, equanimity, turning away from the sense-objects, forbearance, concentration, and faith. The paradigm for the six treasures is in the *Upaniṣads.*[4] The Advaita tradition usually depicts these as tranquility *(śama)*, self-control *(dama)*, withdrawal of the sense objects from the sense organs *(uparati)*, forbearance *(titikṣā)*, the perfect establishment of the intellect in the Absolute *(śamādhana)*, and faith *(śraddhā)*.[5] It is this requirement that concerns ethical behavior. According to the tradition, only that individual who possesses this four-fold requirement, which includes virtuous behavior, is qualified to study the Vedanta texts under the guidance of a teacher *(guru)* who is not only learned in Scripture but also well-established in Truth. A *guru* is defined as a spiritual master who has attained oneness with the Self and without whom a disciple cannot attain liberation.

Advaita philosophy teaches that, for almost all individuals, the practice of the virtues is indispensable for knowledge of the Self. "Self-knowledge is denied to him who has not first turned

---

[1] Nagamma, *Letters from Sri Ramanasramam*, 65.

[2] Venkataramiah, *Talks with Sri Ramana Maharshi*, 462.

[3] *Sādhana catuṣṭaya* or '*nityānitya vastu viveka, iha amutra artha phala virāga, śama damadi sādhana sampatti*, and *mumukṣutva*.

[4] BU 4.4.23.

[5] See also chapter 16 of the *BG* wherein the divine virtues are listed.

away from wickedness, who is not tranquil and subdued, and whose mind is not at peace." The *Upaniṣads* say that the sense-organs naturally move outwards towards externals and have an inclination towards material pleasures and hence worldly individuals become entangled in worldly life. "The Self-existent Lord of all things created the sense organs with a powerful tendency to go outwards, and thus individuals see external objects and not the internal Self."[1] The ideal of 'pleasure' and the ideal of the 'good' are sharply distinguished and compared to darkness and light. Yama tells Nachiketas: "One thing is the good and quite another thing is the pleasant, and both seize upon a man with different meanings. Of those who take the good, it is well with them; that individual falls from the aim of life who chooses the pleasant."[2]

What is the rational for cultivating the virtues? To seek the Self, an illustration of a chariot is given.[3] The body is compared to a chariot, the senses to the horses, the intellect to the charioteer, the mind to the reins, the sense objects to the road, and the embodied soul to the master of the chariot, who is desirous of reaching the goal of Self-knowledge. The chariot can take the master to his destination only when the vehicle is well built, when the driver knows the way, and when the reins are strong, the horses held firmly under control, and the roads well chosen. What is emphasized here is the need of a healthy body, controlled sense-organs, a strong mind, and an intellect which will choose only those material objects conducive to a person's spiritual quest. Thus, virtues like truthfulness, non-injury, forgiveness, good conduct, non-appropriation of others' property, control of the senses, absence of anger, equanimity, detachment, charity, compassion, and the like are extolled. However, it should be noted that Ramaṇa, unlike Advaita theory, mainly taught ethics through his own personal behavior and very rarely spoke of ethical issues.

Ramaṇa's love for all creation was natural and spontaneous. He was an embodiment of love. He always acted ethically in

---

[1] KU 2.1.1.

[2] Ibid, 1.2.1.

[3] Ibid. 1.3.3. *śreyas* and *preyas.*

any given situation, not because he ought to, not because of a cultivated standard imposed upon him, but because it was his very nature. The sun's nature is to shine. It shines on the good and on the bad; on the rich and on the poor. It doesn't shine for any particular reason, e.g., so that the grass may grow or to provide warmth to the earth. It shines because it is its nature to shine.

A Sage is not an inert rock. A Sage is aware of individual differences such as whether a person is tall or short, fat or thin, male or female, this is a peacock and that is a cow, and so on. Further, a Sage is aware of people's merits and faults, shortcomings and weaknesses as they come within his orbit and go about their daily routines. The Sage keenly observes the world around him. At the same time, the Sage is conscious of the underlying essential quality of life as the one Self. No one is essentially, really, an 'other'. The Sage loves all because the Sage is all, the Self is love, love is the Self. Thus, the Sage does not base his or her life on desires and expectations, rules and regulations, give and take. A system of ethics tells a person what they ought to do. It does not concern factual questions or information but concerns how one ought to act, what one should do. There is no 'ought' in the life of a Sage. The Sage acts spontaneously, ever manifesting his essential nature, naturally and without effort. Ramaṇa said: "What is once a means becomes itself the goal. When that happens, that which was at one time a conscious and painful effort, becomes the normal and natural state, spontaneously and without effort."[1] "Sri Bhagavān said that in the whole *Thayumanavar* literature, he preferred one stanza that says: "Ego disappearing another 'I-I' spontaneously manifests in full glory."[2]

The *Śrīmad Bhāgavatam* declares: "It is improper to ask those whose sole delight is in the Self about their welfare, since they are strangers to thoughts of differences between happiness and sadness." What a strange paradox that Ramaṇa, who was totally unconcerned about his own welfare, should concern himself with every small detail of the happiness and sadness of

---

[1] Mudaliar, *Day by Day with Bhagavan,* 20.

[2] Venkataramiah, *Talks with Sri Ramana Maharshi*, 68.

his devotees' lives and even the lives of the plants and animals around him. To illustrate this, let us look at various incidents in the life of Ramaṇa that not only forcefully demonstrate his views on ethics, but also reveal that he was truly an embodiment of virtue.

Virtue Incarnate

There he was, firmly established in the state of steady Self-abidance *(sahaja-samādhi).* He was one with everything, free from all thoughts, desirable or undesirable, happy or sad. His eyes were glittering, unblinking, full of overflowing love for all creation, firmly fixed in the Self alone. He saw no external objects with a desire to receive any impression from them. He asked for nothing. Ever-full, he reveled in the spontaneous bliss of the Heart. Truly he was an embodiment of serenity, full and complete. Such was the Maharshi.

1. Once, two years after Ramaṇa had shifted from the Skandāśrama to the present Ramaṇāśrama, a robbery took place.[1] In those days the *āśrama* consisted of only two rather meager huts, one in front of the mother's *samādhi* shrine and the other to the north of it. Three robbers came, burst fire-crackers, shouted threats, and attempted to break in through the window of one of the huts. While the few devotees present attempted to latch the door, Ramaṇa remarked: "Let these robbers play their role; we shall stick to ours. Let them do what they like; it is for us to bear and forebear. Let us not interfere with them."[2]

The door of the hut was opened so that the robbers could enter and Ramaṇa and the devotees attempted to proceed to the other hut. However, once outside, one of the robbers beat each of them with a stick including Ramaṇa who was beaten on his

[1] Full particulars of this event are available in the authentic court proceedings of the Criminal Court in Tiruvannamalai, Crime NO.52/1924.

[2] Narasimha Swami, *Self-Realization*, 153.

thigh. Ramaṇa remarked to the thief: "If you are not satisfied yet you may strike the other leg also."[1]

The robbers ransacked everything in the hut but could not find anything of value. They demanded to know where the valuables were kept. Ramaṇa told them: "We are poor *sādhus*, living on alms and never have cash."[2] When Ramakrishna Swami saw the swollen leg of Ramaṇa, he grabbed an iron bar and asked permission to attack them. Ramaṇa said: "We are *sādhus*. We should not give up our *dharma*. If you go and strike them some may die. That will be a matter for which the world will justly blame us and not the thieves. They are only misguided men."[3]

The following day the police came and investigated the crime. Ramaṇa did not mention his injury. Interestingly, over the years Ramaṇa would recall and explain in graphic detail many incidents in his life. But we find that there has been not one single reference to this incident made by him. By his example, Ramaṇa demonstrated the need for strict adherence by renunciates to the principle of *ahiṁsā,* non-injury—to never harm another living being. Ramaṇa didn't judge them and as far as he was concerned the event was a non-event.

The equality that Ramaṇa insisted upon in the dining hall was an aspect of his universal love. There are numerous instances one could quote and most of them revolve around the attempts by the kitchen staff, as well as devotees, to show him preferential treatment. Share and share alike was his golden rule, a rule that he never once broke in over fifty years at Tiruvannamalai.

2. One day Ramaṇa suddenly stopped drinking buttermilk. He was asked, "Bhagavān, we eat all the items sumptuously. But you keep giving up one item or the other. How can we bear this?" Ramaṇa replied: "They (the kitchen staff) are only too ready to give me extra helpings. But when it comes to the

---

[1] Ibid, 154.

[2] Ibid, 155.

[3] Ibid.

devotees their hands are paralyzed." It seems Ramaṇa was provoked into making this remark because a young girl in the dining hall had been refused an extra quantity of *sambar* for her rice that she had asked for. In a similar way, the kitchen staff took great care of old devotees, those sitting near Ramaṇa, and Ramaṇa himself while neglecting those who were seated farther away or were newcomers. Repeatedly Ramaṇa would tell them that service to his devotees was the best form of service to him, all to no avail. So he would stop eating or drinking some item to draw their attention to their impartiality.[1]

3. Once, some bananas were brought to the dining hall. Ramaṇa was served first and then the others. Ramaṇa noticed that as time passed, the staff began cutting the bananas into smaller and smaller bits so that the last few people would also receive some. Ramaṇa said in disgust: "This is what I don't like. Why do you serve me when you cannot give the same quantity to all the people? That is why I am telling you. If you serve Bhagavān after you serve all others, there will be equal distribution. If by chance nothing remains, it does not matter if I do not get anything; if all eat, I am satisfied even if I do not get my share."[2]

Once, a member of the kitchen staff noticed that Ramaṇa used to add a little quantity of sweet buttermilk to his *rasam* rice. It so happened that for a few days there was no sweet buttermilk available, only sour buttermilk. Then, one day someone brought a small quantity of sweet buttermilk. Thinking that Ramaṇa ate so little, it would not be wrong to give him the sweet buttermilk even though there was not enough for all to share equally. Ramaṇa remarked to her: "All are equal here." On another occasion, the cook noticed that the vegetables in the *sambar* had not been cooked properly. He gave them to everyone but Ramaṇa. Ramaṇa remarked: "If something is considered unpalatable for me, it should be considered the same for others also."[3]

---

[1] See Natarajan, *Unforgettable Years*, 72.

[2] See Nagamma, *Letters from Ramanasramam*, 291-92 for this reference.

[3] See Natarajan, *Unforgettable Years*, 71.

If something was not equally shared by all it would be considered like poison in Ramaṇa's view. For him, the rule of sharing equally was never to be broken under any circumstances.

4. Ramaṇa was an embodiment of compassion and kindness. "On one occasion the Maharshi and Mudaliar Swami were walking together on a hill, a little above Virupākṣa Cave where there was a huge rock about 15 feet high and with a cleft at the top. A little shepherdess stood there crying. On the Maharshi asking her the reason, she said that one of her sheep had slipped into the cleft and she was unable to retrieve it. He at once descended into the cleft, took the sheep on his shoulders, climbed up and delivered it to the overjoyed girl."[1]

Ramaṇa's love for all creation was natural, spontaneous, and full of compassion. As we observed earlier, it is a common misconception that when a person attains Self-realization, because duality has been destroyed, because there is a total absence of difference in perception, love is not possible. What a marvel that Ramaṇa, though totally unconcerned about his own body, should concern himself with even the minutest details of others' lives. Though there was no sense of difference for Ramaṇa, he seemed to have a special identification with the poor, the humble, the downtrodden and meek.

5. During the summer months when there was no water available at the Virupākṣa Cave, Ramaṇa would shift to the Mango Tree Cave. In those days the caste system in India was strictly enforced. Women from the lower caste would roam the hill in search of grass. Heavy with their loads, they would be hungry and thirsty. Ramaṇa once reminisced about them:

> Poor people, they start from their homes early in the morning after taking a little gruel, go up the hill and secure a head-load of grass. As soon as they come to the cave they throw down their bundles, bend down and

[1] Swaminathan, *Ramana Maharshi*, 34.

say, 'Swami, Swami, first throw a vessel full of water down our spines.' I used to stand on the verandah there and when I threw water on them as desired, they used to recover from their exhaustion, saying, 'Oh, how good this is!' Then, cupping their palms they used to drink water until their thirst was satisfied, wash their faeces, take some rest in the shade of the trees and then depart. They alone could experience the happiness of it all. It is only when one experiences the oppressiveness of the heat that one knows the relief of the coolness of water. I knew they would be coming at that hour and so would sit there with the water ready. What could they do? They should not touch the water in the Mulaipal Tirtham (holy tank) and there is no water anywhere on the hill. The heat is unbearable. They cannot have food unless they sell the grass and get some money. They have children at home. They must reach home quick to look after them. What can they do, poor people! They used to come to the cave with the hope that the Swami would supply water. We were not cooking at that time. If any day we did cook, I poured a lot of water into the rice while cooking, took out the gruel, poured it into the pot, mixed water with it liberally, and added salt. If dry ginger was available I would mix it in also. By the time they came, the gruel water would be quite cool. When a tumbler full of it was poured into their hands, they used to drink it like nectar and go away. The taste of that gruel and the happiness of drinking that water they alone could know.[1]

6. On special occasion like Ramaṇa's Birthday or *Mahāpūja* day, the poor people were fed. Once, Ramaṇa noticed that one of the poor men had not received any of the food. The next day when the dinner bell was rung, Ramaṇa got up and went outside to the tree where the poor were gathered and said: "If you will not give them food first, I will not come to the dining hall at all. I will stand under the tree and stretch out my hands for food like

---

[1] Nagamma, *Letters from Ramanasramam*, 326-27.

them and when I am given a bowl of food I will eat it, go straight to the hall and sit."[1]

7. Once, while attempting to save a squirrel from a dog, Ramaṇa accidentally broke his collarbone. It took sometime for the collarbone to heal and Ramaṇa was considerably weakened by the accident. Having hardly healed, Ramaṇa heard that some devotees were going to Skandāśrama and said that he wanted to go along. Ramaṇa was told that a three-hour walk up the hill, under the blazing sun, with frail health would be inadvisable. Nonetheless, to their surprise, Ramaṇa went. Why? Soon they found out. There was a mason doing some odds jobs at Skandāśrama. Ramaṇa said to him: 'I came for your sake. Your prayers dragged me here.' It seems that four days earlier, in connection with the raising of the pillars for the New Hall, a special worship had been conducted. Ramaṇa had attended this function with the doctor's permission. The mason had also attended the function. There, the mason had silently prayed, 'How lucky are these people who are constructing this hall! Ramaṇa, himself, has come to see their work. Ramaṇa is weak so how could he come and see the work that I am doing at Skandāśrama with such patient care? Besides, it has been a year since he last came to Skandāśrama. It would be too much to hope that he would do so now. How wonderful would it be if he did.' Thus, the reason Ramaṇa went up the hill was revealed and he then personally inspected the mason' work. Such is the compassion of Ramaṇa.[2]

Ramaṇa's identity with all creation and all life forms was total. There were no 'others' for him. Though he perceived all the differences in all the various forms, he was simultaneously aware that each form was none other than the one indivisible Consciousness. How marvelous and mysterious! What a wonder! To see diversity and yet, the diversity in no way breaking the unity of the Self. The essential unity of all life was experiential to him. As a result, Ramaṇa was a loving friend to humans, to animals, to birds, to plants, to all of life alike. His

---

[1] Ibid.

[2] Natarajan, *Unforgettable Years*, 32-34.

compassion led him to plead on their behalf whenever he noticed or felt any kind of discrimination or harm to them. Stories of this compassion for animals abound in Ramaṇa's life and I will mention but a few of them. Each is so illustrative of the virtues that elucidation and commentary seems unnecessary to say the least.

8. One day a devotee and a friend, not finding Ramaṇa in his usual place, wandered around the *āśrama* when they heard a childlike voice *"Chee, asatte"* (stupid fellow). Looking in the direction from which the sound emanated they saw a small goat, a little monkey, a squirrel and Ramaṇa. Ramaṇa was sitting on his haunches with his legs folded up to his chest. The goat rested between his knees, the monkey had its head resting on his right knee and the squirrel was perched on his left knee. Holding a packet of groundnuts in his left hand, Ramaṇa picked groundnuts from it with his right hand, one by one, and was feeding the goat, monkey, squirrel, and himself by turns. It seems his remarks had been addressed to the monkey who had tried to snatch a nut as Ramaṇa was about to place it in the squirrel's mouth. All four seemed to be enjoying the nuts, equally happy, from the way they looked at each other and kept close together. The goat, the monkey, the squirrel and Ramaṇa appeared to have forgotten the differences in their species. All four were good friends despite their differences. Then the nuts were finished and Ramaṇa threw the packet away and said: *"Pongada"* (go away, you fellows) just as an old man talking to his grandchildren. The goat, the monkey, and the squirrel left.[1]

9. Once a devotee brought a big basket of mangoes and offered them to Ramaṇa. He said, "The monkeys are plucking the mangoes one by one. So we hurriedly plucked all of them and brought them here." Ramaṇa smiled and said: "Oh! Is that so? The monkeys take the fruit one by one, while people take them

---

[1] Narayana, *Miracles*, 54.

in one lot. What the monkeys do is petty theft but what we do is regular looting."[1]

10. One day a male monkey snatched some fruits and ran away. Then a female monkey, with her baby on her breast, came near the fruits but was immediately chased away. Ramaṇa said: "It is a mother with child. Why not give her something and send her away. Is this fair? We call ourselves *sannyāsins*, but when a real *sannyāsinī* comes we drive her away without giving her anything. How unfair! We want to eat for years and live. We store things in a room, lock it and keep the keys with us. Has the monkey got a house? Can it put anything by for the morrow? It eats whatever it can get and sleeps on whatever tree is available. It carries the child under the belly wherever it goes until the child is also able to walk about when it leaves the child to itself. Who is the real *sannyāsin*, the monkey or ourselves? That is why the male monkey took its share on the way itself. That was a male and could do it with impunity. This is a female. What can she do?" So saying, Ramaṇa called to her cajolingly. She came to the side of his couch and stood there. In an endearing manner, Ramaṇa gave her all the fruits she wanted and then sent her away.[2]

11. Once a female monkey tried to bring her new-born baby through a window near Ramaṇa's couch. The attendants were preventing her. Ramaṇa chided them as follows: "Don't all of you bring your newborn babies to me? She also wants to do so. Why should you prevent her?"[3]

It is said that in the presence of a Sage, there is no fear. The very word *'āśrama'* literally means 'a place of non-wandering', a place where the lion and lamb lie down together. In 1946, two baby cheetahs were brought to the *āśrama*. The wonder is that while they were there, squirrels, birds, monkeys, peacocks, snakes, and other creatures came and went, moving about

---

[1] Nagamma, *Letters from Ramanasramam*, 24th October, 1947.

[2] Ibid, 26-8-48.

[3] M. N. Swami, "The Call Divine," *Bombay*, 52.

together without any fear or animosity. There are stories told in the *Purānas* of such things happening in the *āśramas* of the ancient *ṛṣis.* What a wonder to behold such before one's very eyes in Ramaṇa's *āśrama.*

12. Once, a snake slithered over Ramaṇa's body. He remarked that snakes seem to know when they need not be afraid. "It did not strike me either that I should be afraid or do anything to it." Another time, noticing that a snake was near the hall, people were shouting, 'beat it, beat it'. Ramaṇa protested but the snake was killed. Then Ramaṇa remarked: "If these people are beaten like that, then they will know what it means." Regarding snakes that infested the *āśrama*, Ramaṇa said: "We have come to their abode (Aruṇācala Hill) as guests and so we have no right to molest them. Let us leave them in peace."

Ramaṇa treated dogs with the same loving care and respect that he gave to human beings. He was so considerate, looking after their food and cleanliness, talking to them and giving them advice. He always saw to it that they were fed before he was. Whether it was coffee, sweets, or food, these 'children' of his would always be served first. When they died, like any of the animal inmates of the *āśrama*, they were always given a decent burial, either near the *āśrama* or in special cases, inside the *āśrama* itself.

13. In his 'Reminiscences' about Ramaṇa, Kunju Swami recalls his first meeting with Ramaṇa at Skandāśrama. Though they were alone, there was no conversation. He observed that Ramaṇa took some flour from a small tin and put it in a vessel and poured water from his *kamaṇḍalu* and stirred it and placed the vessel on the charcoal stove. Kunju Swami thought to himself that Ramaṇa was making some elixir and looked forward to it in silence. It was actually some gruel. Ramaṇa poured a little of it on a plate, got up and lifted a bucket. Four pups with joy came out to the plate to drink the gruel. Ramaṇa tried to restrain them as he thought the gruel might be too hot for them. Ramaṇa, who had not spoken until then, said: "Catch the four". I caught hold of the four pups. After the gruel had

cooled, Ramaṇa said: "Release them one by one." I released them one by one. The pups, with their stomachs full, tottered along. One of them passed urine. Ramaṇa got up, washed the spot with water, and wiped it with an old gunny sack.[1]

14. Among the *āśrama* animals, Jackie the dog, Valli the deer, and Lakshmi the cow have a special honored place. They are all buried inside the *āśrama* beside each other. Jackie never mixed with other dogs nor did he play much. He would sit in front of Ramaṇa on an orange cloth and stare intently at Ramaṇa's eyes. Jackie always behaved in an exemplary fashion. Whenever food was distributed, Jackie would not eat until Ramaṇa began to eat his own portion. On such occasions, he would watch Ramaṇa's face intently As soon as Ramaṇa put a morsel into his own mouth, Jackie would start to eat his own portion. Jackie was very ill during his final days and emitted a foul odor. Ramaṇa looked after him tenderly, providing him with a soft bed and attending to his needs. As he grew weaker, Ramaṇa would hold him in his arms and gently caress him with great love. His life force left his body even as Ramaṇa was holding him.

When Valli the deer lay dying, Ramaṇa sat next to her and put one hand on her head and one hand on her heart-center. Ramaṇa occasionally did this to devotees who were dying. His aim was to make the mind go back into the heart and die there. When this technique was successfully applied, the devotee attained Self-realization. He successfully applied this technique to both his mother and Lakshmi the cow. While Valli lay dying, Ramaṇa kept his hands in this position for about an hour. Once, during this period, Valli urinated on him but he paid no attention to it. After dying, Ramaṇa himself, along with Annamalai Swami built her *Samādhi*. Ramaṇa then asked Annamalai Swami to install a *liṅgam* in the *Samādhi* shrine and offer worship to it.

The cow, Lakshmi, has a special place in the history of Ramaṇa. In Indian thought it is usually stated that liberation is attainable almost exclusively by human beings since they possess a discriminative mind. Throughout history there have

[1] Kunju Swami, *Reminiscences*, 16-17.

been few instances where an animal is said to have achieved liberation. The divine power of Ramaṇa's grace, flowing through his hands, was responsible for the liberation of his mother, the cow Lakshmi, the deer Valli, and the dog Jackie.

Ramaṇa often praised Lakshmi as acting as intelligently as a human being. She used to come to the *āśrama* regularly at meal time and accompany Ramaṇa to the dining hall. She was so punctual that if Ramaṇa was engaged in anything else and had forgotten the time, he would turn and look at the clock when Lakshmi came in. He would know that it was mealtime. When Lakshmi fell ill and was dying, Ramaṇa sat by her side and when the end was near, he put one hand over her head and the other over her heart, just as he had done for his mother, and the deer Valli. Later, when devotees asked Ramaṇa whether he had used the term (liberation) euphemistically, Ramaṇa said that he literally meant that Lakshmi had in fact been liberated.

It is said that though Ramaṇa was compassion incarnate, he generally tried his best not to show any outward signs of it. However, the two notable exceptions to this were his relation to his mother and his relation to Lakshmi. A few minutes after Lakshmi's liberation, Ramaṇa came to her side, bent down and took her face in both his hands as though she were a little child and said: Oh Lakshmi, Lakshmi!" Then, controlling his tears, he said, "Because of her our family has grown to this extent."[1]

For a number of years after the young Ramaṇa took up reside in the Arunācaleśvara Temple, he displayed incredible virtues which included: fortitude, forgiveness, compassion, peacefulness, patience, self-control, steadfastness, fearlessness, tranquility, renunciation, modesty, austerity, non-violence, lack of pride, and freedom from fault-finding. It was not as if he was trying to practice to virtues, they just manifested themselves spontaneously and in full and complete manner. In the following few incidents one can see actual living instantiations of all these virtues.

---

[1] Venkataramiah, *Talks with Sri Ramana Maharshi*, 328-29. There is an Indian belief that having a cow reside in a house or *āśrama* brings great prosperity to that place.

15. Whether Ramaṇa was residing in the thousand-pillared hall in the front part of the temple, the Paṭalaliṅgam (an underground vault under the thousand-pillared hall), the adjoining flower-garden, the Subramaṇya shrine, the Vāhana Manṭapam (the place reserved for keeping the temple vehicles) or in Gurumūrtam, young urchins used to try to disturb Ramaṇa by pelting him with stones. Without a word he would simply move to another location. Large sores developed on either side of his legs, thighs and back, with blood and pus flowing from some of them. He never said a word. Once a mischievous young boy eased himself on Ramaṇa. Ramaṇa did not get angry or attempt to retaliate or scold the boy. Ramaṇa said about this period:

> When anyone thought I should have food, I would stretch my hand and something would drop on my hand. My hands were not useful for any other purpose. I would eat and rub my hand on my head or body and drop again into my continuous mood. This was my condition for some years from the time of my arrival. For many years I ate only off my hand without using any leaf plate.
>
> I am ever the same. There is neither willing, desire, nor change in me. There was nothing I wanted to obtain. I am now sitting with my eyes open. Then I sat with my eyes closed. That is all the difference. I was not practicing spiritual disciplines even then. As I sat with my eyes closed, people thought I was in *samādhi*. As I was not talking, people thought I was observing a vow of silence. The fact is I did nothing. Some Higher Power took hold of me and I was entirely in Its hands.

16. Ramaṇa often narrated a fascinating incident that reveals an incredible fairness, compassion, fortitude, and self-control.

> In those days I used to go all by myself. For answering calls of nature I used to stroll along taking no water with me, but going wherever water may be available. It was on one such occasion, on one morning, that I came across the banyan tree of which I have spoken often. As I was walking on the bed of a hill stream, I saw a big

banyan tree on a boulder, with big leaves. And crossing the stream, I wanted to get to the other bund and view from there this big tree. When I accidentally put my left foot near a bush on the way to the other bank, the hornets clustered round my left leg up to the knew and started stinging it. They never did anything to my right leg. I left the leg there for sometime, so that the hornets could inflict full punishment on the leg which had encroached on their domain. After a time, the hornet withdrew and I walked on. The leg got swollen very much and I walked with difficulty and reached Seven Springs about 2 a.m.[1]

About this incident Ramaṇa composed a verse known as an 'Apology to Hornets.' "When I was stung by hornets in revenge upon the leg until it was inflamed, although it was by chance I stepped upon their nest, constructed in a leafy bush, what kind of mind is his if he does not at least repent for doing such a wrong."[2]

This incident teaches us a great truth about Ramaṇa as a Sage. A Sage is never an agent. Agency is only ascribed to a Sage out of ignorance. Ramaṇa said in this regards:

> If the Self were ever himself the doer the He himself would reap the fruits of actions. But since the sense of doership is lost in the experience of the infinite Self, with it will be lost the three kinds of actions . . . what is said in the books, namely that actions of the future and those of the past, belonging to the Sage, are certainly lost, but that the current karma is not lost, is only intended for the ignorant. Just as one wife out of many cannot remain a non-widow *(sumangalī)* on the death of her husband, so all the three divisions of karma are lost when the doer, the ego, is lost.[3]

---

[1] Mudaliar, *Day by Day with Bhagavan,* 115.

[2] 'Occasional Verses' in the *Collected Works,* 94.

[3] *Forty Verses on Reality,* verses 33, 38.

What does this mean for the hornet incident? A devotee, long after the incident happened, asked Ramaṇa the following question about it. "Since the disturbance of the wasp-hive was accidental, why should it be regretted and atoned for, as if it had been done intentionally?" Ramaṇa replied: "If in fact the regretting and atoning is not *his* act, what must be the true nature of his mind?" The devotee had believed Ramaṇa to be a Sage, but the full truth of what a Sage is, was not fully understood by him. He had *assumed* that the act was performed by Ramaṇa. But Ramaṇa, in his reply, graciously pointed out that his assumption was wrong and indicated that the so-called mind of a Sage is not really mind, but pure Consciousness. Ramaṇa was not obliged to do certain acts or not to do other acts. Whatever a Sage appears to be doing is done spontaneously and automatically, without forethought. A Sage has no regrets. Ramaṇa said: "Can the Sage that dwells in the state of unity with the Truth, which arises by consuming the ego, and is calm, blissful, and beyond relativity and is therefore wantless, be bound to do anything whatever in the world? Since he is unaware of anything other than the Self, how can his state, which is mindless, be conceived by the mind?"[1]

No account of the place of ethics in Ramaṇa's life would be complete without citing instances of the role that issues pertaining to caste and women played. In this context, one should remember that Ramaṇa was born into an orthodox *brahmin* family of South India in the late 1800's. This was a time and a place where ideas of equality were seldom, if ever, seen or practiced.

In South India at this time, and to a certain lesser extent even today, orthodox caste distinctions regulated with whom one was willing to eat a meal with. Ramaṇa had two views on this issue. Here we will see how, on the one hand, he upheld tradition from the worldly point of view and, on the other, how he himself, from his perspective made no such distinction.

A description of the dining hall in the *āśrama* will set the scene. "A partition in the middle of the dining hall stretches

---

[1] Ibid, verse 31.

three-quarters of the width of the hall. At one side of it sit those *brahmins* who prefer to retain their orthodoxy, on the other side non-*brahmins*, non-Hindus, and those *brahmins* who prefer to eat with the other devotees. Provision is thus made for the orthodox, but Sri Bhagavān says nothing to induce *brahmins* either to retain or discard their orthodoxy."[1]

There were many complaints about this seating arrangement and often Ramaṇa himself was criticized for allowing it to continue. After all, wasn't Ramaṇa beyond all dualities including caste divisions? And even more perplexing, Ramaṇa would eat his meal with both sides! Thus, the question was often asked: 'Why does he allow it?' Not only did he allow it, he insisted upon this arrangement.

When *brahmins* would come to *āśrama* and boldly say to Ramaṇa that in Ramaṇa's presence all were equal and sit down on the non-*brāhmaṇa* side of the screen, Ramaṇa would object. He would ask them: "Do you eat with non-*brahmins* in your own home?" When they would reply: "No, but with Bhagavān it is different", he would respond: "So you want to use Bhagavān as an excuse for breaking your caste rules? If you do not observe caste outside, there is no objection to your doing the same here. But you are not going to use us as an excuse for doing something which you consider at home to be wrong."[2] In the dining hall, "only the orthodox *brahmins*, who could not inter-dine at home would not be permitted to do so in the *āśrama* and had to eat in their enclosure. The idea was that if they obeyed caste rules at home, the *āśrama* was not the place to break them."[3]

To reveal how the system worked and Ramaṇa's thoughts on the matter, let us note an incident that happened once. A *brahmin* came to the *āśrama* and sat down to eat with the non-*brahmins*. The *āśrama* manager objected saying that it was against *āśrama* rules for a *brahmin* to take food with non-*brahmins*. The man argued saying that it was his practice for many years to take food with all classes of people and as a result

---

[1] Osborne, *The Teachings of Bhagavan Sri Ramana Maharshi in His Own Words*, 132

[2] Sadhu Arunachala, *A Sadhu's Reminiscences of Ramana Maharshi*, 30.

[3] Sundaram, 'Bhagavan's Cooking', in *Ramana Smrti Souvenir*, 7.

of this, he no longer considered himself a *brahmin.* He flatly refused to eat with the *brahmins.* The dispute continued until Ramaṇa entered the hall. Upon being told what the dispute was all about, Ramaṇa chided both of them. To the *āśrama* manager Ramaṇa said: 'Why do you force him to sit with the *brahmins?'* To the other man, Ramaṇa said: 'You too are wrong. Those people think that they are non-*brahmins;* you do not. Why should you force yourself upon them? I am the only one here who does not think of himself either as a *brahmin* or a non-*brahmin.* So come and sit by my side.' The man felt too shy to sit beside Ramaṇa and joined the *brahmins.*[1]

17. A couple of incidents related by Lokammal provide striking evidence of Ramaṇa's position *vis-a-vis* untouchables, ladies with menses, lying, and the equality of all human beings.

> One day I was asked to cook some *dhal* (split pulses) and some curry for the next day. I came very early so as to have more time, but Bhagavān was quicker than me. He told me the dhal was ready and that I had only to prepare the curry. Tenammal was there, grinding lentils in a stone mortar. Bhagavān asked her what she was doing and Tenammal replied that one of the lady visitors was having her menses and special food was being cooked for her. 'Why should she eat food cooked separated?' asked Bhagavān. 'Why can't she be given some of the food which is served to everyone else? What does it matter that she is unwell. Is it a sin? Make no difference and serve her from the food you have prepared for all. Let her have rice, dhal, and curry from the common kitchen.' After serving the evening meal Bhagavān asked me whether that lady had been given the common food. I assured him that she had.
>
> A young couple had just arrived and Bhagavan asked me if I had served them properly. The *āśrama* manager came near and told me in whispers that in case I was asked what food was served to ladies during their

[1] "The Bhagavan I Knew', in *Ramana Smrti Souvenir,* 16.

period, I should say that they were given separate food prepared elsewhere. Bhagavān overheard it and scolded the manager. 'Why do you ask her to tell lies? The *āśrama* gives food to all and makes no differences. There are no untouchables here. Those who do not like it may eat elsewhere. At Skandāśrama there used to be the same trouble with Mother. Here we have menses and there she had pariahs. She would not give food to the man who brought us the firewood because she was afraid of pollution! She insisted that I must eat first, then she would eat and then the woodcutter could have the remnants left on the ground outside the *āśrama*. I refused to eat until the man had been decently fed. At first she would not yield and would suffer and weep and fast, but I was adamant too, and she came to see that she could not have her way in such matters.

'What is the difference between man and man? Am I a Brahmin and is he a *pariah?* Is it not correct to see only God in all?'

We were all astounded. The rebuke, addressed to the manager, went deep into our hearts. We asked Bhagavān to make our minds clear and our hearts pure so that we would sin no more against God in man.[1]

The South Indian *Brahmana* tradition is very rigid and uncompromising in regards to the rule that women may even enter inside an *āśrama* during their period let alone eat food there. This rule pertained even to a person's house. To break this rule would mean that the entire *aśrama* was polluted and if that were to occur, there would be an outcry not only from the community but also the entire public. On a number of occasions, Ramaṇa broke this ancient rule in order to teach everyone that in spirituality, the human being comes first and that compassion is the supreme law.

Again, regarding untouchability, there is a report of "a man coming to the gate with his family, stopping there and calling out to me. When I went to him he requested me to find out from

---

[1]Lokammal, 'Sri Ramanasramam', in *Ramana Smrti Souvenir*, 2-3.

the swami whether they could approach him to pay their respects. I was surprised and asked: 'Why do you ask permission?' He replied: 'We are untouchables.' I told the man that caste had no meaning for Bhagavān and that they were welcome. The whole party came and prostrated themselves before Bhagavān, and I well remember how for about ten minutes his gracious look dwelt on that untouchable and his family. How many rich and notable people have I seen fall at his feet without being vouchsafed such grace."[1]

Rarely, not more than a few times, did Ramaṇa give initiation *(upadeśa)* in the form of a *mantra* to someone. One such known case was for an untouchable who used to circumambulate the *āśrama* without entering it. One day he saw Ramaṇa at the entrance gate, prostrated before him and humbly asked for an *upadeśa*. With great compassion, Ramaṇa said to him: "Go on saying, Śiva, Śiva, that will save you."[2]

Orthodox Hindu Brāhmana tradition declares that only Brahmins are allowed to chant and listen to the Vedic hymns. In the *āśrama*, only Brahmins were allowed to chant the Vedas but Ramaṇa allowed everyone, irrespective, to listen to the chanting. Ramaṇa said: "The sound of the chanting helps to still the mind." Again, going against orthodox tradition, Ramaṇa allowed food to be cooked and served by both *brahmins* and non-*brahmins* alike, including Moslems and Christians. In the *āśrama* no one was allowed to put garlands on him, though he did allow people to prostrate before him. In this latter regard which some might think as egotistical on his part, Ramaṇa remarked that it is beneficial to one's spiritual practice to humble the ego and place one's head on the ground. Of course many individuals prostrate merely out of custom and to this Ramaṇa remarked: "Men prostrate themselves before me but I know who has submitted in his heart."[3] As well, even if a devotee prostrates before the *guru*, the *guru* him or herself should have a feeling of equality towards all. On his part, Ramaṇa was reluctant to call anyone his disciple because, in

---

[1] Swaminathan, *Ramana Maharshi*, 40-41.

[2] Ibid, 49.

[3] Venkataramiah, *Talks with Sri Ramana Maharshi*, 126.

Ramaṇa's eyes, there were no *gurus*, no disciples, no enlightened beings and no unenlightened beings.

Though a Sage is not really a 'doer', still the sage is not inactive. It is just that the Sage doesn't will the actions that seem to be performed. The *Upaniṣads* say: 'the Sage is a non-doer and a great doer at the same time'. There is no contradiction here because, in Truth the Sage is a non-doer, but appears to be active to those who see the Sage seeming to act. The Sage cannot really be a doer, really be active because, if he were, he would be aware of individuals different from the Self and Ramaṇa has clearly said that this is not the case. Actions are willed out of desire while the Sage is forever desireless.

In this regards Ramaṇa once said: "The egoless state is not one of indolence, but of intense activity." There is another saying, 'The Self is the sleep of Bliss.' The *Gītā* describes the Self as waking-sleep. The sleep-aspect concerns the world of illusion. To that, the Sage is asleep. Ramaṇa said about this: "Just as, to one that is asleep in a carriage, its three states, namely its movement, its standing still, and its being left with the horses unyoked, are all alike, so to the Sage that is in the sleep of Self-awareness in the carriage, the body, the three states of it, namely bodily activity, sleep, and *samādhi*, are alike."[1] Here, the body is compared to the carriage and the sense-organs to the horses. Thus, waking activities are like the movements of the carriage. The states of sleep and *samādhi* are both states of rest. But while *samādhi* is compared to the standing still of the carriage with the horses still yoked (in *samādhi* the sense organs are not detached), in deep sleep the senses are detached. Thus, outwardly there appear to be differences but inwardly there are none. The comparison to a sleeper in a carriage was presented in order to illustrate that the changes of bodily condition, and hence of the world as a whole, do not affect the Sage. Remember, the Sage is not unconscious, as in sleep, but pure Consciousness. The *Gītā* says: "The Sage is awake in the Self which is (as good as) night to all creatures; all that to which creatures are awake is night to the Sage." The Sage, abiding in the Self, is awake to what is Real, while the world is night to him and because it is not real, it is not seen by him at all (as

[1] *Forty Verses on Reality*, verse 31.

distinct independent objects). Thus, the cryptic saying of the Sage 'that the State of the Sage is one of intense activity' should be clear. The Sage is awake in and as the Self, as Consciousness. Consciousness can never become unconscious. Thus, the Sage never 'sleeps'. This never-sleeping, ever-awake in Consciousness is the Sage's 'activity' and it never ceases and it is all the 'activity' there ever really is.

In Ramaṇa one finds a total lack of greed, vanity or self-importance. He was an embodiment of equality, treating everyone and everything, including animals, insects, and objects alike; all with the utmost meticulous care and concern. He ate the same food as everyone, refusing to ever eat something made *only* for him, or eating a larger portion than everyone else received; he wore only a simple loin-cloth *(kaupinam);* he made no distinction between individuals in regards to their wealth or position in society; he was never narrow minded, selfish, judgmental, or harsh. He always spoke softly with a twinkle in his eye and a smile on his lips. One never found him anxious or disturbed, upset or angry. In the *āśrama* he took an active interest in cooking, cutting vegetables, and preparing dishes with the utmost ingenuity and skill.

Q: Does one who has realized the Self lose the sense of 'I'?

B: Absolutely.

Q: Then there is no difference between myself and yourself, that man over there, my servant; are all the same?

B: All are the same, including those monkeys.

Q: But the monkeys are not people; are they not different?

B: They are exactly the same as people. All are the same in One Consciousness.

VI
Ramana, Spiritual Practices and Liberation

Just as rivers flowing to the ocean merge in it, losing their name and form, so the wise individual, freed from name and form, manifests the Divine. Do you identify with the drop of water or the water of the drop?

Self-Inquiry

To put into question the one who is asking the questions is to put into motion an enquiry that may end in the veritable destruction of the questioner. The consequences of this may not be, need not be, what they seem. The consequences need not entail the destruction of whom one really is, but merely the destruction of whom one thinks one is. The riddle of who I really am involves the enigma of existence.

If my name is something that belongs to me, but is not an essential part of who I am, then am I my physical body? Obviously, the same logic holds good here too. The physical body is also something that belongs to me. We all say, "this is my body, this is my hair, these are my hands." But I am not my body, my hair, nor my hands, nor my gender, nor even the sum total of all these physical parts. Even a little reflection reveals that I could change my hair color or the shape of my nose (or my gender and so on) and I would still remain me. A change of the mere surface appearance does not fundamentally, essentially, alter who I really am.

Then am I my thoughts? Thoughts come and go. Thoughts belong to me. The thoughts I had as a child are no longer my thoughts. Does this mean that I am not who I am? Obviously not. Even as the body continually undergoes change, one's thoughts are continually changing. They come and go. They belong to me, but the one that they belong to does not change. Even a little reflection reveals that there must be an unchanging substratum to support, to maintain that which is ever-changing. One's faculty of memory reveals that there must be something permanent which strings together the ever-changing

Somewhere, behind the walls of one's ignorance, concealed within the labyrinths of one's mind, beyond the known and the unknown, lies the Self, waiting to be found. Nobody can build the bridge over which you must cross the ocean of life, nobody but you alone. Each path is unique. Standing at the crossroads, how to know which path is truly yours?

Transformation is at the heart of the quest for the Self. Transformations take different forms. "Thinking like the prey" is an ancient game. One cannot hunt that which one does not know. Things in the physical world change physically. Thoughts in the mental world change mentally. Feet-fleeing, thought-flickering, where is the bedrock upon which I may make my stand? When life proves bitter, know that there were too many sidelong glances at the gutter where drunken desire beckoned, forgetful that glances are waiting rooms to nowhere.

Thus, we come to Ramaṇa's path of Self-enquiry, to asking the question, "Who am I?" Ramaṇa replied, when asked which is the best method of spiritual practice *(sādhana)*, "That depends on the temperament of the individual. Every person is born with latent tendencies *(saṁskāra)* from his past lives. One method will prove easy to one person and another to another. There can be no general rule."[1] There are many methods. You may practice Self-enquiry asking yourself, "Who am I?" or if that does not appeal to you, you may meditate on "I am *Brahman*", or some other theme; or you may concentrate on an incarnation or invocation. The object in every case is to make the mind one-pointed, to concentrate it on one thought and thereby exclude

[1] Venkataramiah, *Talks with Sri Ramana Maharshi*, 580.

the many other thoughts. If we do this, the one thought also eventually goes and the mind is extinguished at its source."[1]

While Ramaṇa authorized many different methods for spiritual practice, the one he said was most effective and the one he, himself, advocated was Self-enquiry. "For the subsistence of the mind there is no other means more effective than Self-enquiry. Even though the mind subsides by other means, that is only apparently so, it will rise again."[2] This practice was the cornerstone of his practical teachings and his restoration of this ancient technique was perhaps his greatest contribution to Indian philosophy. "Self-enquiry is the direct method. All other methods are practiced while retaining the ego and therefore many doubts arise and the ultimate question still remains to be tackled in the end. But in this method the final question is the only one and is raised from the very beginning."[3]

Why should Self-enquiry alone be considered the direct path to Self-realization? Ramaṇa replied:

> Every kind of path except Self-enquiry presupposes the retention of the mind as the instrument for following it and cannot be followed without the mind. The ego may take different and more subtle forms at different stages of one's practice, but it is never destroyed. The attempt to destroy the ego or the mind by methods other than Self-enquiry is like a thief turning policeman to catch the thief that is himself. Self-enquiry alone can reveal the truth that neither the ego nor the mind really exists and enable one to realize the pure, undifferentiated Being of the Self or the Absolute.[4]

The aim of Self-enquiry is to discover, by direct experience, that the mind is really non-existent. That is, the very existence of the mind is called into question. For most individuals, the existence of the mind, which is but a bundle of thoughts, is

---

[1] Mudaliar, *Day by Day with Bhagavan,* II, 30.

[2] *Who am I?* p. 42

[3] Venkataramiah, *Talks with Sri Ramana Maharshi,* 146.

[4] Venkataraman, *Maharshi's Gospel,* 48.

taken for granted as a real entity. To further complicate the problem, every conscious activity of the mind (and body) revolves around the tacit assumption that there is an "I" who is doing something. It is this "I" who makes the assumption that it is responsible for all its activities. The individual's "I" naturally though mistakenly, assumes "I" am thinking my thoughts; "I" am performing various actions. In each and every activity Ramaṇa called this common factor the "I"-thought or *aham-vṛtti*, a mental modification of the "I".

Everyone in the entire world says "I", but who is making an effort to know what that "I" exactly is? One usually means by "I" this "body." On a deeper level, individuals mean their faculties of thinking/feeling/willing. One can easily understand that the body is not "I", since it is insentient and inert. The *Upaniṣad* describes it: "The body is built up with bones, smeared over with flesh, covered with skin, filled with faeces, urine, bile, phlegm, marrow, fat."[1] By this analysis one can understand that the body is always what is known and not the knower. A similar analysis applies to one's thoughts. If the body were you, why do you say, "My body?" If the thoughts are you, why do you say, "My thoughts?" Does anyone ever say, "I am my shirt, I am my gold ring?" "My" is a personal possessive pronoun. These things belong to "me", the owner, the perceiver, the experiencer. So who is this "I" who possesses all these various things? One mistakes this superimposition of one's body and mind for a fact and thereby thinks that their body and thoughts are what one refers to as "I." Further, not only does the mind perpetuate this delusion by superimposing the body and thoughts upon the Self, one's mind deceives the individual into becoming attached to sense-objects thereby forgetting their real nature. The Self is never deluded, just as a person awake is not deluded by the dreams of the dreamer. The Self (the real "I") never imagines that it is doing anything. The "I" that imagines it is a doer, a thinker, a perceiver, is a mental fiction, a mental modification superimposed upon the Self.

Then, what is this "I"? In the body arises a sense of awareness. As a collection this is usually called the mind. What is the mind but a collection of thoughts. And this collection is

---

[1] MU 3.4.

where the "I" functions as their basis. Every thought relates to you, the "I", either directly about you or connected with you as individuals, objects, things, events, opinions. In other words, every thought is rooted in your "I". So what is this "I"—where is it rooted? Track it to its source. This process Ramaṇa called *ātma vicāra* or an enquiry into the Self.

One should realize that no amount of thought will enable one to realize that which is beyond thought. Thus, abide in the Self as it is. What is it that prevents us from doing this? The Self ever shines, ever present. Instead of abiding in the Self, the ego, the "I"-thought arises; the thought that I am a separate individual who believes that I am the body. This ego is the first or root thought, what Ramaṇa calls the "I"-thought. Every other thought, all second and third person pronouns (he, she, it, them) need this "I"-thought to exist, for it is the foundation upon which they rest. To remain as the Self all one need do is to remove this initial obstruction, the first thought, the ego, the I-am-the-body thought, or what Advaita calls "me and mine" *(ahaṁkāra* and *mamakāra).*

Between the ever-luminous Self (which neither rises nor sets) and the non-real, not-Self, the insentient body (which cannot of its own accord say, "I"), arises a false "I" which is limited to the body, the ego, and this meeting place is known as *cit-acit-granthi*—the knot between the sentient Self and the insentient body. When the knot forms, ideas of bondage, desire, the entire world of multiplicity arise. When this knot is cut, liberation happens. Ramaṇa said: "The heart knot is snapped; doubts are set at rest."[1] The *Upaniṣads* say, "The knot of the heart is cut";[2] "When all the knots that fetter here the heart are cut asunder then a mortal becomes immortal";[3] "There is release from all the knots of the heart."[4]

How does this false "I" arise? It grasps a form/a body. By grasping, it feeds upon forms and endures. Leaving one form, it

---

[1] Venkataramiah, *Talks with Sri Ramana Maharshi,* 280.

[2] MuU 2.2.9.

[3] KU 2.3.15.

[4] CU 7.26.2.

grasps another, devouring, growing, enduring. So long as one does not enquire into whom this false "I" is, it will continue to live and thrive. There is a story for this. Once, a man attended a wedding and posed as a friend of both the bride and groom. To the groom's side, he said he was a friend of the bride. To the bride's side, he said he was a friend of the groom. So long as everyone believed he was an invited guest, he got on very happily bossing over both parties and feasting sumptuously. But as soon as an enquiry was started about him, as soon as people began to find out who he was, that he was neither a friend of the bride or groom, he took to flight and disappeared. Such is case with the ego; it poses as both the Self (consciousness) and the body (inert). The ego appears to possess consciousness and shine with the "I"-thought (which really is the Self) and, at same time, the ego is limited to a form and it rises and sets. How clever! Like a ghost in a closet, it survives only until one, not being afraid of it any longer, enquires, opens the closet door, and finds that the ghost has vanished.

Ramaṇa maintained that this tendency towards self-limiting identifications with names and forms, with thoughts can be stopped by enquiring into this "I"-thought, by trying to separate the subject "I" from the objects of thought with which it identifies. Since the individual "I"-thought cannot exist without an object, if attention is focused on the subjective feeling of "I" or "I am" so and so, such and such, with such an intensity that the thoughts "I am this" or "I am that" do not arise, then the individual "I" will be unable to associate with and identify with objects. It will be found that if this enquiry into the "I" is sustained, the individual "I"-thought will spontaneously disappear and spontaneously, instantly, direct experience of the Self will arise. This constant attention to the inner awareness of "I" Ramaṇa called Self-enquiry. Ramaṇa said:

> By steady and continuous investigation into the nature of the mind, the mind is transformed into That to which "I" refers; and this is in fact the Self. The mind has necessarily to depend for its existence on something gross; it never subsists by itself. It is the mind that is otherwise called the subtle body, ego, *jīva,* or soul.

> That which arises in the physical body as "I" is the mind. If one enquires whence the "I" thought in the body arises in the first instance, it will be found that it is from the Heart. That is the source and stay of the mind. Or again, even if one merely continuously repeats to oneself inwardly "I-I" with the entire mind fixed thereon, that also leads to the same source.
>
> The first and foremost of all thoughts that arise in the mind is the primal "I"-thought. It is only after the rise or origin of the "I"-thought that innumerable other thoughts arise. In other words, only after the first personal pronoun, "I", has arisen do the second and third personal pronouns (you, he, etc) occur to the mind; and they cannot subsist without it
>
> Since every other thought can occur only after the rise of the "I"-thought, and since the mind is nothing but a bundle of thoughts, it is only through the enquiry: "Who am I?" that the mind subsides. Moreover, the integral "I"-thought implication in such enquiry, having destroyed all other thoughts, itself finally gets destroyed or consumed, just as a stick used for stirring the burning funeral pyre gets consumed.[1]

Why does ego, the "I"-thought, disappear when enquired into? It exists only when grasping forms. Without names and forms it cannot live. All thoughts, all objects, all knowledge are only name and form, whether gross or subtle. The "I"-thought has no form of itself. To attend to itself, that is, to investigate and enquire into its source makes it lose strength, subside, and finally disappear without a trace. There are not two "I"s, the ego and the Self. There is not duality during spiritual practices and non-duality during liberation. There is only the ocean of Consciousness, one and non-dual, the Self. It is in this ocean of Consciousness that all ideas/feelings/ thoughts/names and forms arise. Are they real? No. Do they appear? Yes.

---

[1] *Who Am I?* 42.

Moreover, thoughts arise because we think them, we accept them, we let them in. They do not impose upon us. They have no power of their own. They gain power only by our attending to them. Pay them no attention and they will subside. Whether they come or whether they go, what does it matter. To accept them, and then to struggle with them, is to give them life. You will never win. It should be noted that the mind functions only when the "I"-thought functions. Deep sleep reveals the truth of this. All thoughts function only when the "I"-thought is there. When the "I"-thought is not there, the world, the mind, and the body do not exist. Anyone can observe that the mind is quiet, that it disappears, when one is deep asleep and that it only reappears upon waking. This means that the "I"-thought daily rises and sets. Follow the "I"-thought back to its point of rising. See where it sets. This "I"-thought is the one necessary clue one has to discover who one really is.

Ramaṇa's method of Self-enquiry is often misunderstood. People think that it implies rejecting all thoughts as they come tumbling in. He remarked: "I do not say that you must keep on rejecting thoughts. You are not to occupy the mind with other thoughts such as "I am not the body". If you cling to yourself, to the "I"-thought, and your interest keeps you to that single thought, other thoughts will get rejected and will automatically vanish."[1] The question "Who am I?" is not an invitation to analyze the mind and to come to conclusions about its nature. Nor is Self-enquiry a *mantra* to be repeated again and again. It is simply a tool, a method, which Ramaṇa gave which will facilitate an individual in redirecting their attention away from the objects of thought and perception back to the thinker and perceiver of all thoughts and perceptions.

For a person to eliminate the body as not "I", the mind as not "I", and so on is a beginning and this method has often been mentioned in Advaita in order to guide a seeker to the Self. This is the time honored *"neti-neti"* (not-this, not this) technique. It is well known that the Self cannot be directly indicated. The Self is unknowable, not because it is unknown, but because it is the basis of all knowledge. It is knowledge (Consciousness) itself.

---

[1] Mudaliar, *Day by Day with Bhagavan,* II, 44.

"Words return along with the mind, not attaining it."[1] "The eye does not go there, nor speech, nor mind. The Absolute is not to be known as such and such."[2] Ramaṇa's technique uses the mind to eliminate the mind – for there is no other way as the Self is beyond thought. A person who eliminates all the "not-I" cannot eliminate the "I". In order to be able to say, "I am not this", there must be an "I" to say it. This "I" is only the ego. But if one uproots the ego, all else will automatically be uprooted. Therefore, Ramaṇa advocates seeking the root "I", find the source of the "I", question who this "I" really is.

Ramaṇa sometimes compared the process of Self-enquiry to a dog tracing its master by his scent. The master of the dog may be at some distant unknown place but that will neither prevent nor detour the dog from tracing him. The master's scent is the infallible clue for the dog and nothing else, be it the master's clothing, build, gender, profession, etc., are important or necessary. The dog undistracted holds onto that scent while searching for his master and finally succeeds in tracing him. Likewise, a seeker should undistracted continuously follow the "scent" of the "I"-thought to its source and thereby discover the Self.

When a practitioner begins the process of Self-enquiry, it starts as a mental activity. The mind commences its enquiry into the "I"-thought again and again, but is often distracted by other habitual thoughts that arise throughout the day. As the practice deepens and the seeker is able to hold onto its investigation into the source of the "I"-thought, there arises a subtle subjectively experienced feeling of "I" that persists. When this feeling ceases to connect and identify with thoughts and objects, even this feeling subsides. Then, what remains is direct experience of Being in which all sense of individuality temporarily ceases to operate. At first, this feeling will be intermittent, but with repeated effort it gradually becomes easier and easier to maintain. At this level, Self-enquiry has become as effortless awareness in which individual effort is no longer possible since the "I" who makes effort has temporarily ceased to exist. This is

---

[1] TU 2.4.1.

[2] KeU 1.3-5 Also KeU 3, "It is other than all that is known, and It is also beyond the knower."

not yet full and complete Self-realization since the "I"-thought periodically reasserts itself. When this experience is repeated as often as is necessary, it begins to weaken, and often destroy, the latent mental tendencies that were causing the "I"-thought to reappear. Finally, when the latent tendencies are sufficiently weakened, the power of the Self destroys them all and, being destroyed, they will never rise again. This is complete Self-realization.

One may observe how practical and easy Ramaṇa's technique of Self-enquiry is. There is no struggling with the mind. There is no suppression of thoughts. All it requires is for the seeker to keep an awareness of the source from which all thought springs. Abiding in the source of the "I"-thought is the method. Abiding in the source of the "I"-thought is the goal. Effort in the beginning is essential, but once awareness of the "I"-thought has been firmly established, further effort is counter-productive.

> A seeker remarked, "When I cling to the "I"-thought, other thoughts come and go. When this happens I say to myself, "Who am I?", and no answer is forthcoming. To be in this condition is the practice, is it not?" Ramaṇa replied, "This is a mistake that people often make. What happens when you make a serious quest for the Self is that the "I"-thought disappears and something else from the depths takes hold of you and that is not the "I" which commenced the quest. That is the real Self, the import of "I". It is not the ego. It is the supreme Being itself . . . I did not say that you must go on rejecting thoughts. Cling to yourself, that is, to the "I"-thought. When your interest keeps you to that single idea, others thoughts will automatically get rejected and they will vanish . . . It may be necessary for a time to reject other thoughts. You fancy that there is no end if one goes on rejecting every thought when it rises. This is not true. There is an end. If you are vigilant and make a stern effort to reject every thought when it rises you will soon find that you are going deeper and deeper into your own inner Self. At that level it is not necessary to make an effort to reject

> thoughts. Not only will it be possible to be without effort, without strain, it is impossible for you to make an effort beyond a certain point. At first it is impossible to be without effort. When you go deeper, it is impossible for you to make any effort. If the mind becomes introverted through enquiry into the source of *aham-vṛtti*, the latent tendencies become extinct. The light of the Self falls on the latent tendencies and produces the phenomenon of reflection we call the mind. Thus, when the latent tendencies become extinct the mind also disappears, being absorbed into the light of the one reality, the Heart[1]

A remarkable feature of the path of Self-enquiry is that it can be practiced any time and any where, while driving the car, while eating, while at work, while taking a bath, and so on. Traditionally, in Advaita Vedānta, the path of knowledge *(jñāna-mārga)* was considered to be the path for world-renouncers. Thus, Ramaṇa was often asked whether one should renounce the world if one were to practice Self-enquiry. As well, there was the additional fact that it appeared to others that Ramaṇa was a renunciant *(sannyāsin).* After all, others could observe that he wore only a loin cloth, was homeless and penniless, and for some time begged his food or at the least, ate only what was given to him. Per this last point one can't help but observe: "Who is the real renunciant? A person who has given up the immortal, eternally blissful Self for a handful of sense-objects or one who has renounced a few trinkets of pleasure for eternal Bliss?"

To address the latter element first, in Ramaṇa's own case one should note that he had his "great experience" while living in his uncle's house in Madurai. He was not a renunciant but a young school-boy. When the Maharshi was asked when he himself renounced the world and went forth to the homeless life, if he did not approve of that path for his followers, he merely said that such was his destiny. "This is my *prārabdha.* One's course of conduct in this life is determined by one's *prārabdha.* My *prārabdha* lies this way; yours lies that way."[2] Further, he,

---

[1] Venkataramiah, *Talks with Sri Ramana Maharshi,* 25.

[2] Ibid, 251.

himself said that he did not classify himself as a *sannyāsin* but as an *āryāśrami* or one who has either bypassed or transcended the "stages of life" classification altogether.[1]

In reply to the question whether one should renounce the world or not, Ramaṇa replied that the work was internal and had to be done in the mind, whatever one's conditions of life. Sometimes he would reply:

> Why do you think you are a householder? The similar thought that you are a *sannyāsin* will haunt you even if you go forth as one. Whether you continue in the household or renounce it and go to live in the forest, our mind haunts you. The ego is the source of thought. It creates the body and the world and makes you think of being a householder. If you renounce, it will only substitute the thought of renunciation for that of the family and the environment of the forest for that of the household. But the mental obstacles are always there for you. They even increase greatly in the new surroundings. Change of environment is no help. The one obstacle is the mind, and this must be overcome whether in the home or in the forest. If you can do it in the forest, why not in the home? So why change the environment? Our efforts can be made even now, whatever be the environment. It is the feeling "I work" that is the hindrance. Ask yourself, "Who works?" Remember who you are. Then the work will not bind you. It will go on automatically. Make no effort either to work, or to renounce; your effort is the bondage. What is destined to happen will happen. I you are destined to work, you will not be able to avoid it; you will be forced to engage in it. So leave it to the higher power. It is not really your choice whether you renounce or retain.[2]

On other occasions, Ramaṇa would reply:

---

[1] Swaminathan, *Ramana Maharshi*, 27.

[2] Venkataraman, *Maharshi's Gospel*, I, 6.

> There is no conflict between work and wisdom. One can continue all one's old activities in one's profession, for instance. But in that case one will not think that it is the old personality that is doing the work, because one's consciousness will gradually become transferred until it is centered in that which is beyond the little self. Setting apart time for meditation is only for the merest spiritual novices. A man who is advancing will begin to enjoy the deeper beatitude whether he is at work or not. While his hands are in society, he keeps his head cool in solitude.[1]

Finally there is the issue of Ramaṇa's path of Self-enquiry as compared with the traditional Advaita Vedānta view. We already touched on this briefly and while it should be pointed out that Ramaṇa and the Advaitins agree on many theoretical matters, they differ in regards to the practice of the spiritual path. In a nutshell, Advaita advocates: (1) the four-fold proximate aids to Self-realization; (2) the three-fold primary means to Self-realization; (3) meditation on the great sayings; (4) the not-this, not-this method; and (5) the prior superimposition and subsequent denial method. As well, there are some Advaitins who say that the path of devotion will also bring about Self-realization if practiced by their definition of what constitutes devotion.

The Advaita Vedānta system lays down an oft-quoted, well-known, four-fold requirement qualifying an aspirant to pursue the path of knowledge.[2] These qualifications are: (1) discrimination of the eternal from the non-eternal; (2) non-attachment to the enjoyment of the fruits of one's actions either in this world or in any other; (3) possession in abundance of the six virtues, *viz.*, calmness, equanimity, turning away from the sense-objects, forbearance, concentration, and faith; and (4) a longing or intense desire for liberation. According to the tradition, only that individual who possesses this four-fold requirement is qualified to study the Vedānta texts under the

---

[1] Ibid, 85.

[2] *Sādhana catuṣṭaya*

guidance of a teacher *(guru)* who is not only learned in Scripture but also well-established in Truth.

A guru is defined as a spiritual master who has attained oneness with the Divine and without whom a disciple cannot attain liberation. The direct path of knowledge *(jñāna)* itself consists of three steps: (1) hearing *(śravaṇa);* (2) reflection *(manana);* and (3) contemplation *(nididhyāsana).*[1] Success will depend chiefly upon the qualification of the seeker. Place, time, and other such circumstances are merely auxiliaries to success. It is said that when the Guru's initial instructions do not result in a permanent and complete manifestation of one's true nature, the *Guru* takes recourse in instructing the student to perform some prerequisite actions which will have the effect of purifying the intellect and removing the defects which hide one's inner Self. Thus, according to Advaita, *sādhana* or spiritual practices are not performed in order to gain the great inner Self, for one is already That, but to remove the impurities which cover it up and hide its presence from the seeker.

Ramaṇa is not actually opposed to these prerequisites for a spiritual aspirant and most likely would agree that without them, it is unlikely that a person would even begin a spiritual discipline, let alone be successful. "The very fact that you are possessed of the quest for the Self is a manifestation of divine grace . . . but such grace is vouchsafed only to him who is a *true* devotee or *yogi* . . . effort is necessary up to the state of realization". These disciplines help to purify the mind and without them being present in at least some degree, practicing a spiritual discipline would be like pouring water into a pot that has holes in the bottom. No matter how much water is poured into such a pot (be it Self-enquiry, meditation, etc.), the fruits of such practices will just run out the holes at the bottom of the pot. But, as we earlier observed, Ramaṇa did not emphasize prerequisites, but would advise seekers to directly enquire into the source of the "I"-thought.

In regards to Advaita's direct path, the situation is a bit more subtle and complicated. Advaita's three-fold scheme is usually described as: *śravaṇa* or hearing the Upanisadic text or

---

[1] BU 4.iv.22; VP 8, 211.

Sages' words of wisdom, which informs a seeker of the Self. "Hearing" removes any doubts that an aspirant may have in regards to the correct source of knowledge *(pramāṇa). Manana* or reflection is employed so that one becomes established in an intellectual conviction about the reality of the Self. It removes any doubts one may have in regards to the correct object of one's knowledge *(prameya),* i.e. "O.k., there is *Brahman* but what is this *Brahman,* with or without attributes?" Finally, *nididhyāsana* or contemplation is a continuous, unbroken stream of awareness of the Self. It removes any last lingering errors or the "opposite stream of thought" (one's latent tendencies). It makes the mind firm in its one-pointed fixity upon Brahman.

To quote the *Vivekacūḍāmaṇi:*

> Reflection is a hundred times superior to hearing; meditation is a hundred thousand times superior to reflection; impartite one-pointed absorption of the intellect in That is infinitely superior to all.
>
> By impartite one-pointed absorption of the intellect in That, the Truth that is the Absolute is clearly and definitely realized, but not otherwise, for then, the mind, being unsteady, will become mixed with other modifications.
>
> Therefore, remain in one-pointed absorption of the intellect in That, with the sense-organs controlled, with a tranquil mind ever turned within, and, through the realization of your identity with the Absolute, destroy the darkness of beginningless ignorance.[1]

Ramaṇa would agree that "hearing" *(śravaṇa)* the sacred word(s) is indispensable. Without hearing of the existence of the Self, no one would know of its existence, let alone seek it. As the Self is utterly beyond conceptualization, beyond the mind and the senses, unless a person is told about it, it would remain unknown and unknowable.

---

[1] V verses 365-367. The paradigm reference is the BU 2.4.5; 4.5.6, "Verily, Maitreyī, by the seeing of, by the hearing of, by the thinking of, by the understanding of the Self, all this is known".

Where the major difference lies in is that while the Advaita tradition posits that the Self can be discovered by the use of the mind, whether through affirmation or negation, Ramaṇa said, "The text is not meant for thinking "I" am *Brahman*". The mind, whether thinking thoughts such as "I" am *Brahman*" or "I" am not this body," requires the "I"-thought. Can the mind, by employing the "I"-thought, transcend itself? This is a debatable issue, but what we can be sure of is that Ramaṇa's path of Self-enquiry was emphatically different from Advaita's, if not in all details, most certainly in its emphasis and understanding.

We have already noted that Ramaṇa's path of Self-enquiry does not affirm the reality or real existence of the "I"-thought. On the other hand, in the Advaita practices this "I"-thought is affirmed and employed to focus, discriminate, concentrate, contemplate, meditate, chant, and so on in the quest for Self-realization. Though Advaita accepts all paths and the particulars in its path as tools or methodological devices in this quest for "obtaining the already obtained", it obviously differs from Ramaṇa's path in that it, even if provisionally, accepts the "I"-thought of the spiritual practitioner in his or her quest and it is with this "I"-thought that the goal will be reached. Ramaṇa's path was not one in which the correct answer to the question "Who am I?" was "I am *Brahman*" which should then be mentally repeated like a mantra. Ramaṇa said that if the mind is constantly engaged in asking the question and then repeating the answer, the mind would never sink into its source and disappear. This very practice, in fact, was keeping the mind alive and well, fully engaged. On this point Śaṅkara agreed for he said: "A disease is not cured by the mere repetition of the word "medicine". One must imbibe it. Similarly, without direct realization, liberation does not arise merely by uttering the word *"Brahman"*.[1]

Likewise, to repeat "Who am I?" as a *mantra*, again and again, will never serve to redirect the "I"-thought away from names and forms. The most such a practice can do is to purify the mind but it will not serve to cut the "I"-thought off at its source. Ramaṇa's rejection of the *neti-neti* approach was for the same reason. Such intellectual activity wherein the "I"-thought

---

[1] V 64.

is sustained by repetition of a *mantra* or repetition of "I am not the body", "I am not the mind", only sustains the "I"-thought and will never eliminate it. Some of Ramaṇa's words about this bear repeating:

> The one who eliminates all the "not-I" cannot eliminate the "I". To say "I am not this" or "I am that" there must be the "I". This "I" is only the ego or the "I"-thought. After the rising up of this "I"-thought, all other thoughts arise. The "I"-thought is therefore the root thought. If the root is pulled out all others are at the same time uprooted. Therefore seek the root "I", question yourself "Who am I?" Find out its source, and then all these other ideas will vanish and the pure Self will remain.[1]
>
> An enquirer said: "I meditate *neti-neti.*" Ramaṇa replied: "No—that is not meditation. Find the source. The false "I" will disappear and the real "I" will be realized. The former cannot exist apart from the latter."[2]
>
> To enquire "Who am I?" really means trying to find out the source of the ego or the "I"-thought. You are not to think of other thoughts such as "I am not this body". Seeking the source of "I" serves as a means of getting rid of all other thoughts.[3]
>
> "Who am I?" is not a *mantra.*[4]
>
> The text is not meant for thinking "I am *Brahman*". *Aham* ("I") is known to every one. Brahman abides as *aham* in every one. Find out the "I". The "I" is already *Brahman*. You need not think so. Simply find the "I".[5]

---

[1] Venkataramiah, *Talks with Sri Ramana Maharshi,* 62.

[2] Ibid, 217.

[3] Ibid, 235.

[4] Mudaliar, *Day by Day with Bhagavan,* 68.

[5] Ibid, 192-93.

One final aspect we may note concerns the neo-Advaita practice of concentrating on the Heart-center (sometimes even erroneously thought of as the heart *cakra*). There is a mistaken belief that Self-enquiry involves concentrating on the Heart-center as the location of the Self. How this mistaken belief came about is most likely due to a misinterpretation of Ramaṇa's comments on the Heart and its location.

Ramaṇa, in describing the origin of the "I"-thought, sometimes said that it rose to the brain through a channel that started from a center in the right-hand side of the chest. Upon Self-realization, there is an awareness that this center is the source of both the mind and world and when the "I"-thought subsides into the Self, it goes back into this center and disappears. He called this center, the Heart-center. However, Ramaṇa was also quick to add that the Heart is not really located in the body and that from the highest standpoint no "I"-thought really ever rises or subsides. In this regards Ramaṇa said: "You cannot know where the Heart-center is with your mind. You cannot realize it by imagination, when I tell you here is the center (pointing to the right side of the chest). The only direct way to realize it is to cease to fantasize and try to be yourself. When you realize, you automatically feel that the center is there. This is the center, the Heart, spoken of in the scriptures[1] as *hṛt-guha* (cave of the heart)."

> Long after I came here I chanced upon a verse in the Malayalam version of *Aṣṭāngahṛdayam* wherein the source of bodily vitality or place of light is mentioned as being located in the right side of the chest and called the seat of consciousness. But I know of no other work that refers to it as being located there.[2]
>
> It is perhaps more proper to say that the Self is the Heart itself than to say that it is in the Heart. Really the Self is the center itself. It is everywhere, aware of itself

[1] MU 6.38; BU 4.4.2; 5.3.1; CU 3.1.4.3; 8.1.1-3; 8.3.3; TU 1.6.1; 2.1.1; KU 1.2.12; 1.3.1; 2.1.7; 2.1.12-13; BSB 1.3.24-25. V 191, 219, 257, 267.

[2] Venkataramiah, *Talks with Sri Ramana Maharshi,* 378.

> as "Heart", the Self-awareness. Truly speaking, pure consciousness is indivisible; it is without parts. It has no form and shape, no "within" and "without". There is no "right" or "left" for it. Pure Consciousness, which is the Heart, includes all, and nothing is outside or apart from it. That is the ultimate truth. From this absolute standpoint, the Heart, Self, or Consciousness can have no particular place assigned to it in the physical body.[1]
>
> Heart is no conception, no object for meditation. I ask you to see where the "I" arises in your body, but it is really not quite correct to say that the "I" arises from and merges in the Heart in the right side of the chest. The Heart is another name for the reality and it is neither inside nor outside the body. There can be no in or out for it, since it alone is.[2]

The following personal experience of the author seems to confirm Ramaṇa's statements about the location of the Heart (as well as many of his other statements).

I had been chanting a hymn in praise of the *Guru* since 6 am and it was now around 7:30 am. The sun had just come over the horizon. I was sitting cross-legged on the floor. Suddenly, spontaneously, without any effort on my part, there was a sudden shift in my perception. I felt as though there was just a "slight shift" in my consciousness, really ever so slight and yet I went from feeling limited to limitlessness. It began with tears spontaneously flowing from my eyes, almost in a continuous stream rather like a faucet that had been left open, and an awareness of what seemed to be a thumb-sized cave just to the right of the center of my chest. I could observe this thumb-sized cave and noted that, in fact, it was the center of everything, it was everything and yet, how is it possible, it was simultaneously experienced to be "located" in the right side of my chest. This sounds not only contradictory but logically contradictory and yet, it was directly experienced.

---

[1] *Sat-Darshana Bhasya*, viii-ix.

[2] Venkataramiah, *Talks with Sri Ramana Maharshi*, 202.

I marveled that the word "vision" was perfect. "Seeing," sight was it exactly; sight as in knowing, wisdom. I could "see" everything clearly, clearer than normal vision. This was sight in the true sense of the word, vision of the universal all-pervading Self, everywhere the gaze turned. I looked at the walls—I looked at the sunlight—I looked at other individuals chanting—I looked at my hands—I looked (how I don't really know, but somehow I could look because I was everywhere!) around the entire universe and it was all the same, all One, all That. I was not looking as in a subject-looking-at-object way. I was everything, everywhere. And this included me, though not me as "ego-me" but "me-as-Self". There was not an iota of difference anywhere and yet, mysteriously I could make out distinctions "within" That, which in no way broke the Oneness of That. I found myself expanded in an indescribable manner. I was an all-encompassing consciousness. Not theory, not intellectual—I *was* That. There was an immediate and direct contact with an intensely conscious universe and I was that universe. I was unbounded consciousness. I was no longer John, but That, That immensity that was incredibly blissful; it was full, complete. I was immanent in every single part of it. The body, the ground I was sitting on, everything including the building, the sky, the entire universe appeared to be distinguishable appearances in this real, interpenetrating, and all pervasive ocean of consciousness, which, to explain the most incredible part of it, as best I can, seemed to be simultaneously unbounded, stretching out immeasurably in all directions, and yet no bigger than a tiny, thumb sized cave in the right side of my chest. From this tiny cave, the entire universe, of which my body and its surrounding were a part, poured out and yet, somehow, there was not an iota of separation anywhere. The thought appeared that this heart cave was described by some individuals as an ocean (of consciousness) and that this too was an accurate, perfect description. Still, I preferred(!) the image of the heart cave better. How strange! Both descriptions fit perfectly, and yet I resonated to this one. Thoughts rose up and yet there was no thinker – how wonderful. There was no entrance to the "cave". Inside and outside disappeared. Tears were pouring down my face and continued to do so for as long as the experience lasted. There was no emotion, none, and not the least bit of an increased pulse or heart rate as the tears flowed. I just observed them cascading down my cheeks as if a faucet had been left open. I am absolutely enchanted with the silence. The silence was immense, overwhelming, all-pervasive. There were no questions and thus no answers. There was no noise. None. To say the silence was deafening would not do it justice. It was both humbling and empowering at the same time. A thought appeared bringing to my attention how noisy the mind is, even when one thinks it is silent. There was nothing left to know; nothing separate that was unknown. All was oneself and thus the silence. It was sweet. So unbelievably sweet. To say anything, anything at all, seemed stupid. Words could never come close to approximating This. This was Full and I was This. I was full. This ocean of Consciousness was both infinitely large and infinitely small at the same time. It was ever-new and ancient at the same time. Each moment was unique and yet, at the same time, each moment was eternity. The thought crossed my mind, again and again, this is what the texts describe. I had no idea. I knew and loved and had some inkling of the texts and what they were conveying—but this experience was about me, me as I truly am. I was That. Not theory, I am That. That was not a magnificent That I had previously thought about, prayed to, worshipped. This That was I. I was That. How it was possible to have a sense of me, and know that me is everything, and still not get lost in everything I do not know. It is a mystery and a seeming logical impossibility and yet, I was experiencing I was That. I, as John, this little physical body was not me. John, who John really is, was That. John was observable as a body sitting there crying and yet I was not limited to that body. All bodies were mine. Mine is not a good word for everything was mine and thus not mine—but everything. I was intensely aware of a Being who was so concentrated and massively conscious as to be the source and manifestation of everything. The phenomenal world receded into the background and yet could be observed without breaking the non-duality of That. How is it that this blissful, and at the same time absolutely motionless state, eradicated the up-to-that-moment all-too-familiar line which demarcated the material world and the boundless, all conscious reality? There was no longer two. I wouldn't say that the two had fused into one—there was only one and yet I could distinguish forms that in no way broke the oneness of the one. How is that? But it was so.

The entire universe was in a tiny grain of sand. And it was not strange, but oh so familiar.

In an instant, the time it takes for one moment to pass into the next, I slid into a state of Being in which I was profoundly, immediately, directly, and completely aware of what I really am. It was an absolute and total awareness, a direct knowledge of Consciousness itself—devoid of any conflict, drama, incompleteness, dilemma, lack. It was pure Consciousness itself without any addition of a communication from any other source. There was no other source. All that was, was consciousness, one and indivisible, and I was that. I knew what I am, for the first time, directly, and completely, I am the one being. There was no thought in all this, as before this moment I had known and experienced thoughts moving through the mind and I am somehow apart from them. Now there was no knower apart from the known. There was nothing more to realize, nothing more to think, nothing more to search for. I was complete. I was not merely cognizing an "other". I was all that is. Thus, there was nothing more to realize, nothing more to gain, nothing lacking in any way. There is nothing with which to compare this Reality. There is nothing else, period. It is unique. It is complete. It is ever-new and yet ancient. Whatever one says is simply this and nothing more. As I entered this state, there was no excitement, no surprise it was merely Yes, this is home, this is who I really am. Once I slipped into this state, I could clearly see that all efforts to be this were doomed to failure. Seeking was a direct denial of what one is and no path, no seeking could ever rid oneself of suffering, separation, doubt, incompleteness. Every effort entails identification with some sort of body or another. Every effort involves separation and a goal. Every effort involves seeking completeness. But one is already complete. No amount of mis-identification with something separate will ever reveal This. Seeking may purify the seeker, or strengthen the seeker, or pacify the seeker, but it cannot give what it cannot give. This is not something to be given. It always is, cannot be divided. Self awareness or Self realization is to be aware of, to realize This Self. It is not something outside one's being. It is not an object of experience. It is always present. There is no gap, no separation, from This. I am not in a body, any body, the physical, the subtle, the causal. Never have I ever been in a body or in any realm, or involved in any experience. Experience appears apart but it is not so. It only appears so to seekers—so that they can pursue forms of energy, visions, powers, experiences, liberation, God. True knowledge is free of all bondage to an "other". Ignorance and suffering are merely dependence on experience.

Then, after an hour or so passed, that incredible Oneness was gone—only the memory of it remained. I wondered, how to get it back—all the while knowing that That was not something that could be lost, nor regained, nor even gained. One is always That and only That. After this experience, life went on, just as before, and yet, and yet, the events of one's life are now understood in a revolutionary new way.

The Advaita Vedānta system advocates hearing the Great Sayings *(mahāvākya)* as its primary means of liberation. Each of the *mahāvākyas* imparts a three-fold knowledge that Advaita seizes upon as the key to Self-realization. First, they remove a person's deep-seated misconception that they are a finite, bound, imperfect mortal being, and conversely, they reveal that the true Self that everyone is infinite, ever-free, ever-perfect, immortal. Second, they remove the deep-rooted misconception that the supreme Reality is remote, hidden, unattainable, and declare that it is immediate, direct, the innermost Self of all. Third, they reveal that there are not separate individuals and an Absolute and that each individual is somehow part of the whole. Instead, they declare, unequivocally, that, there and now, "You are That", without an iota of difference.

To hear the statement, "someone won the lottery" invokes mediation. A few of the myriad indirect by-lanes the intellect explores include: "Who is that someone?"; "have they been notified?"; "how much did they win?", etc. But when one is told, "you are that someone who has won the lottery", the understanding is direct and immediate. Such a statement presupposes that one has bought a lottery ticket, that that lottery drawing was just recently conducted, etc. But given the necessary context, such a statement becomes directly and immediately meaningful. Likewise, with an identity statement, granting the context and preparedness of the individual hearing it, it too will give direct and immediate knowledge.

There is an Advaita story about Śaṅkara:

> The young, eight year old boy walked north until he reached the banks of the Narmadā River. There, he encountered his *Guru*, Govinda Bhāgavatpāda, who asked him, "Who are you *(kas tvam)?"* Tradition declares that Śaṅkara burst forth with a hymn, "Six Stanzas on Liberation,"[1] which begins, "I am neither the mind nor the intellect, neither the ego nor the mind-stuff . . . I am consciousness and bliss; I am Śiva, I am Śiva!" Legend also says that he composed the "Hymn of Ten Verses" on one's true identity. "That ultimate reality is not even One, then how can it be dual? It is neither aloneness nor the opposite. It is neither void nor the opposite. It is pure Advaita. In fact, words cannot encompass its meaning."[2]

Once, many years ago, I had a chance meeting with an Indian monk:

> He asked in a type of broken English, "Been India?" Since I had been in India for a number of years, the best, most easily demonstrable answer was to wobble my head in the characteristic side-to-side manner known to most Indians. The moment he saw that "wobble" he got a big grin on his face, entered the room, and closed the door behind him. He asked me, "Who you?" Having lived in India and being used to this type of English and being young and polite I began to answer him, "I am John Grimes" but just as I reached the "G" of Grimes, he said, *"Bas*, family name, who you?" *("bas"* is Hindi for "stop, enough"). Again, since I had lived in India and studied Indian thought, I very confidently and boldly began to reply, "I am the immortal Atman" but just as I reached the "A" of Atman, again he stopped me with another *"Bas*, who you?" With the first

---

[1] *Nirvānaśatkam.* This hymn is also known as *Ātmaśataka* (Six Verses on the Self).

[2] *Dāsaśloki.*

"stop", he wiped out the idea that I am my physical body. With the second "stop", he wiped out my entire mental universe. What was left? With two small words he had succeeded in conveying to me that I was neither my physical body nor my mental knowledge. How to answer him? So I said, "I do not know." Quick as a wink, he responded, "Find out". I replied, "How?" He responded, "Not how, find out." Again I asked, "How?" He was holding a handkerchief in his hand and he opened his fingers and let the handkerchief drop to the ground and as it fell he said, "Let go". Again I asked, "How (to let go)?" He responded, "Not how, let go". And then he turned and left the room.

Almost twenty years passed before I learned that this monk spoke very few words of English. How interesting! A person who did not speak much English magnificently managing to teach the Vedāntic truth that one is neither one's body nor one's thoughts, all in two words. As if that was not enough, he then proceeded to teach me how to "find out who I really am" with another two words ("let go"). We all know how to let go. We do it every night when we go to sleep. We never asked our mother, "Mom, how do I go to sleep?" We just "let go" and sleep came. However, we become confused, mental, when someone asks us to "let go" of all of our preconceived notions as to who we are. Like this, we look for a technique in order to meditate or to find an answer to the question, "Who am I?"

According to Advaita Vedānta, the Self is one and non-dual. The pluralistic universe of an individual's day-to-day experience, which appears to one as real, is an illusory superimposition that is neither real nor unreal. This appearance is rooted in ignorance that conceals the real *(Sat)* and projects the unreal *(asat).* One's entire experience of life seems to involve differentiations like, "I am male, I am old, I am hungry, I am meditating, I am seeking liberation, I am having a vision" and so on. These differentiations are based on the superimposition of one thing on another or the attributes of one thing on another due to ignorance.

> Upon the same tree there are two birds on one branch. One is calm, silent, majestic, immersed in his own glory. The other bird is eating sweet and bitter fruits by turns, hopping from one branch to another, becoming happy and miserable consequentially. After some time, the restless bird eats an exceptionally bitter fruit, becomes disgusted, and for the first time sees the other bird who appears impartial to sweet or bitter fruits, who is neither happy nor sad but serene, who resides content in its own Self. The restless bird longs for this condition but soon forgets and restlessly begins searching for sweet fruits, and hoping to avoid bitter ones again. After another extremely bitter experience, he again attempts to get closer to the other bird. And so it goes, again and again, until at last, the restless bird begins to feel a change about himself. All he thought himself to be has faded away and he realizes that he was only mistaking a substantial looking shadow for his real self. He was, in essence, the other bird all the time. This eating of fruits, bitter and sweet, and this weeping and happiness, rotating by turns, was all a dream, a vain chimera, an illusion. All along he was a majestic bird, calm and silent, glorious and majestic, beyond grief and sorrow.[1]

If the Self is one and non-dual, what is the status of the world, what is the status of all this multiplicity, including myself—what I think I am and what I think the world is? Even if it is true that appearances are illusory superimpositions, it still appears that there is a duality. The Self may exist, and I seem to exist, and this "I" may even be the Self. But there seems to be something else, an "other" or second, if you will. Even if what I think I am is illusory, still it is "something" illusory. To put it another way, if the Self and the world are non-dual, one and the same, then there is no reason to seek the Self (for there is nothing that it is not). Yet, if that is the case, why am I miserable and happy, by turns? That seems to imply duality. On the other hand, if the world and the Self are different, then

---

[1] Paraphrase of MuU 3.1.

surely that is duality. To answer this question, Advaita relates a tale about ten simpletons that reveals the truth of Advaita in seven easy steps:

> It seems that, once upon a time, ten simpletons set out on a journey. Eventually they came to a large, swollen river. The current was strong and there was no bridge available with which to cross the river. Thus, they decided to swim across. When they reached the other side, their leader decided to count their number to determine whether they all made it safely or not. His worst fears we confirmed. He counted only nine members present. He asked each of the other simpletons to count and they reached a similar conclusion, there were only nine of them present and thus one of them must have drowned. They looked high and low, upstream and downstream, but no trace of the missing person could be found. That could mean only one thing. He had been drowned while crossing the river. They began to weep and their grief was inconsolable. Soon a wandering pilgrim came by. Wondering why these individuals were weeping, he asked them what the matter was. Their leader related the entire tragic story of how ten of them had started out on a journey and, after crossing the swollen river, only nine of them had remained, with the tenth man drowned, dead, and gone. The pilgrim was a wise person and a quick glance revealed to him that there were still ten of them present. He guessed how each one of them counted only nine. Obviously, every fool had counted all except himself. Thus, the pilgrim announced, "the tenth man is not dead, but alive". The simpletons began to excitedly crowd around the wise pilgrim and shout, "Where is he, where can we find him, please take us to him." The pilgrim pointed his finger at the leader and said, "You are the tenth man". At once the mystery was solved. The tenth man the leader was searching for was none other than himself. The redeeming knowledge came in a flash: "I am that missing tenth man!" All their sorrow immediately

disappeared and their tears of agony were replaced with waves of bliss.

All human beings are on a journey, as it were, the journey of life. At some stage each individual suddenly becomes aware of someone or something missing. Each person thinks, "there must be more to life than this". What or where that something is one does not know. But deep down, everyone intuitively has this feeling. (The knowledge that the tenth person/*Brahman* is one's own Self is obscured. "I do not know where the tenth man/ *Brahman* is"—ignorance arises). Thus begins the search to discover if there is someone or something that can bring fulfillment, which can make render one's incompleteness, complete. But, at this stage, one does not know who or what it is or even if it really exists. (The existence of the tenth person/*Brahman* is concealed, the tenth person/ *Brahman* seems absent—"I do not see *Brahman* nor do I know if *Brahman* exists or not"). Some people just give up at this stage and discontinue their search for ultimate, eternal, unceasing bliss and settle for momentary pleasures and pains. Others begin to notice their sufferings and feelings of incompleteness and begin to search for a solution. (One has the feeling that the tenth person is dead. One has the feeling that one is an ordinary human being subject to birth, death, fear, ignorance, delusion, pain, finitude and so on). A wise person or teacher enters the scene and reveals that the tenth man/*Brahman* is living/exists. (This is indirect knowledge). This wise person then reveals to the leader of the ten simpletons that you are that tenth man. (Direct knowledge) This knowledge immediately destroys the grief and suffering caused by the thought that the tenth man was missing. It destroys the individual's sense of fear, finitude, sorrow, and mortality. At the same time, this knowledge produces bliss at the discovery of the missing man. Thus, the individual experiences ineffable bliss that arises from one's own innermost Self.

Generally, the human being directs all their thoughts, actions, everything, outwards. This is because the sense organs are turned outwards and attuned to contacting things from the outside. To turn within is the first requirement regarding the question, "Who am I?" An individual whose attention is turned outwards, by that very act, excludes any possibility of discovering who they really are. An object, the known, will never be the knower. Yet strangely, even in the act of turning outwards, the divine consciousness within one is not excluded. It is merely unnoticed.

Whether an individual knows it or not, Vedānta says, they are this divine inner consciousness. That which conceals this truth from an individual's conscious experience is one's ignorance, one's age-old habit of clinging to externals. If one were to dive deep within, it is impossible not to find the so-called secret heart-cave, the ocean of consciousness, the mysterious Self, the source of one's very being. God dwells within you as you. "That thou art." "I am *Brahman.*" One understands such scriptural declarations when one comes to experience, first hand, the divine essence which is within one, which one really is and always has been.

This Reality that exists within each and every person is Pure Consciousness, Pure Awareness, the Self. The name does not matter. It is what the various names are pointing towards that is of paramount importance. No person can even say that they do not know it. In the very act of denying its existence, one must presuppose it to deny it! No one can say, "I do not exist". Who is the I who is saying that they do not exist? Of nothing else in the universe, or beyond the universe, can this be said of. This is the uniqueness and specialty of this consciousness, though until it is experienced it might as well be said to not exist at all. The Self is nearer than the nearest and yet seemingly farther than the farthest. "It is only when you search for It, that you lose It. You cannot take hold of It, but then you cannot get rid of It."

The mark of this ocean of consciousness is that it always exists and it exists by and in itself. It is totally independent, neither needing effort nor support for its existence. To seek it within oneself, all that is necessary is to understand who or what is doing the seeking. One's habitual pattern is to go in search of it as if it were just another object, even if the greatest, grandest object of all. But that is precisely the problem.

The only thing that one knows for certain, with absolute certainty, is the fact that "I Am". Nothing else has this certainty. But, the problem is, one does not know *who* this "I Am" is. Are you the physical body or is it you who has the body? Do you know the body or does the body know you? Be clearly aware that the body is an object and that you who knows of, and can observe the body, are quite apart from it. You pervade the entire body and are aware of every part of it, but it does not know you. Even the feeling that you have a particular name and form belong only to the mind, and you as the knower of the body and the mind, are apart from both.

You are That, that Reality which cannot have a seer to see it as an object. That, which remains after all knowledge and all ignorance has vanished. You are That reality where all that is illusory has been absorbed, where the duality of a "Thou" and a "That" cannot survive. When the source of consciousness itself has been reached, consciousness disappears. Then, the source of consciousness and all that appears within consciousness is the Self.

According to Advaita, a Great Saying *(mahāvākya)* is an identity statement that reveals the non-duality of the Absolute *(Brahman)* and the individual *(Ātman)*. How can there be any understanding of this statement so long as the identification with the body as a separate entity does not cease or, of the understanding that others are not different from oneself?

Who is the "me" who is going to have this understanding? If the one who wants to "achieve" this understanding is none other than the "me" or "ego" or the mind, it cannot be achieved. The thief cannot become a policeman to catch the thief. The mind cannot destroy the mind. The mind or me is a creation within space and time, and it is only that kind of understanding which is not of space and time that can destroy the time bound mind or ego.

The statement *"tat tvam asi"*—"that thou art", appears nine times in the *Chāndogya Upaniśad.* Advaita contends that the individual soul is nothing but pure Consciousness that appears not by itself, but in association with the psycho-physical apparatus. This association is but an illusory appearance due to ignorance. In the statement, "That thou art", "That" refers to pure Consciousness.

This brings us to the heart of the matter. The Great Sayings appear to be unintelligible in their primary meanings. The word "That" *(tat)* primarily refers to *Brahman* (which is omnipresent, omniscient, omnipotent, etc.) and the word "thou" *(tvam)* primarily refers to the individual self (which is finite, limited, mortal, etc.). Thus, it is with the above stated interpretive tools that Advaitins attempt to overcome this dilemma and demonstrate that the Great Sayings do, in fact, coherently signify that the individual Self is non-different from the Absolute.

In the statement, "That thou art", one may claim that "thou" refers to one's ego-nature on the grounds of grammatical co-ordination.[1] Just as there is grammatical co-ordination between the words "I" and "fair" in the expression, "I am fair", so too, there seems to be grammatical co-ordination between the words "thou" and "That".

However, grammatical co-ordination need not *necessarily* imply identity. There are two types of grammatical co-ordination: co-ordination in the sense of sublation and co-ordination in the sense of oneness. One should employ this grammatical principle carefully. In the expression, "I am fair", "fairness" is a characteristic of the body, but, the body is not "I".

Just so, one may interpret this *mahāvākya* by means of the grammatical principle, co-ordination in the sense of sublation.[2] For instance, there is the example of the judgment, "this post is a man".[3] In one's earlier judgment, one believes that an object (a man) is a post. But a subsequent judgment, upon closer scrutiny, reveals that it is post. Likewise, one's original judgment believes that the "I" refers to one's ego-nature, while a subsequent judgment sublates this earlier view and reveals that "I" is the Absolute. Upon realization, the ego-nature is sublated. The "I" with adjuncts is not the Self; the "I", in its essential nature, is the Self.

---

[1] NS 2.28.

[2] Ibid, 2.29.

[3] See PD *8*.42f. and *Siddhāntaleśa-sangraha* 1.34 where this verse is discussed.

Another way in which to interpret this *mahāvākya* is also possible. In its primary meaning, "thou" equals one's ego-nature. Because this primary meaning is unintelligible, one must resort to a secondary meaning. The type of secondary meaning that is sometimes invoked in such a situation is "exclusive". The primary meaning of "thou" (consciousness with attributes) is completely given up and a secondary meaning (consciousness without attributes), other than, but nonetheless related to the primary meaning, is accepted.

There is still another way in which *tat tvam asi* can be interpreted. There exists a similarity between the Self and the ego. Both have the common qualities of subtlety, inwardness, and behave as if they are the perceiving Self. On this account, one may interpret the text by means of signification based upon the knowledge of similarity of qualities. Thus, the Self is implied by a word ("I") that primarily refers to the ego—even though the ego is material and insentient and cannot be equated with *Brahman*.

Finally, one may interpret *tat tvam asi* directly or in a primary sense to mean "thou or the individual self" is the "That or the Absolute" on the strength of the knowledge that the ego-notion cannot exist without the Self.[1] All that is not the Self, is not Consciousness, is not-real and therefore cannot even appear to exist without the aid of the Self. Thus, in a peculiar and interesting twist, "I" (or any word for that matter) must refer to the constitutive being of anything whatsoever and as such designates that which is self-evident, immediate, direct, and certain, i.e. the Self.[2]

We have observed that the knowledge that is derived from *tat tvam asi* is immediate and non-relational. Normally sentences are relational and yet we observe that a relational sentence, *tat tvam asi,* gives a non-relational meaning. The relational, verbal sense of the text will give a non-verbal, unitary, impartite meaning. Interesting, isn't it, that non-

---

[1] Ibid. 2.56.

[2] This is the central topic of *Problems and Perspectives in Religious Discourse: Advaita Vedanta Implications.*

relational Brahman-knowledge can arise from a relational sentence.

According to Advaita, there are three steps/considerations which must be taken into account in the understanding of a *mahāvākya:* (1) grammatical co-ordination or the relation which exists between two terms, i.e. "blue lotus"; (2) subject-predicate relation; (3) indirect implication. The meaning of a sentence is of two types: (1) relation of duality in which the meaning of a sentence is conveyed through a relation obtained among the words conveying the difference, i.e. "bring the cow with a stick" (wherein, from the usage of the various words, difference is known—stick/cow/bring/etc.; (2) relation of non-duality in which oneness is known through the relation of the words, i.e. "blue-lotus" or *"tat tvam asi"*. This is said to be of two kinds: (1) relation with oneness in which there is oneness with relation, the object is one though it has multiple meanings or attributes; and (2) identity statement in which a non-relational sentence with two entities referred to are actually identical/one.

Before we actually interpret the *mahāvākya "tat tvam asi"*, it should be noted that an understanding of a *mahāvākya* involves a two-fold benefit. Even in an empirical statement that involves grammatical co-ordination, there is this two-fold benefit. For instance, in the statement, "blue lotus", both the color "blue" benefits as well as the flower "lotus". The idea of `blueness" removes all other possible colors from the lotus and "that" which is blue is precisely a "lotus". Thus, each is enriched and benefits from their association.

In a similar manner, *"tat"*, by its association with *"tvam"* removes the misconception that it is remote, unattainable, hidden, etc., and reveals itself as that which is ever-manifest, immediate, direct, and the inner-most Self. In a similar manner, *"tvam"*, in its association with *"tat"* removes the misconception that it is mortal, finite, bound, and imperfect and reveals itself as that which is self-existent, ever-pure, ever-free, and immortal. Thus, what was conceived of as the farthest of the far is revealed as nearer than the nearest; what appeared to be unattainable is already attained; what is ever hidden is really self-manifest.[1] Or, as Gauḍapāda said: "This view (that there is

[1] See MuU 3.1.7-8.

duality) is only for the sake of instruction. When the truth is known, all this duality is gone."[1]

According to some Advaitins, there are three steps or considerations to take in interpreting the meaning of *"tat tvam asi"*:

1 – *Sāmānādhikaraṇya:* The connotations of the two terms "That" and "thou" are different. "That" refers to *Brahman* which is omnipotent, omnipresent, omniscient, etc., and "thou" refers to the individual self which is finite, bound, limited, etc. When the meanings of two words are different, one usually thinks that their denotations are also different. However, where there is grammatical co-ordination present in a sentence, the things referred to are not different. The words "That" and "thou" are in grammatical co-ordination and thus refer to the same object, even as "blue" and "lotus" refer to the same object.

2 – *Viśeṣaṇa Viśeṣya Sambandha:* In order to do justice to the different connotations of, and the co-ordinate relation between, these two terms, one must invoke the subject-predicate relation. In the expression, "the blue lotus", one object is denoted while, being a flower, also possesses a blue color. Thus, though the two terms have different connotations, they have the same denotation. This way of construing the meaning is known as "identity which involves relation".

3 – *Lakṣya Lakṣaṇa Sambandha:* There is a difficulty involved in interpreting *"tat tvam asi"* by "identity which involves relation". It works well with "the blue lotus" because there is a "subject-predicate relation". But with the *mahāvākya*, there is an identity wherein "Thou" cannot be an attribute of "That". Thus, one must apply the relation of non-duality. It would be unintelligent to identity "That" with "thou" in view of the fact the determinants of the two terms are mutually

---

[1] MK 3.18.

incompatible. In other words, this statement cannot be treated as an attributive judgment. The import of the statement is identity—but not a relational identity. Thus, the non-relational meaning of the text can only be revealed by a recourse to its implied meaning. Thus, according to Sureśvara,

> In our view, the relations such as *sāmānādhikaraṇya* (which connect words and their meanings) directly bring out the non-verbal import of *"tat tvam asi"* like the identity of ether through the cancellation of the different adjuncts.[1]

What has been emphasized is that, in employing the secondary meaning of the terms in the *mahāvākya*, one has removed the incompatible determinants of each term. By removing omniscience, omnipotence, etc., from "That" and by removing limitedness, boundedness, fallibility, etc., from "thou"—while retaining the common element between them, i.e. consciousness, he has demonstrated that *tat tvam asi* conveys a sense of non-relational identity.

Some implications from this interpretation include: What we usually associate with "thou" (suffering, etc.) is cancelled by its association with "That" and what we usually associate with "That" (remoteness, etc.) is cancelled by its association with "thou".[2]

After explaining the meaning of the great Vedic statement "That thou art", the *Guru* exhorts the aspirant to meditate on his real nature:

> That which is beyond caste and creed, family and lineage, which is devoid of name and form, merit and demerit; That which transcends space, time, and sense-objects, that *Brahman* thou art. Meditate on this in thy mind. That Supreme *Brahman*, which cannot be comprehended by speech, but is accessible to the eye of

---

[1] NS 3.9.

[2] Ibid, 3.10.

> pure illumination; which is stainless, the Embodiment of Knowledge, the Beginningless Entity, that *Brahman* thou art. Meditate on this in thy mind. That which is untouched by the six-fold wave of decay, death, hunger, thirst, grief and delusion meditated upon by the yogis in their hearts, but never grasped by any sense-organ; which the intellect cannot know, that unimpeachable *Brahman* thou art. Meditate on this in thy mind. That which is the Ground of the universe and its various parts, which are all creations of *māyā*; which Itself has no other support; which is distinct from the gross and the subtle; which is part-less and peerless, that *Brahman* thou art. Meditate on this in thy mind. That which is free from birth and growth, development and decline, disease and death; which is indestructible; which is the cause of the projection, maintenance, and dissolution of the universe, that *Brahman* thou art. Meditate on this in thy mind. That which, though One only, is the cause of the many; which refutes all other causes and is Itself without a cause; distinct from *māyā* and its effects, the universe, and ever free, that *Brahman* thou art. Meditate on this in thy mind. That which is free from duality; which is infinite and indestructible; which is supreme, eternal and undying; which is taintless, that *Brahman* thou art. Meditate on this in thy mind. That which, though One, appears manifold owing to ignorance, taking on names and forms, attributes and changes, Itself always unchanged, like gold in its modifications, that *Brahman* thou art. Meditate on this in thy mind. That beyond which there is nothing; which shines above *māyā*, and is infinitely greater than the universe; the Inmost Self of all; the One without a second; the true Self, Existence, Knowledge, Bliss Absolute, infinite and immutable, that *Brahman* thou art. Meditate on this in thy mind.[1]

The words are there, but because the individual has only intellectual knowledge using the mind, there is also deafness to

---

[1] V 254-63.

the true meaning of the sacred words. These words should not be the "starting point" of one's spiritual journey, but the crowning affirmation of one's plenary experience.

For those who are eminently qualified to realize the truth of non-duality, even one hearing of the *mahāvākya* will be enough. Once there was a great sage, Uddālaka. He had a son, Śvetaketu, who was extremely intelligent, clever, and alert. When Śvetaketu was twelve years old, Uddālaka sent him to a teacher for instruction saying: "Everyone in our lineage is a knower of *Brahman.*" Śvetaketu studied for many years and returned to his father, proud and arrogant. He thought that his knowledge was greater than his father's. He had studied so much; he knew so much. But Uddālaka was a sage. He had experienced the Truth. So he let his son behave like that for a while and then one day he called him and said: "You have learnt so much. But tell me, did you learn That by learning which all things are known?" Śvetaketu replied: "No, I don't know That. My teacher must not have known That for he didn't teach it to me." His father said: "Return to your teacher and ask him to teach you That." Śvetaketu returned to his teacher but was told that only his father knows the Self. So Śvetaketu returned to his father, feeling much humbler. Now he asked, in all humility: "Dear father, will you teach me That?" Uddālaka gave him the teaching "That thou art", *"tat tvam asi"*.[1]

He who realizes the Truth is liberated from bondage. What is the Truth? It is that there is nothing other than the Self. The Self is not something and the individual another. God dwells within you as you. That thou art. If one is not the body, then neither is God or anyone else the body. The Self is not in some remote region, unknown and unrealized. Uddālaka points to his son and says, That thou art.

Śaṅkarācārya declared that the object of the story of Uddālaka and Śvetaketu was to show the oneness of the Self. One may be extremely learned in sacred lore, but if one has not known the truth about the Self, one lives but in vain. The truth is that the Self is extremely subtle, distinctionless, all-pervading, One, undefiled, indivisible, Pure Consciousness.

---

[1] CU 6.1.1; VI.16.3.

This revelation is ultimately based on one's own personal experience. To say that there is only non-duality is but second-hand information. To repeat what others have said, is second-hand information. It is only when one has the experience of *tat tvam asi* for oneself that one can truly say that they are That and that That is they. All else is so many words. Thus the saying, "Those who know do not say and those who say do not know." When all has become That, who is to say what? "Words turn back."

Surrender

We have observed that Ramaṇa, when asked, advocated a path of Self-enquiry. There is an Advaita tradition that states there are two ways to gain Self-realization. The analogy presented is of a person in chains. On the path of knowledge one identifies with the Absolute thereby becoming larger and larger until the chains snap. On the other hand, on the path of devotion, one declares "not-me, O Lord, but you" and thus one becomes smaller and smaller until one is able to slip through the links of the chains. Either one becomes everything or else one becomes nothing – in the end, both are the same. Ramaṇa remarked:

> The "I" casts off the illusion of the "I" and yet remains "I". This is the paradox of Self-realization. The Realized do not see any paradox in it. Consider the case of the worshipper. He approaches God and prays to be absorbed in Him. He then surrenders himself in faith and by concentration. And what remains afterwards? In the place of the original "I" self-surrender leaves a residuum of God in which the "I" is lost. That is for the highest form of devotion or surrender and the peak of detachment.[1]

Religious traditions around the world, especially the theistic traditions that acknowledge a personal God, advocate devotion and surrender to God as a means of salvation. A basic presupposition of all theistic systems, be they dualistic or quasi-non-dualistic systems, is that there is posited a gap between the

---

[1] Ibid, 28.

human and the Divine. Somehow, the theistic systems must find a "bridge" which will enable these two separate entities to commune with each other. If one sets up God as an "other", remote and estranged, a link must be found which will somehow tie the physical to the supra-physical. This link is devotion or surrender. Devotion is called the path of love, an intense love of God wherein the devotee says, "Let that constant love which the ignorant have for objects of the senses, let me have that constancy in my love for Thee." Note that devotion, as it is traditionally known, involves not the disappearance of the ego, the "I"-thought, but its release from all limiting barriers. No matter how high the soul moves, God is always higher – the soul may attain a God-like nature, but never God's identity.

In Śrī Vaiṣṇavism of South India and its philosophical system, Viśiṣṭādvaita Vedānta, a distinction is made between devotion *(bhakti)* and surrender *(prapatti/śaraṇāgati).* Devotion is said to be "formal". It is like a ladder with a gradual movement upwards toward communion with God. It has qualifications and is dependent on external aids. Formal devotion begins at birth and culminates at death. Thus, the devotee must have an unflagging will to undergo all the disciplines needed and a patience to endure. It is described as a long, step-by-step, moment-to-moment, long path to God. It is a long hard path, full of pitfalls, and not open to everyone as rituals, *mantras*, and temple worship are required and mandatory, and such are not open to all the Hindu castes. This path of devotion is called the "way of the monkey". A baby monkey clings to its mother's chest as she moves about the forest. If the baby monkey lets go at any time, the little monkey will fall and die. Thus, in this path, the devotee must exert continual *self-effort* as well as having faith in God.

Surrender, the path of self-surrender, on the other hand, is a path open to everyone. The only prerequisite needed is a complete change of heart, an absolute confidence in the saving grace of the Lord. It has no rules. It said to be a direct and easy path for once taken, all is then left in the hands of God. It is known as the "way of the kitten". A baby kitten puts forth no effort when the mother cat moves it from place to place. In fact, it just goes limp and if it were to struggle, this would actually make the mother's efforts much more difficult. This path preserves the essentials of formal devotion, but dispenses with its conditions and non-essentials.

The path of (complete) surrender implies abiding by the will of God in all things. There will be no grievances about what may or may not take place. Even when things turn out differently from the way one would have once-upon-a-time, before surrender, wanted, everything is left up to God. Surrender means abiding by God's will whether God appears or not. One awaits His pleasure, at all times, in all circumstances. To ask God to do as one pleases or desires is not to surrender, but to command. One cannot demand that God obey you and still think you have surrendered. God knows what is best and when and how to do everything. Surrender means leaving everything, everything inclusive, entirely up to God. God carries such a person's burden even as a lawyer, whom one has signed over a "power of attorney" contract to, carries one's burden. In the truly surrendered devotee, the ego, the "I"-thought is also surrendered.

It is often remarked that Ramaṇa advocated two paths to Self-realization: primarily Self-enquiry, but also the path of surrender. He said:

> There are only two ways in which to conquer destiny or be independent of it. One is to enquire who undergoes this destiny and discover that only the ego is bound by it and not the Self, and that the ego is non-existent. The other way is to kill the ego by completely surrendering to the Lord, by realizing one's helplessness and saying all the time: "Not I, but Thou, O my Lord", and giving up all sense of "I" and "mine" and leaving it to the Lord to do what he likes with you. Surrender can never be regarded as complete so long as the devotee wants this or that from the Lord. True surrender is love of God for the sake of love and for nothing else, not even for the sake of salvation. In other words, complete effacement of the ego is necessary to conquer destiny, whether you achieve this effacement through Self-enquiry or through *bhakti-mārga.*[1]

---

[1] Mudaliar, *Day by Day with Bhagavan,* I, 57.

This needs a little analysis because, when push comes to shove, I think it can be shown that what Ramaṇa does with surrender is to redefine it in terms of the Self thus rendering the path of surrender nothing more than a "reworded version" of Self-enquiry. This should be obvious since Ramaṇa unwaveringly stressed that any dualistic (devotional) practice could at best only be of secondary importance. To worship or surrender to a God who is other than the individual necessarily involves a subject-object relationship as well as the continual use of the "I"-thought.

It has been said that Ramaṇa recommended two distinct versions of the doctrine of surrender: 1) Holding on to the "I"-thought until the one who imagines that he is separate from God disappears; 2) Completely surrendering all responsibility for one's life to God or the Self. For such self-surrender to be effective one must have no will or desire of one's own and one must be completely free of the idea that there is an individual person who is capable of acting independently of God.[1] Ramaṇa said about this:

> There are two ways to surrender; one is looking into the source of the "I" and merging into that source; the other is feeling "I am helpless by myself, God alone is all-powerful and except for throwing myself completely on Him there is no other means of safety for me," and thus gradually developing the conviction that God alone exists and the ego does not count. Both methods lead to the same goal. Complete surrender is another name for *jñāna* or liberation.[2]

As Godman remarked, the first method is clearly nothing but the path of Self-enquiry masquerading under a different name. The second method, of surrendering responsibility for one's life to God, is also related to the path of Self-enquiry since it aims to eliminate the "I"-thought by separating it from the

[1] See Godman, *Be As You Are: The Teachings of Sri Ramana Maharshi,* 78.

[2] Mudaliar, *Day by Day with Bhagavan,* II, 175.

objects and actions that an individual is constantly identifying with.[1]

The path of devotion or surrender is usually thought of as the very antithesis of Self-enquiry since it is based on the presumption of duality, of worshiper and the worshipped whereas Self-enquiry presumes absolute non-duality. So, if Ramaṇa proposed surrender as a path, it is his particular definition of what surrender entails. For instance, he remarked about surrender:

> The spark of spiritual knowledge will consume all creation like a mountain of gunpowder. Since all the countless worlds are built upon the weak or non-existent foundations of the ego, they all disintegrate when the atom-bomb of knowledge falls on them. All talk of surrender is like stealing sugar from a sugar image of Gaṇeśa and then offering it to the same Gaṇeśa. You say that you offer up your body and soul and all your possessions to God, but were they yours to offer? At best you can say: "I wrongly imagined till now that all these, which are Yours, were mine. Now I realize that they are Yours, and shall no longer act as though they were mine." And this knowledge that there is nothing but God, or Self, that "I" and "mine" do not exist and that only the Self exists is spiritual knowledge *(jñāna)*.[2]

> Do not delude yourself by imagining the original source to be some God outside you. Some contend that just as sugar cannot taste its own sweetness, but there must be someone to taste and enjoy it, so an individual cannot both be the Supreme and also enjoy the Bliss of that State; therefore the individuality must be maintained separate from the Godhead in order to make enjoyment possible. But is God insentient like sugar? How can one surrender oneself and yet remain one's individuality for supreme enjoyment? Furthermore,

---

[1] Ibid.

[2] Mudaliar, *Day by Day with Bhagavan*, II, 53.

> they also say that the soul, on reaching the divine region and remaining there, serves the Supreme Being. Can the sound of the word "service" deceive the Lord? Does He not know? Is He waiting for these people's services? Would He not – the Pure Consciousness – ask in turn, "Who are you apart from Me that presume to serve Me?"[1]

To quote but one example from the Vaiṣṇavite saint Nammālvar: "I was in a maze, clinging to "I" and "mine"; I wandered without knowing myself. On realizing myself I understand that I myself am You and that "mine" is only Yours." "Ramaṇa remarked: "To say that one is apart from the Supreme is a pretension and to add to it that one divested of the ego, the "I"-thought, becomes pure and yet retains their individuality only to enjoy or serve the Supreme is a deceit. What duplicity this is. First to appropriate what is really the Supreme and then to pretend to experience or serve this Supreme! Is not all this known to Him?"[2]

Devotion requires a God and a devotee, a worshipped and the worshipper. About this relationship Ramaṇa remarked:

> God is required for devotional spiritual practice *(sādhana)*. But the end of the *sādhana*, even in the path of devotion *(bhakti mārga)*, is attained only after complete surrender. What does it mean, except that effacement of the ego results in the Self remaining as it always has been? Whatever path one may choose, the "I" is inescapable, the "I" that does the selfless service *(niṣkāma karma)*, the "I" that pines for joining the Lord from whom it feels it has been separated, the "I" that feels it has slipped from its real nature, and so on. The source of this "I" must be found out. Then all questions will be solved.[3]

---

[1] Venkataramiah, *Talks with Sri Ramana Maharshi,* 208.

[2] Ibid.

[3] Mudaliar, *Day by Day with Bhagavan,* II, 157.

To conclude, Ramaṇa remarked to the theists who advocate surrender to the worshipped by the worshipper, who staunchly advocate the reality of the subject-object relationship, "Whoever objects to his having a separate God to worship so long as he needs one? Through devotion he develops until he comes to feel that God alone exists, and then he himself does not count. He comes to a stage when he says, "Not I but Thou, not my will but Thine." When that state is reached, which is called complete surrender in *bhakti mārga*, one finds that effacement of the ego is attainment of the Self. We need not quarrel whether there are two entities or more or only one. Even according to dualists and according to *bhakti mārga*, complete surrender is necessary. Do that first and then see for yourself whether the one Self alone exists or whether there are two or more. Whatever may be said to suit the different capacities of different individuals, the truth is that the state of Self-realization must be beyond the triad of knower, knowledge, and known. The Self is the Self; that is all that can be said of it."[1] A seeker asked Ramaṇa, "How can it be said that the end of both these paths is the same? Ramaṇa replied:

> Whatever the means, the destruction of the sense "I" and "mine" is the goal, and as these are interdependent, the destruction of either of them causes the destruction of the other; therefore in order to achieve that state of Silence which is beyond thought and word, either the path of knowledge which removes the sense of "I" or the path of devotion which removes the sense of "mine", will suffice. So there is no doubt that the end of the paths of devotion and knowledge is one and the same.

Other Disciplines

Advaita and Ramaṇa are in agreement that the various spiritual disciplines such as rituals, chanting, singing devotional songs, repetition of a mantra or a sacred name, pilgrimage, selfless service, breath control, the various yogas, and the like are

---

[1] Ibid, 195.

helpful, beneficial, and purificatory aids at a beginning level for certain spiritual aspirants. A mother prepares baby food for the baby; she asks the teenager to get his or her own meal; and she leaves it to adults to eat as they wish. What is proper and needful for one person, is not necessarily proper and needful for all. Ramaṇa said:

> Yes, rituals and forms of worship are also necessary. It may not help you in particular, but that does not mean that it is necessary for no one, and are no good at all. What is necessary for the infant is not necessary for the graduate. But even the graduate has to make use of the alphabet he learnt in the infant class. He knows its full use and significance.[1]

Ramaṇa knew that spontaneous and complete destruction of the "I"-thought by either Self-enquiry or surrender was not possible for many seekers and thus he sometimes, depending on circumstances and qualifications, advised various seekers to undertake preliminary practices which would cultivate purity and control of their wavering mind. However, it should be noted that neither Advaita nor Ramaṇa insist that a seeker should change their beliefs or practices if they are not interested in taking to the path of knowledge. Any method is better than no method and both are convinced that in the end, the Self will reveal itself no matter how long that may take. "All methods are good since they will lead to Self-enquiry eventually."

In this regards, we need not go into great detail as to Ramaṇa's comments about every path. A few examples should suffice for, if one has by now grasped the implications of Ramaṇa's path of Self-enquiry and non-duality, the consequences for any external aids or practices which employ the "I"-thought should be obvious.

> This path (Self-enquiry or attention to the "I"-thought), is the direct path, all others are indirect ways. The first leads to the Self, the others elsewhere. And even if the latter do arrive at the Self, it is only because they lead

[1] Ibid, 100.

at the end to the first path, which ultimately carries them to the goal. So, in the end, the aspirants must adopt the first path. Why not do so now? Why waste time?[1]

The goal is the same for the one who meditates on an object and the one who practices self-enquiry. One attains stillness through meditation, the other through knowledge. One strives to attain something, the other seeks the one who strives to attain. The former takes a longer time, but in the end attains the Self.[2]

Who says there is no benefit in repetition of the name *(japa)?* Such *japa* will be the means for purifying the mind. As the *japa* is done repeatedly the effort ripens and sooner or later leads to the right path.[3]

Upāsana (meditation) or *mūrti dhyāna* (adoration of an image with name and form) helps concentration of the mind. Then the mind is free from other thoughts and is full of the meditated form. The mind then becomes one with the object of meditation, and this makes it quite pure. Then think, who is the worshipper? The answer is "I", that is, the Self. In this way the Self is ultimately gained.[4]

Breath control is only an aid for diving inwards. One can as well dive down by controlling the mind. On the mind being controlled the breath is automatically controlled. There is no need to practice breath control; mind control is enough. Breath control is recommended for the person who cannot control the mind directly.[5]

---

[1] S. Natanananda, *Spiritual Instruction of Bhagavan Sri Ramana Maharshi*, 13.

[2] G. Muni, *Sri Ramana Gita*, ch. 7, vv.26, 22.

[3] Nagamma, *Letters from Sri Ramanasramam*, 202-03.

[4] Venkataramiah, *Talks with Sri Ramana Maharshi*, 69.

[5] Ibid, 448.

> For the subsidence of the mind there is no other means more effective and adequate than Self-enquiry. Even though by other means the mind subsides, that is only apparently so; it will rise again. For instance, the mind subsides by means of breath control; yet such subsidence lasts only so long as the control of breath and vital forces continues; and when they are released the mind also gets released and immediately, being externalized, it continues to wander through the force of subtle tendencies.[1]

> Breath control is also a help. It is one of the various methods that are intended to help us attain *ekāgrahā* or one-pointedness of the mind. Breath control can also help to control the wandering mind and attain this one-pointedness and therefore it can be used. But one should not stop there. After obtaining control of the mind through breath control one should not rest content with any experiences which may accrue therefrom, but should harness the controlled mind to the question, "Who am I?" until the mind merges in the Self.[2]

In confirmation of Ramaṇa's position, one can quote the Tamil saint Thayumanuvar who said: "Why all these *mahāyogas?* You are already the Self. Why don't you remain established in your own natural state? Don't forget who you are, don't cease to be aware of it, and don't concern yourself with all these exotic practices."

Satsang

There is one last aid to Self-realization, which in his inimitable way Ramaṇa redefined. In Advaita works, *satsaṅg* is usually presented as an aid to one's spiritual practice and is defined as, "keeping the company of the holy." It entails associating with, and keeping the company of the good, the

---

[1] *Who Am I?* 42.

[2] Mudaliar, *Day by Day with Bhagavan,* I, 4.

godly, devotees of God and God-minded people, the wise, saints, *Gurus*, and especially sages or the Self-realized. However, there are some Advaitins who define the term in a manner similar to Ramaṇa and base as their paradigm for doing so, the etymological meaning of the term *"upaniṣad"*. Generally the term *"upaniṣad"* is said to mean, "to sit close by or near" derived from the verb root *ṣad* = "to sit" + the prefixes *upa* = "near" and *ni* = "down". This, the Upanisads meant teachings given by sages to their disciples who were sitting nearby the teacher. The implication was that in order to receive the wisdom teachings, one had to be in the direct presence of the sage and receive them first hand, experientially. However, some Advaitins interpreted the term upaniṣad to mean, "sitting close by the inner Self", in other words, the wisdom teachings did not apply to an external relationship, but an internal one.

Ramaṇa employed the term in both the above meanings, but he gave priority and preference to the latter meaning. One shouldn't mistake this and think that one definition is greater than the other. For after all, what is the Sage? A Sage is certainly not his body. He is an embodiment of the Self. Thus, if one understands this, being in the presence of an embodied sage is a remarkable thing. One is in the presence of the Self, manifesting itself, whether one realizes it or not and the benefits which accrue from such an association cannot be praised enough. I dare say, and others emphatically declare, "the only gift worth receiving is the Presence, all else is but mere wrapping."

Of all aids to Self-realization, the presence of a *jñāni*, a Self-realized individual is the greatest. This presence is known as *"satsaṅg"* or "holy company" or the association with Being" according to Ramaṇa. Ramaṇa sometimes explained that the real "Being" is the Self and therefore no physical form is needed for *satsaṅg*. Nevertheless, he often spoke of the immense benefit that association with a *jñāni* brings.

Ramaṇa came across five stray verses concerning the glory of *satsaṅg*, of which he was so impressed that he translated them into Tamil and incorporated them in his *Ulladu Narpadu Anubandham* (*Forty Verses on Existence*):

1 – By *satsaṅg* the association with the objects of the world will be removed. When that worldly association is removed the attachment or tendencies of the mind will be destroyed. Those who are devoid of mental attachment will perish in that which is motionless. Thus they attain liberation. Cherish their association.

2 – The supreme state which is praised and which is attained here in this life by clear enquiry, which arises in the Heart when association with a realized person is gained, is impossible to attain by listening to preachers, by studying and learning the meaning of the scriptures, by virtuous deeds or by any other means.

3 – If one gains association with sages, of what use are all the religious observances? When the excellent cool southern breeze itself is blowing, what is the use of holding a fan?

4 – Heat will be removed by the cool moon, poverty by the celestial wish-fulfilling tree and sin by the Ganges. But know that all these, beginning with heat, will be removed merely by having the *darśaṇa* of incomparable sages.

5 – Sacred bathing places, which are composed of water, and images of deities, which are made of stone and earth, cannot be comparable to those great souls. Ah, what a wonder! The bathing places and deities bestow purity of mind after countless days, whereas such purity is instantly bestowed upon people as soon as sages see them with their eyes.

Ramaṇa used to say that the benign influence of a *jñāni* steals into the devotee in silence. The gaze of a *jñāni* has a purifying effect for certain. However, just as a piece of coal takes a long time to be ignited, and a piece of charcoal takes a shorter time, and gunpowder ignites instantly, so too with individuals who come into the presence of a *jñāni*, there are grades of individuals. But none can escape the warmth of the fire of wisdom that is emitted in the Sage's presence.

Then, to cut to the chase, Ramaṇa remarked: "Do you mean "is the physical proximity of the sage helpful?" What is the good of it? The mind alone matters. The mind must be contacted. What *satsaṅg* does is to make the mind sink into the Heart. Association with the sage is both physical and mental. The extremely visible Being of the sage pushes the mind inward. The sage is also in the Heart of the seeker and so he draws the latter's inward-bent mind into the Heart. First, you must decide what is *satsaṅg*. It means association with *sat* or Reality. One who knows or has realized *sat* is also regarded as *sat.* Such association with sat or with one who knows *sat* is absolutely necessary for all. Śaṅkara has said that in all the three worlds there is no boat like *satsaṅg* to carry one safely across the ocean of births and deaths. *Satsaṅg* means *saṅg* (association) with *sat* (Being). *Sat* is only the Self. Because the Self is not now understood to be *sat*, the company of the Sage who has thus understood it is sought. That is *Sat-saṅg*. From that association, introversion results, the "I"-thought dissolves, and Self-realization naturally and spontaneously occurs."[1] Thus, on this point, Advaita and Ramaṇa are in complete accord. As Śaṅkara was to emphatically repeat thirty-two times in his *Guruvāstakam*, *"gurum eva"* (only by the grace of the *Guru*/Sage) does one become liberated, or the Upaniṣads, "Unless taught by one who knows It, one cannot gain access to it"[2] or "One obtains the liberating knowledge from a sage", and "Knowledge obtained from a Sage has the greatest efficiency."

Liberation

This leads us to Advaita's and Ramaṇa's conception of the nature of liberation. On this point they are in complete agreement as to its nature. Perhaps the only difference between the two is that while Advaita, as a philosophy, is not averse in its attempts to describe the goal, Ramaṇa did not, on the whole, approve of questions about the meaning and nature of Self-realization. Ramaṇa's purpose was not to satisfy a person's

---

[1] Venkataraman, *Maharshi's Gospel*, 140; 186, 242; Mudaliar, *Day by Day with Bhagavan*, 236-67.

[2] KU 1.2.7-8; also BU 2.1.14; CU 4.14.1-4, 6.14.1, 7.1.1; TU 1.2.3, 1.3.3, 1.9.1, 3.1.1.

intellectual curiosity, but rather to make them aware of the need to attain Self-realization. In this regards Ramaṇa remarked:

> Questions are endless. Why worry about all these things? Never mind about liberation. First find out whether there is such a thing as bondage. Examine yourself first . . . in a sense, speaking of Self-realization is a delusion. It is only because people have been under the delusion that the non-self is the Self and the unreal the Real that they have to weaned out of it by the other delusion called Self-realization; because actually the Self always is the Self and there is no such thing as realizing it. Who is to realize what, and how, when all that exists is the Self and nothing but the Self?[1]

"Realizing, attaining, reaching" the goal only have a figurative meaning according to Advaita and Ramaṇa. If a goal, Self-realization, is to be reached, it cannot be permanent. The goal must already be there. Why? If an individual seeks to reach the goal with his or her ego, how can they reach it? The goal must have existed before the ego searched for it and when the ego is destroyed, what is there is only the eternal Self, as it ever was! Thus "bondage" and "release" must only pertain to the ego and not to the Self. Where duality exists, there bondage and release make sense. But, if there is no duality, if duality only exists in the mind, or in the ego of an individual, then whom is to be released? When the mind ceases through Self-enquiry, it will be discovered that there is neither bondage nor liberation. Ramaṇa said:

> If the Self were to be reached, it would mean that the Self is not here and now, but that it should be got anew. What is got afresh will also be lost. So it will be impermanent. What is not permanent is not worth striving for. So I say, the Self is not reached. You are the Self. You are already That. The fact is that you are ignorant of your blissful state. Ignorance supervenes and draws a veil over the pure Bliss. Attempts are

[1] Mudaliar, *Day by Day with Bhagavan,* I, 61.

directed only to remove this ignorance, which consists in wrong knowledge. The wrong knowledge consists in the false identification of the Self with the body, the mind, etc. This false identity must go and there remains the Self.[1]

Mokṣa is freedom from all limiting conditions. It is freedom from subjection to time and space. It is freedom from empirical bondage. It is freedom from finitude. Individuals find themselves immersed in finitude. They long to escape. Their difficulty lies in locating a firm reference point in the quicksand of their life. They seem to secrete illusion from their very pores. In desperation, they yearn to escape illusion into Truth, into bliss. For this, Ramaṇa directs them to practice Self-enquiry.

The discovery of one's essential nature is freedom. There is no interval between the rise of knowledge and the attainment of freedom. The results of action take place in time, but the results of knowledge are immediate. "Instant is the light with which we see." The consequences of this mean that freedom is possible in this very life. Freedom is "an experience of the present, not a prophecy of the future."

Freedom is here and now. It is not a *postmortem* condition of excellence to which, and in which, the individual revels. Bondage is ignorance and once knowledge dawns, freedom follows as a matter of course. Freedom is now, in this body, just as much as one felt bondage previously. From freedom individuals have come; in freedom they are living; unto freedom they will return. Freedom is an individual's eternal nature. Thus, "there is no dissolution, no origination, none in bondage, and none liberated. This is the absolute Truth."[2]

Bondage is not denied at the empirical level and, at the absolute level, the question of bondage does not arise. When all is one, for whom would there be bondage? The same holds true in regards to the seeking of freedom. It is all a matter of perspective.

---

[1] Venkataramiah, *Talks with Sri Ramana Maharshi,* 207.

[2] MU *Kārikā* II.32.

Śaṅkara defines freedom as "that which is absolutely real, immutable, eternal, all-penetrating like ether, exempt from all change, ever-satisfied, impartite, self-luminous; in which neither good nor evil effect, nor past nor present nor future has any place—this incorporeal state is called freedom."[1] This passage shows that Śaṅkara equates freedom with Brahman or Being. Ontologically, they are the same. The stress is on immutability and this underlines the fact that freedom is not an effect, to be produced from a cause or causes that are ephemeral.

Freedom is not a goal to be reached in some remote space by an actual movement—either mental or physical. The state of freedom is exempt from all change. This means that its character is noumenal and not phenomenal. It is independent and has its own intrinsic value. It does not need to be illumined for it is a light unto itself. As well, it does not fall within time. It is the eternity of which time is the moving image. "*Mokṣa* is the state of freedom where the stream of time has stopped."[2]

The *Upaniṣads* describe the *mukta* as: "Him who is the bodiless among bodies, stable among the unstable, the great, all-pervading Self—on recognizing the Self, the wise man sorrows not."[3] Freedom is the abolishment, once and forever, of ignorance and the accompanying idea of embodiment. Free, one no longer suffers the bondage of the body. One realizes that now, in the past, and in the future, one was never bound. "Due exclusively to the right knowledge born of the great saying *(mahāvākya)", tat tvam asi*, one sees that ignorance with its manifold effects (such as embodiments, etc.) was not, is not, and will be not."[4]

Individuals are neither bound nor free. Śaṅkara does not deny the human experience of bondage. What he does is to relegate it to the realm of empirical reality. It is really but a figure of speech to say that individuals become free. The true nature of the individual is always free and a real alienation is

---

[1] BSB I.1.4.

[2] CU *Bhāṣya* 8.12.3.

[3] KU 2.22; MuU 2.1.2; & 4.3.15.

[4] BU *Vārtika* 1.183.

impossible. If alienation were real, it could never be overcome. However, due to the confusion born of ignorance, conscious realization of this nature is not effected. Thus, a spiritual discipline is laid down in order to dispel the clouds of ignorance that (seemingly) cover the Self. The illusion of the loss of one's Self is removed and its seeming recovery is spoken of as the attainment of freedom.

Śaṅkara uses a parable to describe this process:

> There was a king who was at war with his foe, a neighboring king. As this king was about to lose the battle, he fled with his pregnant queen and his minister? He was chased by his enemies, caught and killed. But before he was caught, he chanced upon the hut of a hunter in the forest and left his pregnant queen and minister there. The queen died giving birth to the prince and he grew up leading the life of a hunter totally ignorant of his real identity. The minister fled fearing for his own life Later, upon attaining manhood, the prince felt a novel and noble spirit striving within himself, and there grew a sense of total estrangement from his immediate environment. Now it happens that, as these feelings were emerging in the prince, the kind and trustworthy minister from his father's court meets him and reveals to him his royal status. His artificial and unbecoming status as a hunter falls off, and he recognizes his innate royalty. He plans for war, defeats his enemy and assumes the throne.[1]

This parable reveals the real nature of realization. The knowledge gained is merely a shedding of the ignorance that had been mistaken for the truth. Nothing new is gained. Merely the covering that was obscuring what was already there has been removed. When one is caught in the fetters of ignorance, illusion is not seen for what it is. It is only when ignorance is removed that it is seen to be mere illusion. Its truth never was, nor will be—except in the imagination of those under its spell. How ironic. It is one's fertile imagination that has all along been

---

[1] MK with Sankara's *Bhāṣya* 4.93.

calling the kettle black.

"The truly existent *(Sat)* cannot suffer to be negated."[1] If bondage were real, it could never be destroyed. Knowledge neither creates nor destroys reality. One may do, or may not do, or may do otherwise—any action that they so desire. Actions are person-dependent. But objects of knowledge are not person-dependent—they are object-dependent. Knowledge can remove illusory presentations of ignorance but it cannot change an actual object. The "snake" in a rope-snake perception may be removed because it is a product of ignorance. But knowledge can never remove the "rope". "The goal of life cannot be attained unless the individual gets rid of agentship which is full of pain; and agentship cannot be natural to the self because it would make release an impossibility."[2]

The continuance of the physical body is in no way incompatible with the status of freedom. All that happens is a change of perspective. Before freedom, one takes the world, of which the body is a part, as real. After knowing the Truth, one realizes that the world is but an illusory appearance superimposed upon the Truth. The person who has realized himself has nothing more to achieve and no end to gain. All his desires are fulfilled and his duties are done.

The most important question raised in Vedāntic philosophy is this: Can you attain and keep what you haven't already attained, or, to put it slightly differently, can you attain what you already have? If you are going to get something that you didn't have before, what good is it? Since you didn't have it before and get it now, there is every possibility if not actuality that you'll lose it at some time in the future. Anything that comes, necessarily goes, that is the law of the universe. And the question of getting what you already have is ridiculous, isn't it?

In Advaita there are said to be two types of attainment: attainment of the not-yet-attained and attainment of the already attained. What has not-yet-been-attained, say the attainment of a new automobile, is achieved in space and time. It may be

---

[1] BG 2.16.

[2] BSB 2.3.40.

attained by a limited effort and will produce a limited result, e.g., a new car. This type of attainment always involves both gain and loss. One gains a new condition and loses their old condition.

However, Vedānta also talks about another type of attainment. It is called, "obtaining the already obtained" *(praptasya praptiḥ)* or, "getting rid of what you haven't got". To obtain the already obtained, there is neither space nor time involved. One can obtain only that which one does not already have. Since one always is the Self, when one realizes this fact it is designated as "obtaining the already obtained".

In the *Muṇḍaka Upaniṣad* there is the statement, "The knower of *Brahman* becomes *Brahman*."[1] The question may be posed, is the Absolute known or not? If it is known, then it must be the object of a valid means of knowledge, for, according to the Advaitin, the distinctive cause of valid knowledge is proof or evidence. And if it is an object of a valid means of knowledge, then it follows that the Absolute is neither the innermost Reality of all things nor is it self-luminous. Why? The sole function of a valid means of knowledge is to make known what was hitherto unknown. How can a self-luminous self be unknown? As the innermost Reality of everyone, if it is self-luminous, it must surely be known. And yet, if the Absolute cannot be known, then the Scripture will be proven untrue and liberation will be rendered impossible.

Śaṅkara replies to this dilemma: "*Brahman* is not a non-object in an absolute sense." Why? It is the object of the notion of the ego, and is immediately known by everyone. No one says, "I do not exist". To do so would be self-contradictory. Thus the "I-notion" of everyone proves that *Brahman* is not unknown entirely. This "I" will be revealed as the innermost self of all and self-luminous by a proper analysis.

In connection with this dilemma, the Advaitin points out that even though all knowledge of the myriad things of the world comes through some means of valid knowledge, a means functions as a means only through the help of consciousness. This consciousness is presupposed in all acts of knowing and it

---

[1] MuU 1.2.23 "*Brahmaveda brahmaiva bhavati*".

is the basis of all knowledge. It is only indirectly that all objects are established through a means of knowledge. They are established directly through consciousness. And consciousness is self-established. Everything shines only after that shining light. Even as a light is needed to reveal objects in a dark room but no further light is needed to reveal the light itself, so too is consciousness self-luminous and self-established.

The question whether *Brahman* may be known or not has been posed in another way. If *Brahman* is already known, then one need not enquire into it. And conversely, if *Brahman* is not known, then one cannot enter into such an enquiry. Again Śaṅkara replies: "*Brahman* is known." Not only from the etymological derivation, but also because of the fact of it being the self of all, everyone feels that they exist and no one feels that they do not exist. Then why should one enquire into the already known? Because, though it is known as the self of all things, its nature is not fully understood. Some hold the self to be the body, others take it to be the mind or a void, etc. Thus, it follows the necessity for a deliberation on *Brahman*.

If one says that *Brahman* is known, the question may be asked: Does *Brahman* know itself or is it known by some other object? Obviously it cannot know itself for one and the same entity cannot, at the same time, be both the subject and the object of knowledge. The knower is other than the known. If the knower becomes the known, then it ceases to be the knower, and by definition, becomes the known. If one says that *Brahman* is known by some other object, this is impossible, for all things other than *Brahman* are insentient and therefore can know nothing. Then does it follow that *Brahman* is unknown? This would have the disastrous consequences of rendering release impossible. Also, as *Brahman* is eternally immediate and the innermost self of all, it cannot be logically unknown. Thus the *Kena Upaniṣad* says: "That *(Brahman)* is surely different from the known; and again, It is above the unknown."[1] This has the two-fold effect of asserting that It is not to be rejected (all known things are to be rejected as other than *Brahman*) and that It is not something to be obtained (only unknown things can be newly obtained). As *Brahman* is not an object to be acquired or

---

[1] KeU 1.4.

rejected, one's search for the Absolute can theoretically stop. The inmost self of all alone meets this description.

The Scripture does not seek to establish the Absolute as an entity referable objectively by the word "this." *Brahman* is not described as such and such. Its aim is to remove the ignorance that imagines and superimposes on the Absolute, differences. Knowledge of *Brahman* is but the cessation of identification with extraneous things. *Brahman* is known from the knowledge that arises from hearing the Great Sayings of the *Upaniṣads*. Yet, this *Brahman* is said to be inexpressible and unknowable because It is not understood by the apprehending consciousness. To explain—"apprehending consciousness" is defined as knowledge with the reflection of consciousness in it. When knowledge of *Brahman* occurs, not only is ignorance destroyed, but also the apprehending consciousness that is included in ignorance and is a product of it. Thus, *Brahman* may be said to be known and yet there is no knower, known, nor knowledge in such a situation. Therefore the Scripture says: "Through what should one know that owing to which all this is known?"[1] As well, there are the texts: "*Brahman* is known to him to whom It is unknown, while It is unknown to him to whom It is known,"[2] and "you cannot know that which is the knower of knowledge."[3] So, the statement "the knower of *Brahman* becomes *Brahman*" does not mean a change of state or an attainment. The Sanskrit root *"bhu,"* from which *"bhavati"* (becomes) is derived, means both "Being" an "becoming". In the present context it refers to "Being". One is what one always is. To attain the unattained, action is necessary. But to attain the already attained, no action is required. Knowledge of the fact as-it-is will dispel the darkness of ignorance which covers it.

The heart of Advaita is the Self. This means that a spiritual aspirant must discriminate between the Self and the not-Self.[4] Obviously Advaita's voice is perfect for conveying this idea, as

---

[1] BU 2.4.14.

[2] KeU 2.3.

[3] BU 3.4.2.

[4] *Nitya-anitya vastu viveka*. This idea is so prevalent in Vedānta literature that numerous examples could be quoted from any book chosen.

it emphasizes, "Don't take the world so seriously; beware the not-Self." Its emphasis on "not-this, not-this" *(neti-neti)* is a wonderful corrective or check against desires, against worldliness, against imaginations, against the enemies of ignorance, lust, anger, greed, delusion, and so on.

This so-called gaining of the Self has often been compared by Ramaṇa to the gaining of a necklace supposed to be lost.[1] A person imagines that she has lost her necklace while all the time it is round her neck. She goes frantically searching for it here and there. A friend comes along, enquires as to what was the object of her search, notices the necklace around her neck (the very person who is the victim of a delusion), and points out her error to her. She jumps with glee and joyfully exclaims, "I have got my necklace back." Did she ever lose her necklace? Did she gain it afresh now? She merely obtained the already obtained. Likewise, knowing the Self means being the Self, and not knowing it while being other than it. A person wrongly imagines that something is lost, the Self, and that it must be found. A day will dawn when such a person will laugh at all their futile efforts. That day that you laugh is also here and now.

Advaitins like to tell another story:

> One day a washerman was taking his donkeys to the forest to graze them. He happened to chance upon a new-born lion cub. The lion cub did not know that it was a lion and so the cub grew up with the donkeys. As time passed, by living in their company, the lion began to speak like the donkeys, to eat with them, and to travel back and forth to the river carrying laundry on its back. The lion grew up thinking of himself as a donkey. One day, when he was grazing on the riverbank with his donkey brothers, another lion came down to the river to drink. While he was drinking he caught sight of this young lion and was shocked and puzzled to see him standing in the midst of donkeys in such a pitiful condition. He came closer to the young lion and said, "Brother, what are you up to?" The young lion replied, "I am grazing with my brothers". Shocked, the elder

[1] Venkataramiah, *Talks with Sri Ramana Maharshi,* 297.

lion said, "How can you call them brothers? They are asses and you are a lion. Come with me and look at your reflection in the water. Look at your reflection and then look at my reflection. Is there anything similar about us?" The young lion gazed down at his reflection and saw that he looked just like the old lion. The old lion demanded, "Are they your brothers or am I your brother? Now stop braying like a donkey and roar like a lion." The young lion began to roar. All the donkeys as well as the washerman ran away.

Was the young lion ever a donkey? No. He only thought he was a donkey. The human being is not a limited, unhappy, imperfect being. Human beings only believe they are small, finite, mortal creatures. Once one discards this ignorant superimposition, one will manifest the strength, the glory, the majesty that one is, and always has been. It is only one's awareness that need be changed. Individuals never were limited, and never will be limited, because they are the Self. Though a mirage appears in the desert, there never was, isn't now, nor ever will there be water there. Though subjects and objects appear in one's nightly dreams, they are not real. Upon waking the next morning, one remarks, "Oh, it was but a dream". It is an improper question to ask and no one ever does ask, "Where did the people in my dream go?"

Advaitins (Ramaṇa learned of these analogies and would relate each of them in his own wonderful way) like to narrate four analogies to illustrate this "un-covering" of the always existent Absolute, this "obtaining of the already attained". Two, we already told, is about the woman who, forgetting that her necklace is around her neck, goes anxiously in search of it and about the prince who was abandoned in a forest in his infancy and grew up thinking that he was the son of a hunter. The third is about ten rustics who, upon crossing a river, each counted the other nine, and forgetting to count himself, bewailed the fact that one of their party had drowned. The last is the donkey-lion analogy. In truth, the necklace was never lost, the prince was never not a prince, the tenth man was never drowned, and the lion was never a donkey.

The question of stages in liberation arises. Since all is the Self, there is no common measure between the Absolute and the conditioned. A million is no nearer to infinity than a hundred. Ramaṇa remarked:

> For, as compared with the Self, neither this physical world nor any higher world is inherently real, just as, compared with infinite, a big number has no more meaning than a small one." A saint may attain a lofty grade without ever conceiving of the ultimate Reality of Oneness or having only brief ecstatic intimations of it. That does not matter; the power of his purity and aspiration will eventually sweep him onwards either in this life or beyond. For one who envisages the ultimate Goal, and strives towards it there are no stages; either he is realized or he is not. There are no stages in Realization. There are no degrees of liberation.[1]

A lady cannot be half pregnant. Either she is or she is not. Either one is in New York or one isn't. However, practically speaking, one can also say that it makes sense to say that one is half way or even nearing New York. The former examples are from the perspective of *ajāta-vāda*, of Gauḍapāda, Ramaṇa, and the Vivaraṇa school of Advaita Vedānta. The later example illustrates what many call the compassionate teachings of Śaṅkara (though he made use of both of them) and the Bhāmati school of Advaita. The former is the thundering truth, immediate, direct and without mincing words. The latter example is often called the "gradual path" and leads the seeker from what they know to what they don't.

[1] Mudaliar, *Day by Day with Bhagavan,* II, 110.

VII
Ramana, Jivan-mukti and the Sadguru

When you dream at night, you are a tiger.

Have you ever stopped being a human being?

Jivan-mukti

Ramaṇa was a Sage, a *jñāni*, a *jīvan-mukta*, an embodiment of the one non-dual Self. This is the mystery and the wonder, that a person can be both beyond and *seemingly* within duality at the same time. A Sage is thus, in what appears to be, two mutually contradictory states at the same time.

Critics say that the concept of being-liberated-while-living is a contradiction in terms. How can the individual, who is embodied, coexist with freedom, which, by definition, is free from embodiment? How can the body, which is due to *prārabdha-karma*, continue after the attainment of knowledge when it is acknowledged that ignorance and all *karmas* are dissolved with the attainment of knowledge? Critics have raised a number of doubts regarding whether Śaṅkara and post-Śaṅkara Advaitins who willingly embrace this concept have the conceptual structure capable of supporting it, and truly understand its implications. To delineate but three of these conundrums: (1) If liberation is the destruction of ignorance, how does the physical body continue to exist and function (since it is the effect of ignorance)? (2) If liberation is an accomplished fact, then why speak of the destruction of bondage and the attainment of liberation? 3) Why is a distinction made between liberation-with-form *(jīvan-mukti),* without-form *(videha-mukti),* and with-and-without-form *(adhikārika-mukti),* as well as between immediate-liberation *(sadyo-mukti),* and gradual-liberation *(krama-mukti),* between liberation-for-the-individual *(mukti)* and liberation-for-all *(sarva-mukti)?*

Śaṅkara, as well as Ramaṇa, reply that upon realization, all *karmas* are destroyed. The liberated individual need not wait until his *prārabdha-karma* is exhausted (through enjoyment or suffering) before freedom occurs. Whether the physical body persists or not is of no consequence to the liberated individual. One who is free appears, for all outward appearances, to act in terms of agency and purpose. But, such a one is no longer subject to this delusion. Having no desires, such as individual does not act in the common sense of the term. Latent impressions impel actions, but there is "no one home" to whom such actions can be attributed. Like a fan that has been switched off, momentum continues to impel the blades around until their previous impetus has exhausted itself. When a *jīvan-mukta's karmas* have been exhausted, the physical body will drop. But to attribute actions to a *jīvan-mukta* is to misunderstand their position.

The concept of liberation-while-living *(jīvan-mukti)* is certainly one of the most original and inspirational ideas that India has contributed to the world. Of all the Indian philosophical systems that propound this concept of *jīvan-mukti,* Advaita Vedānta is unique in that it is the only school that must *necessarily* embrace the concept.[1] That is, doctrinally, Advaita's metaphysics has a built-in necessity that *demands* the concept. If one grants Advaita's presuppositions, *jīvan-mukti* is not only a logical consequence, but necessarily so. It is a debatable question as to exactly when and how the term *"jīvan-mukti"* originated. The most commonly accepted designation has post- Śaṅkara Advaita Vedānta propounding the concept with Sāṅkhya-Yoga, Śaiva Siddhānta, and Kasmiri Śaivism following thereafter. However, the concept itself, if not the term, has ancient roots.

The word *"jīvan-mukti"* itself does not occur in the canonical texts of Vedānta. It is not found in the *Vedas* or in the earlier *Upaniṣads,* the *Bhagavad-Gītā,* or the *Brahmasūtras.*

However, the concept of liberated-while-living can be found scattered throughout the literature that either directly or indirectly point to the idea. To mention but a few references:

> While I *(Vāmadeva)* was in the womb I realized (the Self and subsequently lived a long and productive life). (AitUp 2.1.5-6)
>
> Verily, while we are here we may know this. (BU 4.4.14)
>
> A mortal becomes immortal, attains *Brahman*, even here, when the knots of the heart are destroyed. (KU 2.3.14)
>
> He who knows that which is set in the cave of the heart, he, here on earth, cuts the knot of ignorance. (MuU 2.1.10)
>
> When, to one who knows, all beings have, verily, become one with his own Self, then what delusion and what sorrow can be to him who has seen the oneness? (ĪśaU 1.7)
>
> The man free from desires realizes Brahman even here. (Śaṅkara's comm. on BU 4.4.6)
>
> Brahman-knowledge takes place even in this life. (BS 3.4.51)

This being said, the final position of Ramaṇa states that the Self and liberation *(mukti)* have the *same* meaning. This implies that the term *"jīvan-mukti"* is both relative and redundant. The qualifier *"jīvan"* is unnecessary. A *mukta* is a *mukta*, with or without a body. It has been said that a knower of the Self with a body is a *jīvan-mukta* and when that person sheds the body, such a one attains *videha-mukti*. But this difference exists only for the onlooker, not the *mukta*. As Ramaṇa remarked, "*Mukti* is synonymous with the Self. *Jīvan-mukti* and *videha-mukti* are all for the ignorant. The *jñāni* is not conscious of *mukti* or *bandha*. Bondage, liberation, and orders of *mukti* are all said for an *ajñāni* in order that ignorance might be shaken off. There is only *mukti* and nothing else."[1]

The distinctive insight of Ramaṇa is simple to state and even more devastating in its implications: "Liberation is our very nature. We are That."[2] To unpack this *sūtra*-like insight is to make explicit what is implied. In other words, the individual is the Absolute, the seeker is the sought—not sometime later, in a place above and beyond, but here and now. Thus, the concept of liberation-while-living *(jīvan-mukti)* is spoken of to an ajñāni, but in actual fact there is only the Self and all such designations are but for those who do not know and experience this. Any seeking obviously manifests a denial of the presence of the sought and necessarily implies ignorance of what-is. As the *Vivekacūḍāmaṇi* says, "It can be neither thrown away nor taken up."[3]

The *Bhagavad-gītā* gives a description of a *jīvan-mukta*—the person who is liberated while living in a physical body. Such a person is one who has gained steady wisdom; who has transcended the three qualities *(guṇas);* who is free from desires; who has no sense of agency or enjoyership—for he has ceased to identify with the mind-body organism; who is beyond the dual extremes of pleasure and pain, heat and cold. Such individuals are spontaneous expressions of innate goodness and their very presence is a blessing to the world.[4]

The *Uddhava-gītā*, the quintessence of the *Bhāgavata Purāṇa*, records the lives and behavior of several Sages and their teachings in order to explain the attitude of the *jīvan-mukta*. The author cites the incident of the *avadhūta* Dattātreya and his twenty-four teachers. It reveals at once both the means to the attainment of freedom and the end achieved. That the human body is the best instrument for the attainment of freedom is

---

[1] *Letters from Ramanāśramam*, 310-11.

[2] Mudaliar, *Day by Day with Bhagavan*, 65.

[3] V 242. See *BSB* III.4.52. Śaṅkara defines embodiedness not as a physical state so much as a matter of false knowledge. BSB I.3.19 states, "Unembodiedness or embodiedness for the Self follows respectively from the fact of discrimination or non-discrimination." See KU I.2.22 and BG XIII.31.

[4] BG 5.25.

indicated in the *avadhūta's* teachings:

> The wise man, after many births, obtained this extremely rare human body which though frail is yet conducive to man's supreme welfare, should quickly strive for liberation before the body which is always subject to death chances to fail for sense-enjoyment is obtainable to any body.[1]

This passage goes on to describe the *jīvan-mukta:* "The wise one, even though in the body, is not of it like a man awakened from a dream."[2]

The *Aṣṭāvakra-gītā* describes the *jīvan-mukta* as: "He realizes that the worlds are but the waves of the boundless ocean that he is—their rise and fall do not affect him."[3]

There are sixteen verses[4] in the *Vivekacūḍāmaṇi* describing the characteristics of the *jīvan-mukta.* Here are some of them:

> Completely freed from all awareness of external sense-objects on account of always remaining established in the Absolute; only consuming what is necessary for bodily sustenance, as provided by others, like one asleep or like a child; perceiving this world as one seen in a dream, this rare person enjoys infinite merit. Such is to be honored on earth.
>
> This spiritual aspirant, whose mind has merged in the Absolute, enjoys eternal bliss, is changeless, and free from all activity, is a person established in wisdom.
>
> One is said to be liberated-while-living-in-a-body who, while having one's mind merged in the Absolute, is nevertheless awake yet at the same time free from the characteristics of the waking state, and whose awareness is free from residual tendencies.

---

[1] *Śrīmad Bhāgavatam* 11.ix.29

[2] Ibid, 11.ix.8.

[3] *Aṣṭavakra-gītā* 5.74.

[4] See V verses 72, 318, 429-41, 452.

The mark of one liberated-while-living-in-a-body is an absence of any sense of “I” and “mine” in this body, though it follows like a shadow.

The mark of one liberated-while-living-in-a-body is seeing with an eye of equality everything, though its nature is otherwise, being qualified by auspicious and inauspicious characteristics.

The mark of one liberated-while-living-in-a-body is being changeless in respect of both the favorable and the unfavorable due to seeing everything with an eye of equality.

The mark of one liberated-while-living-in-a-body is an absence of all ideas of interior and exterior because their mind is completely engrossed in experiencing the ambrosial bliss of the Absolute.

One is said to be liberated-while-living-in-a-body who is free from all sense of "I" and "mine" with regard to the actions of the body and its sense organs, and so on, and remains indifferent to them.

One is said to be liberated-while-living-in-a-body who never again has a sense of "I" with regard to the body, the sense organs, nor the sense of "this" in other things.

One is said to be liberated-while-living-in-a-body who has perfect equality whether adored by the good or tormented by the wicked.

Accumulated-past-actions which have now begun to fructify are very strong indeed. For the wise, they are destroyed only by enjoying them. Of the accumulated-past-actions-which-have-not-begun-to-fructify and of actions-yet-to-come, their destruction takes place in the fire of perfect knowledge. But none of these three affect those who realize their identity with the Absolute, and who are always established in it. They are verily the attributeless Absolute.

Similarly, one absorbed in the Absolute remains forever established in that Self and does not see anything other. Like a remembrance of objects seen in a dream, so are the reactions of the wise regarding eating, expulsion, and so on.

The body is created out of an accumulation-of-past-actions which may be imagined with reference to it. But such is not appropriate with reference to the beginning-less Self, for the Self is never the outcome of an accumulation-of-past-actions.

Accumulated-past-actions-which-have-begun-to-fructify are meaningful only so long as there is an identification with the body. But the sense of the body being the Self is not valid, hence the accumulated-past-actions-which-have-begun-to-fructify has to be rejected. Attributing accumulated past actions which have begun to fructify to the body, too, is a delusion.

When the limiting adjunct moves, the movement of its reflection is ascribed by fools to the original, like the sun which is unmoving. Likewise, one thinks "I am the doer", "I am the enjoyer", "I am lost", alas!

The Great-One, who has perfectly realized the Truth, whose mental modifications have been rendered ineffective, does not depend upon place, time, posture, direction, abstentions, and so on. What disciplines can there be in knowing one's own Self?

What more is there to say? Both Advaita and Ramaṇa have described the state of the *mukti* in such glowing terms time and again.

Some people believe that a *jīvan-mukta* must live in two states or planes of existence at the same time: the empirical plane and the trans-empirical plane. People observe that a *mukta* moves about in the world and observe that the *mukta* sees the same objects others see, i.e. other individuals, tables, chairs, monkeys, etc. It is not as if the *mukta* does not see them. Thus, they conclude, since he sees both the world and objects therein, as well as the Self, must not he dwell on two planes at once? Ramaṇa replied: "You say that the *jñāni* sees the path, treads it, comes across obstacles, avoids them, etc. In whose eye-sight is all this, in the *jñāni's* or yours? He sees only the Self and *all in* the Self. For instance, you see a reflection in the mirror *and* the mirror. You know the mirror to be the reality and the picture in it a mere reflection. Is it necessary that in order to see the mirror, we should cease to see the reflection in it?"[1] What a wonderful analogy and yet numerous are the individuals who asked such questions. Intellectual curiosity is a hard habit to break and instead of asking what is really important, one's own Self, people ask about others. Ramaṇa said:

> Coming here, some people do not ask about themselves. They ask, "Does the *jīvan-mukta* see the world? Is he affected by *karma?* What is liberation after being disembodied? Is one liberated only after being disembodied or even while alive in the body? Should the body of the Sage resolve itself in light or disappear from view in any other manner? Can he be liberated though the body is left behind as a corpse? Their questions are endless. Why worry oneself in so many ways? Does liberation consist in knowing these things? Therefore, I say to them, "Leave liberation alone. Is there bondage? Know this. See yourself first and foremost.[2]

When asked what the difference between *jīvan-mukti* and *videha-mukti*, Ramaṇa replied:

> There is no difference. For those who ask, it is said, "A *jñāni* with a body is a *jīvan-mukta* and he attains *videha-mukti* when he sheds the body. But this difference exists only for the onlooker, not for the *jñāni.* His state is the same before and after the body is dropped. We think of the *jñāni* as a human form or as being in that form; but he knows that he is the Self, the one reality which is both inside and out, and which is not bounded by any form or shape. There is a verse in the *Bhāgavatam* which says, "Just as a man who is

---

[1] Mudaliar, *Day by Day with Bhagavan,* 144.

[2] Ibid, 534.

drunk is not conscious whether his upper cloth is on his body or has slipped away from it, the *jñāni* is hardly conscious of his body, and it makes no difference to him whether the body remains or has dropped off."[1]

Ramaṇa once said to a seeker asking such questions: "What is your idea of a *jñāni?* Is he the body or something different? If he is something apart from the body, how can he be affected by the body?"[2] Hence, these two, bondage and liberation, are imaginations of *māyā.* They do not pertain to the Self. How can there be any imaginations of the partless, actionless, peaceful, defectless, taintless, non-dual supreme reality that is like the sky? The ultimate Truth is that there is no death, no birth, no bondage and no spiritual aspirant, no seeker with a burning-desire-for-liberation, none liberated.

Some may contend that there is activity even for the liberated, that is, a *jīvan-mukta* may seem to be engaged in various activities. However, this contention is based on a mistaken view. Since ignorance, which is the cause of bondage, has been destroyed, the embodied state of the liberated one and the so-called activities in which he is supposed to be engaged *from the standpoint of others*, do not bind him anymore. Since the root cause of activity has been destroyed, the residual *karmas* that account for the continuance of his body have already been made ineffective. What one sees in not action but a semblance of activity. In reply to the fools who asked how the body continues to live if the effects of ignorance, along with their root, are destroyed by knowledge, the scripture speaks of accumulated-past-actions-which-have-begun-to-fructify from an empirical point of view. But the purport of the scripture relates only to the Absolute. Ramaṇa remarked: "People surmise the existence of the pure mind in the *jīvan-mukta* and the personal God. They ask how he could otherwise live and act. But this is only a concession to argument. The pure mind is in fact the Absolute Consciousness. The object to be witnessed and the witness finally merge together and Absolute Consciousness

---

[1] Ibid, II, 109.

[2] Ibid, 195.

alone remains. It is not a state of blank or ignorance but is the Supreme Self."[1]

Ramana once told a story of a King with three wives. When the King dies, do only two of the wives become widows? No, all three are widows. Likewise, not only one's *sañcita karma* (residual actions produced in this or previous lives) and one's *āgāmi karma* (results of acts performed in this life), but also one's *prārabdha karma* (residue of acts working themselves out during the present life are all destroyed.

The *Aṣṭhāvakra-gītā* ends:

> What need is there for striving or stillness? What is freedom or bondage? What are holy books or teachings? What is the purpose of life? Who is the disciple, and who is the master? Nothing arises in me in whom nothing is single, nothing is double. Nothing is, nothing is not. What more is there to say?

Sadguru

The term *"Sadguru"* means a "true teacher, a perfect Master, a Self-realized spiritual guide". The term comes from *sat* = true, real + *guru* = teacher.[2] Such an individual is one with the Self. The term *"guru"* literally means "weighty", "large", "heavy", "great".[3] In other words, a *Guru* is great; a *Guru* is one who is extremely great within; a *Guru* is one who is large enough to contain the entire universe, a *Guru* is the greatest of the great. For this reason such a one is called *"mahān"* (great). There are *gurus* and *gurus* in India. The term, when applied in everyday discourse, usually refers to a "teacher" and thus there is the music *guru*, the dance *guru*, the school-teacher *guru*, and even the spiritual *guru*, and so on. When the term *"guru"* is qualified by the prefix *"sat"*, it refers to a Self-realized *Guru*. However, in Ramaṇa's vocabulary, he generally used the term *"Guru"*, but by it he meant "the true *Guru*", someone who has

---

[1] Venkataramiah, *Talks with Sri Ramana Maharshi*, 68.

[2] Grimes, *A Concise Dictionary of Indian Philosophy*, 261.

[3] Monier-Williams, *A Sanskrit-English Dictionary* 359.

realized the Self and who is able to use his power to assist others towards the goal of Self-realization. In various places he said, "The *Guru* is the Self . . . God takes the form of a *Guru* and appears to the devotee and teaches him the Truth, and moreover, purifies his mind by association . . . a true *Guru* is one who is endowed with tranquility, patience, forgiveness, and other virtues, is capable of attracting others even with his eyes, who has a feeling of equality towards all."

We may note that Śaṅkara describes the *Guru* as: "One who by their Self-realization is to be equated with Truth"[1]. In this verse Śaṅkara speaks of such a one as *"sat"*. He continues to describe the *Guru*, "That person who desires to know the truth of the Self and possessed of the above-mentioned qualifications should approach the *Guru*, a knower of the Self, who confers freedom from bondage. The *Guru* is one who is well-versed in the (inner meaning of the) scriptures, taintless, desireless, a perfect knower of the Absolute, continually established in the Absolute, calm like the flame when its fuel is consumed, a boundless ocean of spontaneous compassion for which there is no reason, a friend to all good people who surrender to him."[2]

The most oft-quoted "creative" etymology of the word *"guru"* derives the word from the two syllables *"gu"* (which means darkness) and *"ru"* (remover). Thus the *Guru* is that one who removes the darkness of (the disciple's) ignorance.[3] Another etymology of the word says, "The first syllable *gu* represents the principle of illusion and the second syllable *ru* the supreme knowledge that destroys the illusion."[4] Other "creative" etymologies include *"gu"* (beyond the qualities) and *"ru"* (devoid of form). The *Guru* is the one who bestows the formless state that transcends the qualities.[5] Or again, *"gu"* (to sound or speak) and *"ru"* (declaring the way to behave). Thus, the *Guru* is the one who speaks the truth.

---

[1] V 8.

[2] Ibid, 33-35.

[3] *Guru-gītā* verse 23.

[4] Ibid, verse 24 .

[5] Ibid, verse 46.

The *Guru tattva* or *Guru* principle is often spoken of as existing on two levels in the Advaita tradition. In a similar fashion, according to Ramaṇa, the *Guru* is both inner and outer. The outer *Guru* is God in human form and simultaneously, the inner *Guru* is the Self in the Heart of each devotee. The outer *Guru* gives instructions and by his power enables the devotee to keep his attention on the Self while the inner *Guru* pulls the devotee's mind back to its source, absorbs it in the Self, and finally destroys it. Ramaṇa said: "The *Guru* is both external and internal. From the exterior he gives a push to the mind to turn it inwards. From the interior he pulls the mind towards the Self and helps in the quieting of the mind. That is the *Guru's* grace. There is no *difference* between God, *Guru*, and the Self."[1]

As noted earlier, a basic teaching of Ramaṇa was that a *Guru* is absolutely indispensable for virtually everyone who is striving for Self-realization. Ramaṇa said, "The *Guru* is absolutely necessary. The Upaniṣads say that none but a *Guru* can take a man out of the jungle of the intellect and sense-perceptions. So there must be a *Guru*."[2] Which raises the question in many seeker's minds, "but you never had a Guru (at least in human form)".

> That depends on what you all a *Guru*. He need not necessarily be in the human form. Dattātreya had twenty-four *Gurus*, the elements, etc. That means that every form in the world was his *Guru*. A *Guru* is absolutely necessary . . . I might have had a *Guru* sometime or other. And didn't I sing hymns on Aruṇācala? What is a *Guru?* God appears to a seeker in some form or other, human or non-human, to guide as *Guru* in answer to his prayer.[3]

History has recorded a few cases where there was no *Guru*, i.e. Vāmadeva, Śuka, the Buddha—but such instances are so extremely rare that they validate the saying, "the exception proves the rule".

---

[1] Venkataramiah, *Talks with Sri Ramana Maharshi*, 516.

[2] Cohen, *Guru Ramana*, 67-68.

[3] Ibid.

This necessity of a *Guru* is very subtle. According to Advaita, as long as the seeker regards him or herself as a separate individual and the *Guru* as also separate, no matter what one does, it will not help liberation and in fact, will only tighten one's bonds. "Although in absolute truth the state of the *Guru* is that of oneself (the Self), it is very hard for the self which has become the individual *(jīva)* through ignorance to realize its true state or nature without the grace of the *Guru.*" The seeker will only go round and round like a dog chasing its own tail or like individuals pulling on their own bootstraps in an attempt to rise into the air. Remember, the individual is not really a "seeker" and the *"Guru"* is not really someone separate who "knows". Still, the *Guru* provides a strange sort of help. The *Guru* has no power to bring about Self-realization in another. On the one hand, since Reality is non-dual, what could anyone give? There is no giver, no gifts, and no process of giving. On the other hand, if an individual seeker makes an ardent attempt to discover the Self, then the grace and power of the *Guru* automatically begins to flow. If no such attempt is made, the *Guru* is helpless.

According to Advaita, as well as Ramaṇa, destruction of ignorance alone is liberation *(avidyā-nāśa).* White cloth is white. Dirt on it makes it look black. To make it white, all one need do is to wash it. It is not necessary to add whiteness to it.

The *Guru's* help is negative in the sense that nothing is given; only the non-existent delusion of the seeker is removed. It is like a person that wakes up on seeing a lion in their dream. Even as the person wakes up at the mere sight of the lion, so too will a person wake up from the sleep of ignorance into the wakefulness of true knowledge through the *Guru's* benevolent look of grace. Ramaṇa remarked: "Yes, the *Guru* does not bring about Self-realization. He simply removes the obstacles to it. The Self is always realized." A devotee once remarked: "All books say that the guidance of a *Guru* is necessary." Ramaṇa responded:

> The *Guru* will say only what I am saying now. He will not give you anything you have not already. It is impossible for anyone to get what he has not got already. Even if he gets any such thing, it will go as it

came. What comes will also go. What always is will alone remain. The *Guru* cannot give you anything new, which you have not already. Removal of the notion that we have not realized the Self is all that it is required. We are always the Self. Only, we don't realize it.[1]

If the *Guru* is the grace-bestowing power of the Absolute, *what* the *Guru* bestows is *darśan;* it provides the seeker with a direct personal experience or glimpse of the Self, embodied. It is the *Guru's* spiritual power which radiates from, and is transmitted by the *Guru* and which awakens the disciple's own inner power. Obviously, as both tradition and the texts reveal, the *Guru* plays a major role in both Ramaṇa's teaching and Vedānta. And yet, even if one intellectually understands that one is the Self, the senses still lead one astray. One needs some instrument, some device, whereby one can overcome the pull, the tyranny of the senses. That instrument is the *Guru.*

For the *Guru* to awaken the disciple there must be a link between the two. This link is called, in Advaita, grace *(anugraha).* It is like the wire that connects the powerhouse with the light bulb that shines in one's home. Or, it is like the original flame that can then light an infinite number of candles without diminishing itself. The *Taittirīya Upaniśad* says, "The teacher is the first letter; the student is the last letter; knowledge is the meeting place; instruction is the link."[2]

According to Advaita, what has a name must have a form, and *vice-versa.* Every appearance in the universe partakes of these two characteristics. The wonder and power of the physical *guru-paramparā* is in the *special* qualities inherent in its names and forms. The *Guru's* name and form is filled with Bliss. The *Guru's* name and form possess a special power.[3] Somehow the

---

[1] Mudaliar, *Day by Day with Bhagavan,* 13.

[2] TU 1.3.3.

[3] The great sage Vālmiki was liberated even though he uttered the name of God contrariwise. Further it enabled him to write the life-story of Rāma, the *Rāmāyaṇa.* By meditating on the name, Prahlāda was protected again and again. The outcast Ajāmila was made holy by the name. Rukminī balanced the scales against Satyabhāmā. The lists are endless. Even the great God Śiva has been relieved from the torments of poison by the power of the name. Therefore, it is said, chant the name continuously.

mind must be made to sink into the Heart. How to do this? Attach the name and form of the *Guru* to the mind and it will automatically begin sinking, for, the word *"guru"* literally means "heavy", "weighty", and thus it will enable the mind to sink, to journey from the name to the Nameless, from the form to the Formless, from the relative to the Absolute.

A disciple finds that spiritual disciplines are many and varied. Much will depend upon the capacity of a seeker to understand the guidance that the *Guru* provides. While grace is pulling the disciple from within, the *Guru* is pushing the disciple from without. According to Advaita, and I am sure Ramaṇa wouldn't disagree, in order to turn one's mind within and discover the inner Self, the *Guru* may be said to provide three gifts to assist the spiritual seeker. These three gifts (even if they don't directly involve the direct path of Self-enquiry) are: the name of the *Guru;* the form of the *Guru;* and the life/sport *(līla)* of the *Guru.*

The human *Guru*, like every physical entity, has five characteristics: existence, cognizability, attractiveness, name, and form *(asti, bhāti, priyam, nāma, rūpa).* The first three we earlier observed under the names *sat-cit-ānanda* and are but terms for the nameless, formless Self. In addition, the *Guru* also possesses a name and form. The name is pure and auspicious, e.g., Bhagavān Sri Ramaṇa Maharshi. *"Bhagavān"* = "possessor or Master of splendor"; "he who possesses the six divine attributes of wisdom, strength, lordship, power, heroism, splendor". *"Śrī"* = "holiness, glory, prosperity". "Ramaṇa" = "the dear darling", "one who revels in the Self, "one who is the Self". *"Mahārṣi"* = "the great seer". The name contains power when thought of, spoken or chanted. Hanumān leapt across the ocean using only Rāma's name (while Rāma had to build a bridge!). Instances of the power of the *Guru's* name are legion. As Muruganar said: "The Name. It will be doing its job of ripening one to be rid of the dross, so that the inner pull of the Self would be felt strongly. Nurturing and protecting it watches over loving devotees whose delusion is immolated, in the vast fullness of final realization."[1] Constant repetition of the name

---

[1] Muruganar: *Non-dual Consciousness. Seventy Verses in Praise of the Guru's Holy Feet,* verses 625, 629, 106.

has a wonderfully purifying effect. The *Guru's* form is a special form. It fills the devotee with bliss. It has a universal appeal (people from all over the world are attracted to it). His eyes were glittering, unblinking, full of overflowing love for all creation, firmly fixed in the Self alone. His body radiant, wearing but a *kaupina* or loin-cloth. Finally, in order to give the naturally unstable mind that is forever craving variety something to occupy itself with, the life, the sport of the *Guru*. If a seeker is not mature enough to dive deep into Self-enquiry, meditating on the various events in the life of the *Guru* provides it with ample variety, variety that is pure and auspicious and full of wisdom.

These three gifts of the *Guru* are given in order to assist the devotee in seeking Self-realization. One should accept them with reverence, respect them, and utilize them. Once there was a wife of a fisherman. One day she found herself in the house of a gardener who raised flowers as the guest of his daughter. She had come with her empty fish basket and was asked to sleep in a room where many fragrant flowers were kept. Because of their fragrance, she couldn't get to sleep. She tossed and turned. Finally, in a stroke of insight, she asked for her fish basket. As soon as it was brought into the room, she fell asleep. Individuals have become so accustomed to the smell of the fish basket of the world that the fragrance of the divine Self makes them restless. These three gifts of the *Guru* help a seeker to develop the capacity to withstand the fragrance of the Self as well as to begin to seek it, to cultivate it, and to eventually realize it.

VIII
Ramana's Contribution to Indian Philosophy

At times the question is asked: "How does the Sage give instruction? Is it from the state of ignorance?" If this were so, the mind would not have been dissolved, the threefold differentiation of the knower, knowledge, and the known could not have been merged. So what would the Sage be able to give you? Where could he lead you? But there is a stage where this question does not arise. Is it the body that is the obstacle to Supreme Knowledge? Is there even a question of whether the body exists or not? At a certain level this question is simply not there. On the plane where this question arises, one is not in the state of Pure Being, and one thinks this question can be raised and also replied to. But the answer lies where there is no such thing as questioning and answering, where there are no "others", no divisions.

Evaluation

There he was, firmly established in the state of steady Self-abidance *(sahaja-samādhi).* He was one with everything, free from all dualistic thoughts, desirable or undesirable, happy or sad. His eyes were glittering, unblinking, full of overflowing love for all creation, firmly fixed in the Self alone. He saw no external objects with a desire to receive any impression from them. He asked for nothing. Ever-full, he reveled in the spontaneous bliss of the Heart. Truly he was an embodiment of serenity, full and complete. Such was the Maharshi.

Ramaṇa was a Sage, a *jñāni*, an embodiment of the Self, a momentary appearance of the nameless, formless Reality. It may appear as if he had a birth, a personality, a history, spoke, acted, taught—all the raw material which informs a biography and of which comprise all that ordinary people can and do perceive with their mind and senses—but know that all this is but a tale that a mind that is possessed by the defect of duality tells. In whatever way one perceives Ramaṇa, know that Ramaṇa remains what Ramaṇa is, always has been, and always will be, the nameless, formless, indivisible Self.

What were Ramaṇa's contributions to philosophy? He blazed forth anew the path of Self-enquiry. Through it, anyone, at any place or time, can attain Self-realization. No one is excluded. No one is too low or too high, too small or too great for this path. Even as Ramaṇa's Presence was always accessible to all, so were his teachings meant for the good of the entire world.

Ramaṇa's life and teachings were an incredible confirmation of both the Upaniṣadic teachings as well as the teachings of Advaita Vedānta. However, in an interesting twist in this instance, Ramaṇa's teachings are the primary revelation and the *Upaniṣads* and teachings of Advaita are of value because they are found to be in accord with his teachings! It is a wonderful phenomenon that the words of Ramaṇa, in numerous instances, are virtually the exact words found in the *Upaniṣads*, in the teachings of the ancient Sages like Dattātreya, Ribhu, Śaṅkara, and a host of others. What is remarkable is that Ramaṇa had no knowledge of these ancient teachings before his Self-realization and only came to learn of them many years after.

Ramaṇa played the role of a *Sadguru*, as a guide on the spiritual path, as an unfailing friend to all in their inner journey to the Heart. Yet, never once did Ramaṇa refer to himself as a *Guru*. He had transcended the *Guru*-disciple relationship. He had transcended all relationships, all duality.

Ramaṇa did not found any new school of philosophy. He taught the ageless truth of Advaita and even to call that truth Advaita (non-duality) is only a concession to the inherent limitations of language. More than an expounder of Advaita, he was a living, breathing embodiment of it.

Ramaṇa has left an indelible footprint on the sands of time by giving a new exposition of the spirit of contemporary Indian philosophy that will continue to reverberate and inspire generations to come. The tradition of Advaita has been renewed, from time to time by Sages and philosophers. Ramaṇa turned the wheel one more time.

Ramaṇa demonstrated in his life the truth of Advaita. He revealed how it is possible for a Sage to be in the world but not of it. He demonstrated, as well as occasionally explained, how a *jñāni* acts in the world. The objects of the world don't disappear to such a one's perception—though they are no longer objects being perceived by a subject—they are now appearances of the one, indivisible Self. The mind works by division but once the mind is divested of the "I"-thought, reflections are observed as they truly are, nothing but reflections of the prototype, the original, the Self. "The moon shines by reflecting the light of the sun. When the sun has set, the moon is useful for displaying objects. When the sun has risen no one needs the moon, though its disc is visible in the sky. So it is with the mind and the Heart. The mind is made useful by its reflected light. It is used for seeing objects. When turned inwards it merges into the source of illumination which shines by itself and the mind is then like the moon in daytime."[1]

All his life, Ramaṇa had to endure the practical pressures of Swamihood. He once jokingly said: "It is a very difficult job. I am speaking from fifty years experience. They have put wooden bars around me that I may not cross. People are specially deputed to watch me by turns. I cannot move about as I like. What is the difference between this and being in jail?" People wanted to give him special preferential treatment, be it food, clothing, shelter, a massage, prostrations, eyeglasses, medical treatments, animals. Then there were those casual visitors to the

---

[1] Venkataraman, *Maharshi's Gospel*, I, 17.

āśrama who would remark, "What is there about this Bhagavān of yours which makes you think that he is a realized soul? He eats and drinks, and does everything else like the rest of us."

However, even on the physical plane, Ramaṇa did display some rather extraordinary abilities. His endurance of heat and cold were phenomenal. His ability to withstand pain, whether of insects gorging themselves on his flesh, wasps stinging him, cancer ravaging his body, was unbelievable. He could go for hours without blinking or of his body twitching or moving. In the early days, he sat for days, weeks, without moving, deeply absorbed in the bliss of *nirvikalpa samādhi.* It is said he could follow the language of animals. Remember though, however marvelous these phenomena might appear, they are but phenomena *(siddhis).* On this point Ramaṇa said:

> There are two kinds of *siddhis* and one kind may well be a stumbling block to realization. It is said that by mantra, by some drug possessing occult virtues, by severe austerities or by *Samādhi* of a certain kind, powers can be acquired. But these powers are not a means to Self-knowledge, for even when you acquire them, you may quite well be in ignorance. The other kind are manifestations of power and knowledge which are quite natural to you when you realize the Self. They are *siddhis* which are the products of the normal and natural *tapas* of the man who has reached the Self. They come of their own accord. They are God given. They come according to one's destiny but whether they come or not, the *jñāni*, who is settled in the supreme peace, is not disturbed by them. For he knows the Self and that is the unshakable *siddhi.* But these *siddhis* do not come by trying for them. When you are in the state of realization, you will know what these powers are.[1]

Other qualities that Ramaṇa displayed to an extraordinary degree and which could be observed on a daily basis by anyone coming into his presence were virtues like love, compassion, kindness, friendliness, humility, patience, charity, and wisdom.

---

[1] *Sat-darshana Bhasya*, xxii.

So, who was Ramaṇa really? That is, how did Ramaṇa answer this question when it was put to him directly and he responded directly and not in a philosophical sense? This question was first put to Ramaṇa by Raghavachariar around 1910. He asked, "Will you please enable me to see your real form if I am eligible to see it? He wrote:

> I waited with eager mind (for his answer). He was then seated on the porch with a picture of Dakṣiṇāmūrti painted on the wall next to him. He silently gazed on as usual and I gazed into his eyes. Then his body and also the picture of Dakṣiṇāmūrti disappeared from my view. There was only empty space, without even a wall, before my eyes. Then followed a whitish cloud in the outline of the Maharshi and of Dakṣiṇāmūrti, formed before my eyes. Gradually the outline with silvery lines of these figures appeared. Then eyes, nose, etc., other details were outlined in lightning-like lines. These gradually broadened till the whole figure of the swami and Dakṣiṇāmūrti became ablaze with very strong and unendurable light. I closed my eyes in consequence. I waited a few minutes and then saw him and Dakṣ iṇāmūrti in the usual form. I prostrated and came away. For a month thereafter I did not dare to go near him, so great was the impression the above experience made on me. After a month, I went up and saw him standing in front of the Skandāśrama. I told him "I had a question put to you a month back and I had this experience," narrating the above experience to him. I requested him to explain it. Then, after a pause he said, "You wanted to see my form. You saw my disappearance. I am formless. So that experience might be the real truth. The further visions may be according to your own conceptions derived from the study of the *Bhagavad-gītā*. But Ganapati Sastri had a similar experience and you may consult him."[1]

---

[1] Narasimha Swami, *Self-Realization*, 106-07.

Prior to this experience, while Ramaṇa was residing in the Virupākśa Cave, Śrī Kāvyakaṇṭa Gaṇapati Muni and Ramaṇa walked a few steps outside the cave and observed the full moon shining in the eastern sky. The sky was full of stars. Pointing to the moon and beautiful sky, Ramaṇa said: "Nayana! If the sun, the moon, and all the stars have their being in me, and the sun himself goes round my hip with his satellites, who am I? who am I?"[1]

Two other experiences are worth noting in regards to Ramaṇa referring to himself. What is of interest here is that Arthur Osborne, among many others, noticed that Ramaṇa usually spoke impersonally and avoided the use of the word "I" when referring to himself. When Ramaṇa asked a visiting *sannyāsin* who had asked Ramaṇa to put his name in a notebook intended to raise collections for a charity, Ramaṇa asked him, "What is my name?" The *sannyāsin* replied, "Sri Ramaṇa." Ramaṇa replied: "You say so: I have no name."[2] The second experience worth noting is about an experience that Sri Krishna Prem had similar to the experience of Raghavachariar. Krishna Prem narrated it:

> In the evening, I entered the hall where the Maharshi reclines daily on his couch. I sat down in silence, along with the others, to meditate at his feet. But believe it or not, as soon as I sat down I heard a voice questioning me over and over again: "Who are you?" "Who are you?" I tried hard to ignore it, but it went on and on. In the end, I just had to formulate an answer: "I am Krishna's servant." At once the question changed, "Who is Krishna?" I suddenly took it into my head to return the compliment and put a question to him in silence, "And who are you? May I humbly ask?" It so happened that the next moment I had to open my eyes involuntarily when—Lo! I found his couch empty! There was the couch where he had presided two seconds before, but in the twinkling of an eye as it were he had vanished—just melted into thin air! I closed my

[1] Iyer, *At the Feet of Bhagavan*, 49.

[2] Ramananda Swarnagiri, *Crumbs From His Table*, 51.

> eyes once more and then looked again and he was tranquil and beneficent like Lord Siva Himself! A momentary smile flicked on his lips as he gave me a meaningful glance and then looked away.[1]

Ramaṇa saw no differences anywhere. Barely touching the earth; always on the point of almost vanishing. For such a Sage, there was no place to go and nothing to attain. There he sat, immovable like his beloved Aruṇācala. He embodied a transparent, flawless purity. There was no inferior and no superior. Such invented opinions are baseless to such an impeccable one. Life is a succession of events, for both the Sage and the ordinary person. However, the Sage is detached and merely watches the passing show while ordinary individuals, being attached, cling to certain objects and events and shun others. A Sage's attention is on the Self, while ordinary individuals' attention is on things, people, thoughts, ideas, plans, schemes, and objects. An Advaitin's Advaitin. Ramana has been praised as one of the greatest living embodiments of Advaita Vedānta, as great as the greatest of that illustrious group. Such a wonder the world seldom sees. He has often been described as "an incarnation of Advaita". The description is an intriguing philosophical oxymoron as the thunderous truth of Advaita boldly declares that no one has ever been born, lived, or died, and yet it is without doubt an astonishingly powerful image in conveying the profound affinity that exists between the teachings of Advaita and Ramaṇa

---

[1] See Swami Anu Ananda, 'The Siddha Purusha', in *Maharshi Ramana: His Relevance Today*, 98.

The Writings of Ramana

Ramaṇa wrote little, and what he did write, was written to meet the specific needs of devotees. Ramaṇa himself has said on the subject:

> All this is only activity of the mind. The more you exercise the mind and the more success you have in composing verses the less peace you have. What use is it to acquire such accomplishments if you don't acquire peace? But if you tell people this it doesn't appeal to them, they can't keep quiet . . . Somehow it never occurs to me to write a book or compose poems. All the poems I have made were on the request of someone or other in connection with some particular event.

Self-Enquiry (Vicāra-saṅgraham)

This Tamil prose book covers the period 1900-1902 and consists of forty questions and answers covering the entire range of spiritual disciplines *vis-a-vis* Self-realization. The replies to these questions were written out by Ramaṇa (as during this period he was not speaking).

Who am I? (Nān Yār?)

Like *Self-Enquiry*, this book is in the form of thirty questions put forth by M. Sivaprakasam Pillai and replies given by Ramaṇa, either in the form of gestures or, when they were not clearly understood, by writing. Along with *Self-Enquiry*, these two works constitute the first set of instructions in Ramaṇa's own words and are the only prose pieces among his works.

A Garland of Teachings (Upadeśa-mañjarī)

This is an anthology of seventy questions and answers collected and arranged topically by Natanananda. The topics cover virtually the entire range of Vedāntic teachings, with an emphasis on practical disciplines.

Quintessence of the Teachings (Upadeśa-undiyār, Upadeśa-sāram)

This work is a compendium of teachings on Advaita. It came about because Muruganar, an ardent devotee and eminent Tamil poet, put into verse the legendary story of how the ritualists of the Daruka-forest received instruction from Lord Siva. However, Muruganar felt unable to put into verse form Siva's teachings to the ritualists and implored Ramaṇa to do so. In response, Ramaṇa composed thirty verses setting forth the truth of Vedanta and the path that leads to the realization of the truth. This poem was known as *Upadeśa-undiyār.* Later, Ramaṇa translated this poem into Sanskrit, Telugu, and Malayalam verse with the title, *Upadeśa-sāram.*

Forty Verses on Reality (Uḷḷadu-nārpadu)

This is a poem of forty verses on the nature of Existence. It is an authentic exposition of the non-dual experience. Again, the inspiration behind this work was Muruganar.

Five Verses on the One Self (Ekātma-pañcakam)

This short poem in only five verses lucidly teaches the Truth of the one, non-dual Self. Originally composed in 1947 in Telugu, it was later translated into Tamil.

Five Hymns to Aruṇācala (Arunācala-pañcakam)

These five hymns praising the holy hill, Arunācala, are lyrical poems composed on different occasions and under different circumstances. The five hymns are: The Marital Garland of Letters for Arunācala; The Necklace of Nine Gems for Arunācala; The Eleven Verses on Arunācala; The Eight Verses on Arunācala; and The Five Verses on Arunācala.

Glossary

abhāsa-vāda – a causation theory of appearance or manifestation.

adhikarin – eligible person; a qualified aspirant after liberation.

adhisthāna – basis; substratum; ground; support.

adhyāropa – the "method or theory of prior superimposition and subsequent denial".

adhyāsa – superimposition; false attribution.

Advaita – nondualism; nonduality; "not-two;" (from *a* = "not" + *dvaita* = "dual, two").

aham – 'I'; 'I'-thought; 'I'-awareness.

ahamkara – 'I'-ness; egoism; the concept of individuality; lit ṣ the 'I'-maker.

aham-vṛtti – the 'I'-thought.

ajāta-vāda – the theory of non-origination.

ajñāni – ignorant or deluded individual.

akhaṇḍākara-vṛtti-jñāna – the mental cognition through which the Absolute is apprehended.

ānanda – bliss; delight.

anandamayakośa – the sheath of bliss.

anirvacanīya – inexpressible; inexplicable; ineffable.

annamayakośa v the food sheath.

antahkaraṇa – the inner organ comprised of mind, intellect, ego, apprehension.

apavada – subsequent denial; refutation.

Aruṇācala – a holy hill in South India; the physical embodiment of the non-dual reality that transcends time, space, name and form.

āryāśrami – one who has bypassed/transcended the 'stages of life' classification altogether.

asat – non-being; non-existent; false; unreal.

āśrama – a halting place; hermitage; a place of striving.

Ātman – the Self;

avaccheda-vāda – theory of limitation.

āvaraṇa – concealment; veil.

avasthā-traya-vicāra – enquiry into the three states of experience.

avidyā-nāśa – destruction of ignorance. Advaita's definition of Self-realization.

bhakti – loving devotion; the path of devotion.

Bhāmati – One of the two schools within Advaita Vedānta.

Brahman – the ultimate Reality; the Absolute.

Brāhmaṇa Swami – name Ramana was known by after arriving in Tiruvannamalai.

brahmin – member of the priestly caste.

buddhi – intellect; the discriminative faculty.

cidabhāsa – the reflection of consciousness residing in the internal organ; the *jiva.*

cit – Consciousness; Reality; the Self.

citta – apperception; consciousness.

Daksinamurti – Name for Lord Siva as the silent sage.

darśana – to have sight of a revered person, sacred idol, or sacred place.

dhyāna – meditation.

dṛsti-sṛsti-vāda – gradual creation theory.

Gaudapāda – famous Advaitin; author of *Māndukya-kārikās.*

guna – quality; attributes; comprised of *sattva, rajas, tamas.*

Gurumurtam – a small shrine located in a suburb of Tiruvannamalai.

Īśvara – Lord; the Divine with form.

jagat – the world.

jagrat – the waking state.

jīva – the individual human being.

jīvan-mukta – a person liberated-while-living-in a-body.

jīvan-mukti – the state of Self-realization while in the body.

jñānendriya – organs of knowledge (hearingltouch/taste/smell/sight).

Jñāni – a Self-realized person; a sage.

Kaivalya-navanītam – Tamil text on Advaita.

kāraṇa-śarīra – the causal body.

kośa – sheath; cover; the five subtle bodies.

kramamukti – attainment of Self-realization in stages.

Maharsi – Great Sage; part of the name given to Ramana by Kavyakanta Ganapati Muni.

Mahāsamādi – the great union; when the Self-realized leaves their body.

mahāvākya – great sayings of the *Upanisads.*

mamakara – me, mine.

manana – contemplation; reflection.

manas – mind.

manomayakośa – the mental sheath.

mantra – sacred word or phrase of spiritual significance and power.

māyā – illusion; the principle of appearance; that which measures.

mithyā – not real; false; illusory.

moksa – liberation; Self-realization.

mukti – liberation, Self-realization.

mukta – one who is liberated, Self-realized.

neti-neti – not-this, not-this; *via negativa.*

nididhyāsana – profound and continuous meditation.

nirvikalpa samādhi – a state in which no differences are perceived.

pāramārthika – absolute level or Truth.

pariṇamavāda – transformation theory.

pramā – truth; valid knowledge.

pramāna – means of valid knowledge.

prāṇamayakośa – the vital-air sheath.

prapatti – the path of complete and absolute surrender.

praptasya praptih – obtaining the already obtained.

prarabdha karma – action-in-store; accumulated past actions.

prasthana-traya – the triple canon.

pratibhaṣika – apparent or illusory appearance.

pratyaksa – perception.

rajas – energy; active; passion; one of the *gunas.*

sadasadvilaksaṇa – what is other than the real and unreal.

sādhana – spiritual disciplines.

sādhu – a person practicing spiritual disciplines; holy person.

sadyomukti – bodiless liberation; immediately upon attaining Self-realization one gives up one's body.

sahaja-samādhi – natural, constant and innate *samādhi.*

sākṣin – the internal witness; the witness-self.

samādhi – one-pointedness; the state in which the unbroken experience of Existence-Consciousness is attained by the still mind; an advanced stage of meditation.

samskara – latent tendencies; predispositions; residual impressions.

sannyāsin – monkhood; renunciate.

sarvamukti – liberation for all.

sat – Reality; Existence; Being.

satkaryavāda – causation theory that the effect exists latent in its cause prior to its manifestation .

satsang – holy company; association with Being.

sattva – pure; illuminating; one of the *gunas.*

siddha – accomplished; perfect; a miracle-worker.

siddhi – miraculous powers.

śravaṇa – hearing; a primary aid to liberation in Advaita.

sṛṣti-dṛṣti-vāda – simultaneous creation theory.

sthula-sarlra – gross or physical body.

suddha-sattva – pure matter.

suksma-śarira – subtle body.

svarupa-jñāna – the Self; Self-knowledge.

tamas – darkness; inertia; dullness; one of the *gunas.*

tapas – austerity.

Tiruchuzhi – small town in South India where Ramaṇa was born.

trikaraṇa śuddhi – purity in thought, word, and deed.

triputi – the triple form; knower/known/knowledge.

turiya – the 'fourth'; the Transcendental Self; Supreme Reality.

upadeśa – spiritual instruction or initiation.

upādhi – vehicle; adventitious condition; limiting adjunct.

Venkataraman – Ramana's given name at birth.

videhamukti – liberation attained after leaving the body.

vijnānamayakośa – the sheath of the intellect.

viksepa – projection; prior superimposition.

Vivaraṇa – one of two schools of Advaita Vedānta.

vṛtti – mental modification; fluxuation of the mind.

vṛtti-jñāna – empirical knowledge.

vyāvahārika – the relative or empirical standpoint.

Author Biography

John Allen Grimes received his B.A. in Religious Studies from the University of California at Santa Barbara and his M.A. and Ph.D. in Indian Philosophy from the University of Madras. He has taught at universities in the United States, Canada, Singapore, and India. His book publications include: *The Vivekacudamani: Sankara's Crown Jewel of Discrimination; A Concise Dictionary of Indian Philosophy; Ganapati: Song of the Self; Problems and Perspectives in Religious Discourse: Advaita Vedanta Implications*; *Sapta Vidha Anupapatti: The Seven Great Untenables*; *Quest for Certainty; Sankara and Heidegger: Being, Truth, Freedom; The Naiskarmyasiddhi of Suresvara,* and most recently, *Ramana Maharshi: The Crown Jewel of Advaita.* He currently spends his time writing and traveling between California and Chennai.